NICKY SAMUEL
My Life and Loves

NICKY SAMUEL

My Life and Loves

As told to
Richard Perceval Graves
Richard Perceval Graves

Copyright © 2023 Richard Perceval Graves

The moral right of the author has been asserted.

Apart from any fair dealing for the purposes of research or private study, or criticism or review, as permitted under the Copyright, Designs and Patents Act 1988, this publication may only be reproduced, stored or transmitted, in any form or by any means, with the prior permission in writing of the publishers, or in the case of reprographic reproduction in accordance with the terms of licences issued by the Copyright Licensing Agency. Enquiries concerning reproduction outside those terms should be sent to the publishers.

Troubador Publishing Ltd
Unit E2 Airfield Business Park
Harrison Road, Market Harborough
Leicestershire LE16 7UL
Tel: 0116 279 2299
Email: books@troubador.co.uk
Web: www.troubador.co.uk

ISBN 978 1805140 566

British Library Cataloguing in Publication Data.
A catalogue record for this book is available from the British Library.

Printed by TJ Books Limited, Padstow, Cornwall
Typeset in 12pt Adobe Jenson Pro by Troubador Publishing Ltd, Leicester, UK

Matador is an imprint of Troubador Publishing Ltd

For all those for whom celebrity
has been a mixed blessing,
as it has for me.

Contents

	Prologue	ix
1	Howard and Jane	1
2	Bowing to the Indian	8
3	Downs, Fountain House and Henniker Mews	15
4	Death Comes Calling	23
5	Drawn Curtains	30
6	Lonely and Abandoned	36
7	Adolescence and a Leap from the Window	43
8	Sexual Assault and Becoming a Superstar	49
9	Working for Yoko Ono	58
10	The Arts Lab and Queen's Gate	66
11	Monty Berman and Making New Friends	74
12	Reaching San Francisco	87
13	Seducing Jim Haynes	96
14	Chesil Court and a Bunch of Violets	106
15	David Litvinoff and Nigel Waymouth	116
16	The Black House and Modelling	128
17	The Isle of Wight Concert	141
18	The Chelsea Hotel, the Chateau Marmont, and Mexico	148
19	An Inheritance and a Wedding	165
20	The Trouble with Nigel	181
21	Donald Cammell and Myriam	

		188
22	An Interlude in Venice; and Meeting Bill Willis and Victoria Brooke	196
23	A Blind Date in Rajasthan	203
24	Travelling with Christopher Gibbs and Bill Willis	217
25	Partying in New York and London	230
26	Paul Getty, Nicholas Gormanston and Harry Hyams	246
27	Friends and Lovers	257
28	Andy Warhol and his set	269
29	Kenny Jay Lane	280
30	A Cabinet of Skulls	287
31	Breakdown	294
	Postscript	305
	Acknowledgements	309

Prologue

Psychiatrists have heard it all before. They look at you sadly, listen to you patiently, and after exactly sixty minutes they remind you to pay on the way out. Nothing seems to touch them. But this time it's different. By the time I have finished telling my story, Sir Martin Roth looks pale with shock.

It's his turn to talk now, but I'm tired, and not very interested any longer. I didn't even send for him. That was Arnold Goodman, rallying round as usual. So I settle myself slightly less uncomfortably in my hospital bed, and close my eyes and try to imagine that I'm back in the Ritz, instead of this dingy little sick-room in St. George's. Back in the Ritz, with another bottle of pills to be swallowed, please, and washed down in whisky five or ten at a time; and this time, with luck, no-one will find me until too late.

For weeks, I've been feeling desolate, absolutely desolate. The only life I have ever wanted is over. Or is it? Perhaps a letter… Please Ken, please my love, I could be well, I feel well, I *am* well! But I don't know if I can ever persuade you that this is true… Anyhow I can't beg, it's your decision now. I'll go to a doctor *every day* if that's what you want! **LOVE LOVE LOVE NICKY…**

Sir Martin is saying to the nurse that sleep is the best thing for me; and I hear the door closing behind him, and his feet walking heavily away down the corridor. I would like to forget; but images from the past flicker unwanted across the screen of memory. Turning over in bed, with my eyes tightly shut, I see a hand reaching out to a glass-fronted cabinet full of skulls; which shimmers and fades and becomes one of the whores' cages in Bombay; and then a tangle of bodies, friends out of wholesome need, strangers to be seduced for darker purposes... Further back, to a kaleidoscope of faces, to Mick Jagger, Paul Getty, Donald Cammell, to a whirl of parties and drugs, punctuated by the sudden sinister glare of flash-bulbs; and all the time Andy Warhol is whispering flatly but insistently in my ear: 'Who did you sleep with last night, Nicky? Did he have a big prick? What did you do to each other?' Further, further, to the first man whom I desired, who sucked me to orgasm after orgasm, but always left before morning. Still further, to a deserted church at midnight, under a full moon; to a pocket-watch held against my ear, tick, tick, tick; to my mother's glazed, indifferent eyes; to my father's body floating face-downward in nine inches of water...

CHAPTER ONE
Howard and Jane

Howard Samuel was my father: a stylish man who had been born in February 1914 at the tail-end of safe, secure Edwardian England, just a few months before Europe went up in flames. When I was a child of seven or eight, he would come to my bedroom to say goodnight, his face pale and drawn, a large glass of whisky in his hand; and I would detain him with questions. 'Daddy, tell me about Grandpa and Grandma! Tell me about when you were a boy!'

'Again?' He smiled and sat down on the edge of my bed, and sipped his whisky before beginning. 'They were orthodox: that means candle-lit prayers, and going to the synagogue every Sunday. Business was important, too. When your Grandpa wanted to give us a treat, he'd take your Uncle Basil and me to visit one of his jewellery shops.'

'Why don't we see Uncle Basil very often?'

He looked at me shrewdly. 'Strange, isn't it? We had the same family life, the same schooling at St. Paul's, we were both articled to estate agents; but we could hardly be more different.'

'Don't you like Uncle Basil, then?'

'He's my brother, isn't he? But he's always accepted things as they are. I'm more like your Uncle Nye: I want to challenge everything, and change everything! Very upsetting for Grandpa, especially when I stopped going to the synagogue. I was thirteen, then. He liked me better the next year, when I started my own business, selling rare books. I've always loved books.

Anyway, young lady, it's time I was going down to supper.' He drained his whisky and got up to go, but I called him back.

'Please Daddy, just tell me again about Grandpa Samuel losing all his money! Please!'

As always, he came back, and sat down on my bed again. 'Gambling,' he said thoughtfully. 'It's in the blood, I suppose. It was one morning in 1937 that Basil and I were summoned to Grandpa's office. He was sitting behind his big mahogany desk: the one I've got downstairs in the Library. For once he looked serious, and I noticed that there were none of the usual papers spread out in front of him. "Boys," he said in a quiet, rather sad voice, "Boys, I can't support you any longer." When I asked why, he put his head in his hands, and told us very quietly that he'd been gambling down at Monte Carlo. In a single night he'd lost most of his capital. "Don't worry," he told us, looking up again. "I can't go on with the business, it's true: but I've got enough put by to retire on. And I'm going to give you fifty pounds each, and some advice: go into Property."'

'Sound advice!' I chimed in, as I always did when we reached this part of the story. My father smiled at me and looked ruefully at his empty glass of whisky before going on.

'Yes, Nicola, sound advice. The war was coming, and property prices were rock-bottom. We borrowed another £100, found a basement in Regent Street for our headquarters, and began acquiring properties around Oxford Street, right in the centre of London.

'How we did it, I don't know. But I'll never forget negotiating my first lease. Appearances are important: remember that! I bought the largest cigar I could find, put on my best suit, and took my prospect out to lunch at a good restaurant. When the bill came, I was so horrified by how large it was, that I immediately increased the rent – and then found to my surprise that he was ready to sign!'

Luck was also important: my father seems to have enjoyed a permanent winning streak; and by the time war broke out in 1939, he and Basil had built up a large string of properties. They both enlisted, and Basil was given a commission in the Royal Artillery; but the authorities found that my father had tuberculosis, and he was rapidly invalided out.

Years later I heard from his friend Reg Davis-Poynter what happened next. 'He used some fake medical papers,' Reg told me,

> And that got him back in again; but much to his disappointment he was only accepted as a private soldier. His personal revenge was to lead a double life. In the evenings he would put on a dinner-jacket and go to Claridge's, where a table was permanently booked in his name and where (as in all the establishments which knew him well) two bottles would rapidly appear upon his table: one of HP sauce, and the other of Johnny Walker whisky!

Sitting on the end of my bed, my father would leave out this part of the story, and jump from his first enlistment to when he was 'searching Piccadilly Circus for unexploded bombs. Someone needed to do it, I suppose. At least there were still parties. That was how I first met your mother.'

※

Jane Willington Lane, my mother, was almost exactly ten years younger than Howard and a great beauty. As for her parents: her father, Reginald, was a successful businessman who had been a captain in the Royal Naval Air Service during the First World War; but by the time that I knew him, he was chiefly famous for being deaf. Her mother, Ailsa, was a terrible snob. They were a family of beauties and Ailsa's sister had managed to snare as her second husband Lord Howland, who later became the Duke of Bedford. 'Never forget, Nicola, ' Ailsa told me once, when we were playing Happy Families, 'that your Great-aunt is a Duchess.'

As well as being beautiful, my mother was intense and artistic. After only a year at Queen's Gate, she won a scholarship to the Slade; but then, during the very first year of the War, when she was still only sixteen, Jane was raped in a London taxi by one of her art teachers. This led first to a complete nervous breakdown, and then to the discovery that she was pregnant. Reginald and Ailsa, sick with worry, arranged for an illegal abortion; and that breakdown would be only the first in a series that plagued my mother for the rest of her life.

When my father met Jane for the first time, he saw only a witty, lively and astonishingly beautiful young woman; and he fell in love immediately, beginning a pursuit so determined that once (as he told my brother Nigel): 'I jumped into her taxi just as it was pulling away from the kerb. The result was that I knocked her portfolio out of her hands; and in an instant we were knee-deep in pictures of naked models!'

Jane was deeply flattered by Howard's almost obsessional interest, and began introducing him to her friends. Chief among these were Nye Bevan and his wife Jennie Lee, in whose house Jane had been renting a room. Howard and Nye took to each other at once. My father had always longed for excitement; and in Nye Bevan he found the most exciting and charismatic of men, the finest Welsh orator of his generation, and a politician with radical ideas who cared passionately about the welfare of the poor.

Another close friend was the French patriot Emanuele d'Astier de la Vigerie, known simply as Mani d'Astier. He came from an aristocratic French family; but after the fall of France he was so disillusioned with the class from which he sprang that he became a communist. When Hitler's attack on the Soviet Union in June 1941 brought the communist party into the Resistance, the 'Red Baron' (as he became known) was one of its most important figures. Having disguised himself by growing a beard, he wandered freely through France recruiting and organising; and then crossed by submarine to England, where he joined de Gaulle's government-in-exile.

At that time, Jane had been designing costumes for a theatrical agency in Savile Row; and when Mani d'Astier fell in love with Luba Bergery, sister of the proprietress, my mother met him, and was immensely struck by his charm, his strength of character, and his political principles. So in the summer of 1944 she told Howard that he must be approved by Mani before she would agree to get married.

She had already introduced him to her parents, who were far from impressed. Ailsa wanted her daughters to marry into society, not into the ranks; as devout members of the Church of England, neither she nor

Reginald were keen on their daughter marrying an atheist Jew; and it was quite evident that my father was not in the best of health.

Nye Bevan solved the first of these problems by taking Howard to see an eminent specialist who immediately spotted the tuberculosis, and had him invalided out of the army a second time. No longer a humble private, Howard treated Reginald to an excellent dinner, and formally asked for Jane's hand in marriage. Apparently, my grandfather consented by examining his glass of wine very carefully, sniffing it thoughtfully, and then saying with great satisfaction: 'A jolly good year for claret!'

All that remained was for my father (who had virtually no French), to meet Mani d'Astier (who spoke very little English.) Fortunately for Howard, they communicated so well over a game of chess and a bottle of whisky, that they became firm friends. Soon afterwards, Jane agreed to a wedding-date; and she and Howard were married in London at Caxton Hall Registry Office on 26 October 1944.

The wedding-photos tell their own story: my mother looks radiant; she holds Howard's arm lovingly and protectively, and in spite of her black war-time clothing manages to be a beautiful pre-Raphaelite bride with a veil in her hair, and a mass of orchids at her breast. My father, though he is smiling, appears strained and ill, and leans upon a walking-stick, seeming much older than his thirty years. One set of grandparents, deprived of their kosher wedding ceremony, look slightly bemused; while Reginald looks miserable; and Ailsa, whose dreams of a society wedding at St. Margaret's have finally been shattered, looks furiously angry. Perhaps they all cheered up at the wedding luncheon at Claridge's. After which my parents retired to their suite in the same hotel, where my father drank so much that his bill for spirits and liqueurs came to three times the cost of their rooms.

※

With the end of the war in sight, property was already booming, and my father was once again out in the market-place, where his touch continued to be golden. Before long, he and Jane had acquired not only a house in Queen's Gate; but also a Buckinghamshire country retreat at Bedlow

Ridge in the Chilterns, where on 11 March 1946, Jane gave birth to my brother Nigel.

My mother found this experience so shattering that she determined to have no more children. Instead, she dedicated herself to her art and her socialist principles, and she began to hate it when my capitalist father showered her with expensive presents from Cartier's. Not surprisingly, their paths began to diverge, although one thing they still had in common was that they admired Nye Bevan: Howard almost to the point of idolatry. His eyes would light up whenever Nye came into the room, and he began showering him with money. Thanks to Nye, their home was always full of left-wing politicians (some from as far afield as Russia); and my father became a close friend of Michael Foot, poured a great deal of money into the left-wing magazine *Tribune*, and also propped up *Liberation*, the neo-communist journal owned by Mani d'Astier, who would rarely leave my father's office empty-handed.

Not that his admiration for socialist politicians meant that Howard had softened in his business dealings. To his associates, he seemed to be constantly on the move, always pacing up and down, and smoking as he paced: putting one cigarette down, lighting another and putting that down, until there were lit cigarettes all around the room. And, as Reg Davis-Poynter recalls:

> The brain was working. Howard had an extraordinary memory, and if you walked with him round the whole of the Oxford Street area, taking Oxford Circus as its hub, he would know the details of the lease of every building that mattered: who had it, when it was due to fall in, and what it was worth. He also had immense charm and flair; and he was tremendously quick with figures, which he seemed to juggle in his head without ever needing a pencil and paper.

However, my mother increasingly disapproved of her husband's property business; and her particular bête noire was Arthur Wallace, a large man who had come through the war with a decoration, and was as tough as hell. He was my uncle Basil's man rather than my father's; but Jane knew that both brothers used him when necessary as their hatchet-man.

By the spring of 1951, when Nigel was four years old, Jane had become so emotionally detached from Howard that she welcomed a new admirer named Jasper into her circle. My father countered by taking her for a long holiday to Deauville; where he not only kept her away from Jasper, but got her pregnant. This made Jane so deeply depressed that Nye and Jennie (who couldn't have children of their own), offered to adopt. She accepted; and at four o'clock on the afternoon of 22 June 1951, when I was born by caesarian section, she was more than ready to hand me over. Fortunately, my father decided that he wanted to keep me: so that was that. But my mother wasn't pleased.

Perhaps I was aware of these tensions, for I seem to have cried a great deal as a child. The week after I was born, Howard swept Jane off to Deauville for another long holiday, leaving me with a nanny who gave me brandy and milk to stop me crying at night. And later, at my christening (where my godparents included Luba Bergery's son Jean Francois; and Geoffrey Bing, a Labour politician chosen out of the congregation more or less at random when Nye Bevan didn't turn up in time), I cried so much that the Vicar splashed the holy water over me as quickly as he could. Then he sent me out of the church in the arms of my godmother Jennie Lee so that he could continue with the service in peace.

CHAPTER TWO

Bowing to the Indian

In the spring of 1956, when I was four years old, we moved to 'Chuffs' in the village of Holyport, not far from Maidenhead. It was a twenty-five-room Georgian mansion, most of whose enormous, well-proportioned rooms, my mother had filled with Regency and Chippendale furniture: delicate, soft, feminine pieces with no hint of harshness about them. The only really masculine room was my father's Library, full of large solid furniture, including a bookcase on top of which stood a plastic Indian who was so magical that Daddy and I had to bow to him whenever we went in. Outside, there were wonderful gardens and enormous stables in which I could play all day long and, when we first moved there, I felt safe and secure.

I was certainly by myself a great deal: my father went up to London to work every day; Nigel was already away at boarding-school; and I didn't see much of my mother, who always seemed to be painting in her studio at the bottom of the garden. They were curious pictures: one of them is of two rather menacing hospital nurses; another shows me coming down the main staircase clutching my brother's teddy-bear; and, far from being cheerful, the atmosphere is sinister. She seems to be not only painting me, but painting some great gulf between the two of us, an emotional gulf that she knew she would never be able to cross.

At the time, I knew that both my parents were somewhere in the background, and I had a nanny called Pauline whom I adored, a generous woman who gave me physical warmth and endless patience. When Pauline was busy, I slipped out of the house into the garden, and then (if the coast was clear) ran across the front lawn to an old oak tree. Quickly opening a door in the side of the tree, I flung myself into the hollow interior. This was my secret hide-away, my own little house; I kept many of my toys there and, when I was bored with them, I climbed up a ladder into the leafy branches, and spied on everyone.

If I saw Parsons, the gardener, pushing his wheel-barrow across a corner of the lawn, weighed down with plants for spring bedding-out, or dead leaves for aromatic autumn bonfires, I would rush down to help him. But if ever I caught a glimpse of Rita and Jorge (the cook and butler, a Portuguese couple who had come with the house), I lay flat against my branch in panic. I wasn't bothered by Jorge; but I feared that Rita was a witch, because she spoke broken English, and had terrifyingly black hair.

Something else which frightened me was *Alice in Wonderland*, which Pauline insisted on reading to me last thing at night. I liked Alice meeting the White Rabbit, and falling down that long tunnel into the ground; but when she met all those strange creatures it scared me; and after she had read the chapter in which the Queen of Hearts was shouting 'Off with her head!' I had such a dreadful nightmare that I woke up and was literally sick with fear.

I loved the weekends, when my father made a point of spending a great deal of time with me, even when people were staying. Bowing to the Indian was just one of our many private games; another was pretending to be at Rose School, where he was the only teacher, and I was the only pupil: so when we went shopping on Saturday mornings to buy prizes for prize-giving day, it was obvious who was going to be the winner.

Weekends were even better when Aunty Jennie and Uncle Nye were visiting. Jennie, with her grey-white hair, and her bright clashing colours (often pinks and turquoises) was always wanting to be kissed; and Uncle Nye, with his generally unkempt appearance, was just the same. He liked me to sit on his lap while he told stories to me, and he seemed to have endless time for games. They were both physically warm and loving, quite unlike my parents. And if Nigel was at home, although he was five years older than me, and usually very quiet, he was always kind and affectionate and would help me to make clay and plaster animals out in the barns.

Occasionally, Pauline was meant to have a weekend off; but in practice she always took me with her to stay with her family in their small, crowded home; and they were all so welcoming that visiting them became one of my greatest treats. Pauline's father, whom I called Uncle Albert, was especially friendly. He was a bookmaker, and on Saturday evenings he allowed me to help him counting out all the money he had taken, so I thought he was unbelievably rich. I also began to think that it would be the best thing in the world to live in a small house, with lots of other people around. So, one day, when my father was driving Nigel and me to London, I saw a row of terraced houses in Hounslow, and decided that I wanted to live in the one with a bright purple front door. My father seemed amused by this; and on subsequent journeys, whenever we passed by, he promised that one day he would buy it for me.

Our London outings involved either endless presents – we once spent a whole afternoon in Hamley's toy shop – or practical jokes which amused Nigel and my father, but which were sometimes unintentionally cruel. One day, for example, we were taken to the room in the British Museum where the Egyptian Mummies were kept. 'We must hurry,' said my father, 'They'll be closing soon. You've just got time to have a good look at that mask over there: do you see it, all gold and jewels?' I walked forward rather nervously; and then turned to find that the door had clanged shut behind me, and I was alone with the sinister Mummies all around. And then the lights went out. I was just about to scream when the door re-opened, and my father and Nigel re-appeared with broad grins on their faces. And then my father pointed to one of the Mummies and said casually: 'You know of course that it's your mother underneath this one!'

I didn't find that very funny, either. By this time, I already had ambivalent feelings about my mother. In some ways I was fond of her; and I recognised how beautiful she was. Very occasionally she would let me have a bath with her, and touch her breasts, a sensation which I found deeply thrilling. And whenever I knew that she was going out for the evening, I would beg her: 'Please, please come to my bedroom before you go out, and let me see you!' But she was usually so remote, that I had begun to fantasize that she was not my mother at all: my natural mother, I told myself, was a Queen; and therefore I was really a Princess.

Princess or not, when my schooling began, my mother insisted on my being sent to the village primary school. It was only a short distance from Chuffs, and my father used to drive me there every morning, usually seeing if he could do so without putting his hands on the steering-wheel. I liked to arrive as early as possible, so that I could be first into the classroom. This wasn't because I enjoyed being in that large, dismal room, which smelt of disinfectant and dirty bodies, but because I had a passion for blank sheets of paper and, since I knew how to open the classroom cupboard, I could steal unused exercise books without anyone noticing.

※

Chuffs was at its most perfect at Christmas-time. Uncle Nye and Aunty Jennie would come down, and the most distant and deserted rooms were suddenly filled with hosts of relatives. I enjoyed sitting on one of the Regency sofas in the long drawing-room, playing cards with my snobbish Granny Lane, who looked round from time to time at her palatial surroundings with evident satisfaction; or I would put on a coat and go out into the garden for a walk with my deaf Grandpa Samuel, who had a jolly, humorous face, and was always telling jokes.

On Christmas Eve 1956 we all gathered in the drawing-room by a roaring fire; and before I went to bed Grandpa Samuel rang for Jorge, who came in with a cold cup of cocoa with the milky skin on top. 'That's for Father Christmas!' Grandpa said with a chuckle, putting it down in the fire-place; and sure enough, by next morning the cocoa had disappeared.

After going to church we enjoyed a traditional Christmas lunch, and I was allowed to sit next to my father and drink Lucozade, which I liked because it was exactly the same colour as the neat whisky that Daddy sipped from morning to night. In the evening we all took part in a Christmas pantomime at one end of the library. This year, I was the 'Sleeping Beauty,' but we never reached the scene where I was due to be woken up. Uncle Nye was the real star: and after my mother had dressed him up as the Wicked Witch, he was so sinister, and gave such horrid cackles, that he almost frightened me to death, and the pantomime had to be stopped.

※

The following summer, soon after my sixth birthday, Nye and Jennie joined us for a month in an enormous villa in the south of France. It was Uncle Nye, helped by Pauline, who usually seemed to be in charge of us when we went to the sea; and luckily, he didn't seem to mind when I unkindly nicknamed him 'Mr. Rude Man' after catching him changing behind a rock.

The sea turned out to be safer than the swimming-pool which came with the villa. One afternoon, on seeing Nigel jump in, I decided to follow him. He had just learned to swim, but I hadn't, and I was way out of my depth. Soon after the first shock of impact, the waters closed over my head. Slowly I sank to the bottom. I held my breath; but soon my chest was becoming tight, and with both hands I began tugging at my hair, hoping that I could somehow pull myself to the surface. Suddenly there was a massive disturbance in the water above me, with pink legs and thighs at the epicentre, and skirts billowing out in all directions. Then I could hold my breath no longer, my lungs began filling with water, and everything went black. When I came to, I was lying face down on the side of the pool, coughing and retching as Uncle Nye pumped the water out of me. Pauline, who had rescued me, was kneeling close by, wringing out her dress and sobbing with relief.

There wasn't much time for anyone to worry about my near-drowning. My mother, who was on the verge of another breakdown, had taken to disappearing with Jennie for hours on end; and my father's tuberculosis had flared up. Once he began coughing blood into his handkerchief, we all flew home. When we arrived at London Airport there was an ambulance waiting for him; but since my mother had been behaving quite madly on the plane, it was used for her instead. Immediately afterwards, my father had himself taken to St John & St Elizabeth Hospital in St. John's Wood. This was his usual refuge, run by an order of nuns called the Sisters of Mercy.

※

My father returned home before my mother, who disappeared for several months. Whenever I asked about her, I was told that she was very tired, but would return when she had enjoyed a long rest. However, Pauline looked after me as kindly as ever and for a while life went on much as normal.

Then my mother returned; and everything began to change for the worse. She was no longer distant and pre-occupied, which I was used to, but angry and bitter; and I didn't understand why. Was it my fault somehow? And what was going wrong between my parents? Suddenly I could hear them shouting at each other all night long.

For a while I clung to Pauline for comfort; and then, without any explanation, Pauline disappeared and (despite her witch-like hair) I began spending more and more time in the kitchens with Rita. But after each day came another night, and my bedroom was right next to that of my parents, and I could hear them endlessly fighting. I buried my head in my pillow, and tried not to listen; but sometimes I couldn't help it.

First my father's voice, angry and yet also frightened: 'I'm sick of hearing about Jasper: can't you forget him just for one moment?'

Then confusion: both shouting angrily at each other.

Then my mother's voice, unusually shrill: 'Yes, that's what you'd like to do: send me back to that place. Make them give me more electric shocks. I shall never forgive you, never.' And then a storm of weeping, before the shouting began again.

I felt utterly confused, and it made me frightened of them both. Each day, when I awoke, I knew that I must pretend to have heard nothing; otherwise from behind their cheerful day-time faces, their night-time selves might emerge, snarling and screaming at me, and that would be the end of everything. And it would all be my fault.

I felt safer when there were guests in the house. Cocktail parties and dinner parties went on, and I would kneel on the landing, looking down through the bannisters to watch the guests arrive. Sometimes I was even produced, washed and brushed, to say 'hello' to everyone; and one morning my father told me that an extremely fat man was coming to lunch. When he arrived an hour late (I nicknamed him 'Mr. Late Man'), he turned out to be Arnold Goodman, my father's legal adviser. He was certainly very large and rather ugly, which I found alarming at first. But he was also very relaxed.

He smiled warmly at both my parents like an old friend; and I noticed that when he looked at my mother there was a hint of longing in his eyes, like a child looking at a wonderful gift which he knew could never be his.

At nights the shouting continued. I became so unhappy that I grew bad-tempered, and sometime in the spring of 1958 I even picked a quarrel with my only school-friend. That was our daily woman's daughter, who used to come to Chuffs and play with me. "We own the village green", I told her one break-time, "and your mother works for my mother, so I'm better than you!"

I was kept away from school after that; and before any new arrangements could be made for my education, my father said that he had something important to tell me, and asked me to come into his study. As usual, we bowed gravely to the Indian on the bookshelves, and then my father sat down in one of his leather armchairs, and I sat facing him, and he told me very gently that he and my mother were going to live in separate houses from now on.

'That means, Nicola, that you'll have two homes instead of one! And do you know what's going to happen to-day? A Maharajah is coming to look at Chuffs. He's a black man, and he's going to arrive on an elephant with another six elephants behind, and lots of servants wearing turbans covered with precious jewels! What do you think of that?'

A few days later, Nigel came home from school. He was even quieter than usual; but the first thing he did when he saw me was to give me a great big hug and whisper in my ear: 'Don't worry, Nicola: everything's going to be all right.'

I didn't see how it could be.

Our father had disappeared to London by now; and one morning, as we were sitting at breakfast, two huge removal vans roared up the drive. 'I've found a cottage for us,' my mother announced brightly. 'It's at Fulking, a lovely village in Sussex. As soon as you've finished your toast, we'll pack up and leave. More tea for anyone?' So later that day, clutching a doll which my father had given me, I was driven away from Chuffs, never to return.

CHAPTER THREE

Downs, Fountain House and Henniker Mews

When we arrived in Fulking, we moved into a very pretty little Georgian cottage, right in the middle of the village, and with fields at the back which led straight up onto the South Downs. It was known as 'Laurel House' when we arrived; but my mother changed it to 'Downs'; partly because of the view at the back, and partly as a grim joke about her black moods. I was hoping that these black moods would disappear, now that she had the house she wanted; but she didn't seem any happier. Mostly she looked at me with glazed, indifferent eyes; and once Nigel had gone back to school for the start of the summer term of 1958, I felt desperately lonely.

I had missed a month or two of schooling by the time my mother found a place for me at Windlesham, a small private school six miles to the south-east on the outskirts of Hove. I was kitted out with a smart new uniform, but my difficulties with reading and writing made school a constant embarrassment. Worse still, Mr. Grimes, the burly garage mechanic who was paid to drive me there and back, kept forgetting to collect me at the end of the school day. Often, feeling furious both with Mr. Grimes and with my mother, I would still be there at six in the evening when the cleaners were leaving. And when someone finally bothered to fetch me, I would return home to find that there was hardly anything to eat.

This was the first time that my mother had ever had to run a house on her own, and she had no idea how to go about it. She didn't mind running up huge bills on account (though it was a black morning when one of them arrived on the door-mat), but she had decided at an early stage that she could only withdraw £5 a week in cash from the bank; so by Wednesday or Thursday her ready money had usually run out; and this helped to make her culinary efforts the most ridiculous part of our life in Fulking.

When Nigel was home for the weekend, there would sometimes be only one trout to be shared between the three of us for a main course, followed by such a small bunch of grapes that we had only six each. How I used to long for Rita's roast potatoes and Yorkshire pudding! The only ordinary dish that Jane knew how to prepare was cauliflower cheese. This was delicious; but for a while we lived chiefly on small amounts of exotic fare which needed no cooking, such as avocado pears, prawns, stilton, asparagus and patê.

It was only when my father came down from London that these problems vanished for a day and a half. Nearly every weekend he and Nigel and I were installed in the Grand Hotel in Brighton, where my father always took the entire top floor, so that we had somewhere to play; and there was the usual flood of presents.

After these luxurious weekends, it was difficult to understand why we had to go back to our little cottage. It upset me that my father would never even step over the threshold, and once I asked: 'Daddy, why can't you and Mummy talk to each other anymore? What's going on?' It seemed so silly and unfair that they should be living apart, making everyone unhappy. But I saw a look of such misery on my father's face that I never asked again. Instead, I took my anger out on my mother, and we had screaming rows which usually ended up with my running upstairs to my bedroom and slamming the door in her face.

On leaving Chuffs, Howard had taken a flat in Mount Street, where he had been drinking heavily, chasing after other women (including the recently widowed actress Phyllis Calvert), and neglecting his business interests.

One evening, when the opportunity arose, he had even knocked off a policeman's helmet with his umbrella. This was something he had always wanted to do, but he was immediately arrested and marched away to the cells of the Central Police Station in Savile Row, where in the early hours of the morning he was visited by Arnold Goodman and by Nye Bevan's doctor, Dan Davies of Wimpole Street. The three of them had soon established (to their own satisfaction) that Howard hadn't been assaulting a police constable at all: far from it, he had been using his umbrella to hail a taxi, when the constable was stupid enough to get in the way!

Once Arnold and Dan had presented the police with this story, and Dan had added that Howard was seriously ill, my father was released into their custody; and Dan sent him straight to a Nursing Home. Not long afterwards, Howard sold his Mount Street flat, moved to a grand apartment in Fountain House on Park Lane in Mayfair, and returned to work.

In the meantime, my seventh birthday came and went; and then it was the summer holidays, and Nigel was with us again. My mother used his presence as an excuse to behave worse than ever. Arnold Goodman had been sending housekeepers down from London to look after us, but none of them lasted long, and often we were sent out on the Downs at eight in the morning (without any food or money), and told not to re-appear until five in the afternoon, in time for a bath. It was lucky that the people in the village shop just down the road took pity on us, and gave us food.

In addition, my mother began disappearing (sometimes just for an afternoon, but sometimes for days at a time), to see her married lover, Jasper. When I finally met him, he turned out to be a healthy, good-looking man in his late forties, with greying hair and piercing blue eyes. Apparently, he ran a printing company, and my mother told me to be grateful when he heaped children's books on me; but I disliked him instinctively, telling myself that the only books I had ever wanted were the ones given to me by my father.

Instead of taking us to the Grand Hotel at weekends, my father could now drive Nigel and me up to Fountain House, where our own beautiful bedrooms were always waiting for us. Mine was the largest, with pretty Regency furniture, and a single bed at one end with a wonderful view over Hyde Park. I'd been allowed to have it painted in pink, just the way I wanted; and once again we were looked after by Rita and Jorge, just as we had been at Chuffs. In addition to his property interests, my father now owned three small publishing companies: Arco, Staples Press, and McGibbon and Kee; and when we were with him, it became one of our favourite outings to spend a morning at McGibbon and Kee folding book covers.

Then it would be back again to 'Downs'; where I suffered an autumn of ill-health, with a bad throat, a bad chest, and then a bout of glandular fever before having my tonsils and adenoids taken out. Having this operation was almost worth it, because when I came round from the anaesthetic in the private nursing home to which I had been taken, there sitting on the edge of my bed was my father, the one person whom I loved without any reservation, presiding over a huge pile of comics, drawing books, coloured chalks, games, and boxes and boxes of wonderful toys from Hamleys. As always, when I really needed him, he was there for me.

By this time, life in Fulking was improving a little. My mother had made some friends called the Durrants, who lived just across the road. They not only taught her elementary cookery (such as how to make shepherd's pie); but they also brought her into their business, which was converting cottages: something for which my mother had a natural design flair.

Another new friend was Mr. Cornish, the vicar. A slightly eccentric figure, who wobbled uncertainly about the village on an old and battered bicycle, he was one of the kindest and friendliest people I have ever met. I adored him so much that I happily went to Sunday School each week, and at Christmas I even read a passage from the Bible in Church. He came to visit my mother once a week; but somehow he always arrived just when she had washed her hair, and was looking particularly attractive. This had a powerful effect on him, and I noticed that by the time he left he was often looking a little dazed, and once I even heard him muttering that his faith had been severely tested.

By the spring of 1959 the divorce between Jane and Howard had gone through, with unexpected results for them both. Now that Jane was officially a free woman, Jasper, whom she had hoped to marry in due course, began keeping his distance. At the same time, my father's feelings for Phyllis Calvert cooled, and he somehow got it into his head that he and my mother were courting again. Reg remembers a drinks party in Dan Davies's huge sitting room in Wimpole Street, where Howard was pacing up and down, talking to Michael Foot, Nye, and Jennie, and telling them:

> how he was going to remarry your mother. And it went on and on. Everyone was bored to tears. I think Michael finally said something like: 'The trouble, Howard, is that you've told everybody except Jane that you're going to remarry her!' And Nye added: 'The real trouble, Howard, is that your divorce has never been consummated!'

And then my mother, who by this time was half-mad with worry over Jasper's apparent desertion, had a dreadful accident.

I was sitting by the fireplace in Downs when it happened: there was a scream from the back of the house, followed by a terrible thump; and then silence. I stepped anxiously into the narrow corridor, and saw at once that my mother was lying at the foot of the stairs. For a few moments she lay quite still and I thought that she was dead. Then she began to moan, and I rushed through the front-door and over the road to the Durrants to fetch help.

The next few days passed in a blur. I stayed with the Durrants, who told me that my mother had nearly broken her back, but she would be all right. Then my father turned up; and suddenly the news was that my parents had been reconciled.

To begin with, this was just as confusing as their divorce. Howard was certainly financially more secure and more respectable than ever. 1959 was the year when he and Basil, though technically still estate agents, decided to amalgamate their twenty to thirty separate property companies, and the result of the merger was successfully floated on the Stock Exchange as Great Portland Estates. My father had dreamed up this imposing title, ensured a successful launch by securing guarantees from his cousin

Harold Samuel of Land Securities; and he was now one of the twenty or thirty richest men in Britain, continued to finance left-wing causes, and had become part-owner of the *New Statesman*.

At any rate, when the Easter holidays began, Nigel and I found ourselves living with both our parents in Fountain House. Shortly afterwards Jane and Howard re-married in a London Registry Office; after which the four of us set off together for my parents' second honeymoon in an Italian villa near La Spezia; and the months during which they had lived apart would never be mentioned again.

※

The first Sunday morning back in England found us at 'Downs', which had been kept on (at my mother's insistence) as a week-end cottage. Nigel and I were downstairs early, and decided to cook breakfast for our parents. First Nigel lit the fire; then I found two eggs which he dropped into a pan of boiling water, and he saw to the toast. By the time the pan had almost burned dry, the eggs were as solid as rock, and the air was full of fumes from our first attempts at toast, the kitchen looked as though it had been hit by a bomb. But I laid up a tray, and we put the eggs in egg-cups, spread butter on the burnt toast, and carried it upstairs very proudly. My mother turned away when we came into the room, and stared out of the window towards the Downs; but my father thanked us just as warmly as he normally thanked Rita for his usual whisky, raw eggs, and kidneys on toast.

※

Other weekends were spent with Nye and Jennie on their farm in Cheshire. Once Nigel went on a few days ahead of us. When we arrived, I went to look for him, and found him in the farmyard, wearing wellington boots, and turning over some evil-smelling silage with a two-pronged fork. In the background, pigs were squealing, and a spaniel was running up and down, barking fiercely. 'I'm going to become a farmer,' he told me proudly through all this noise. 'Uncle Nye's training me – and paying me proper wages.

Look at this!' He fished in his pocket, and then held out a grubby hand with a pound note and a handful of sixpences and half-crowns.

'Perhaps you'll farm together!' said Nye, who had joined us. 'And to start you off, Nicola, I'm giving you a litter of pigs. Come here, girl, and have a look at them!' I was only lured away from the little pink pigs, so tiny against their mother's enormous bulk, by a smell of baking from the kitchen, where Nye and Jennie kept a warm-hearted Scottish lady who always seemed to be making cakes.

※

That summer there was another foreign excursion, this time to my father's favourite resort Deauville, where we stayed at the Normandy Hotel. My father spent a great deal of time with Nigel and me, encouraging us to run riot in the front lobby of the hotel; taking us over to Trouville to go to the races or play on the slot machines; and (best of all) he granted my dearest wish, and paid for me to have riding-lessons.

The first time I climbed up on a pony I was too excited to be scared. There were no reins to begin with: the assistant placed my hands firmly on the pommel of the saddle. And then the pony was urged round the ring by an excitable Frenchman with a lunging-rein and whip, who stood in the middle crying out instructions to us: 'Prenez garde, Mamselle – 'old tight wiz your knees! Assez juste.' With three lessons a day, I was soon promoted to riding with reins; and within a few weeks I could walk, trot and canter.

My father, having won a good deal of money early on in the holiday, had decided not to go home until he had gambled away his winnings, and could leave with exactly the same amount of money that he had when we arrived. This was difficult, since the more he gambled (either in the casino or at the races) the more he won! The free flowers and fruit from the hotel management grew more and more splendid as our bill grew higher and higher; and our holiday only came to an end when my father became ill and needed another spell in the St John and St. Elizabeth Hospital.

※

I had begun to realize that although my parents were back together again, there were differences from the old days at Chuffs. In particular, my mother seemed far more in control. She talked of opening an antique shop; and when, following her successful work with the Durrants, she asked my father to buy her some properties which she could convert, he immediately bought her the whole of Henniker Mews on the western edge of Chelsea.

CHAPTER FOUR

Death Comes Calling

When in the autumn of 1959 my schooling began again, my mother sent me to Queen's Gate, her old school; and not long afterwards, at her insistence, we moved from Fountain House to 72 Elm Park Road, from where the school was within walking distance. Rita was told to accompany me to school; but now that I was eight years old, I felt that it was babyish to have a nanny: so I insisted on her walking a long way behind.

Despite this show of independence, I was very scared on my first day at Queen's Gate; and it was terrible when I discovered that I was the only one of my class who still couldn't read properly. My teachers assumed that I was dim – no-one had heard of dyslexia in those days – and after a while I decided that if I was destined to be a failure, then I might as well give up work altogether, and enjoy myself.

This made me attractive to some people, including Annie Griffiths, a clever, pretty, kind, sensible girl who was a good listener, and always seemed to be smiling. Her mother had been at Queen's Gate with mine; but she seemed to like me for myself; and almost as soon as I met her (in her usual jersey and tartan skirt, with a neat headband to keep her hair in place) I knew that she was going to be my best friend. Sometimes she reminds me that I rapidly become known as:

the naughtiest girl in the school. You'd never do any prep or anything like that. And you would never learn your tables, ever! You never did what you were supposed to do, but crossed all the barriers and broke all the rules. I was terribly keen to be top, and be the highest up the chart on reading books. You couldn't have given a stuff!

Annie lived only just round the corner in Chelsea Park Gardens; and the first time I stepped through her front-door, I found myself in a world where children were protected and well-organised, an uncomplicated world of birthday-parties, happy laughter, and smiling parents; a world in which I felt that nothing could go wrong. I might have everything a spoilt child could want; but she had all the things she really needed, and that makes a big difference.

By the time of my ninth birthday, in the summer of 1960, Annie Griffiths and I were almost inseparable. My mother was still painting, and her pictures were still being exhibited, and Annie and I would sneak up to her studio to look at them when she wasn't there. We thought they were weird, and getting weirder: so many unhappy self-portraits, with yellow-grey or green and turquoise sky-scapes, and green and turquoise bottles disappearing into the distance as far as the eye could see. 'You see those bottles?' I explained to Annie one day, 'She says they're her nurses!' Then we found the paint-tubes, squeezed out some paint, and began making what we thought were improvements: lots more yellow and grey in the background, lots more green round the edges. Curiously we were never found out.

The first time that Annie was invited to spend a long week-end with us, we took her down to Fulking. My father had never liked 'Downs', and as we were setting out in the Bentley, he announced crossly: 'I'm sorry, Nicola, but we've got to go for another camping weekend with your mother in Sussex!' When we reached Fulking, he convinced Annie that 'Downs' was where our butler lived. At least when we were there he didn't have to drive anywhere for a drink, as 'The Shepherd and Dog' was practically on our door-step. He took me there every lunch-time; and I understood at once why he liked going. Propping up the bar among a crowd of cheerful regulars, was someone whom I'd seen on television:

'Professor' Jimmy Edwards, the comedian with the walrus moustache, busy cracking jokes in his gruff voice, while a pint of bitter spilled down his tweed jacket.

Occasionally, Annie and I lured my father away from the pub, and persuaded him to come with us for a walk over the Downs; and one morning, when Annie was still asleep, I set out on my own. I walked rather slowly through the back-garden, out of the gate and round the edge of the large field. Then, just as I was climbing up the track which led through some trees onto the Downs, I almost stumbled over a dead sheep.

I stared at it for a long time, utterly fascinated. It was alone, like me, and it must have died in agony. Its throat had been torn out by a dog; and now it was lying on its back with its legs in the air. The blood had dried, and I could smell that it was already starting to rot. However, it was free of pain, and I had this revelation: death brings freedom. I found this thrilling; but when I made Annie have a look, all she saw were the rotting remains; and until the corpse had been cleared away, I had to lead her past it with her eyes closed.

※

Most of the time I remained the apple of my father's eye: he promised to buy me strings of emeralds; he promised to buy me the whole of Pelham Crescent; he promised that he would always take care of me. Only once was he angry with me, and I can still hear him, after a weekend with Annie at Downs, asking me:

"Nicola, is it true that you've been letting Annie do all your homework for you?" When I didn't answer, because it was true, I saw a look of fear and unhappiness on his face: the same look he sometimes gave my mother. "Do you realise how stupid that is?" he went on, raising his voice. "Stupid and dishonest! You silly girl!' And then he gave me a half-hearted kind of smack. There was no physical pain; but it was the only time he had ever struck me, and I felt badly hurt.

※

Nye Bevan went into hospital just after Christmas 1959 to undergo surgery for an ulcer, and Jennie Lee came to stay with us at Elm Park Road. My father was also unwell; and when I visited his bedroom in the early evening, I would find him lying in bed watching the news, with Jennie sitting in a chair close by. I couldn't understand why evening after evening there would be news bulletins about what Nye had eaten for dinner: 'Wonderful, Auntie Jennie!' I would exclaim: 'They've just said that Uncle Nye has had some consommé for dinner!'

Tragically, it had been discovered that Nye's problem was not an ulcer, but an advanced case of stomach cancer. In February he returned home, where he died in his sleep on 6 July 1960, just a few weeks after my ninth birthday. When my mother tried to explain what had happened, I refused to believe her, telling myself that Uncle Nye wasn't really dead, but had gone to some distant country from which he would in due course return. My mother herself seemed quite calm, though she had lost one of her closest friends and she was soon sunk in depression.

But it was my father who was worst hit. He was in his office when he heard the news. Immediately, he rushed round the corner to the Spanish restaurant where Reg Davis-Poynter and some other colleagues were having lunch, collapsed into a chair, and sobbed like a broken man. And then a few days later, perhaps in a kind of tribute to the socialist principles of his dead friend, when he saw that his usual news vendor was looking very miserable and cold as the rain poured down, he took off his coat and gave it to him. He himself was then soaked to the skin, with the result that he caught pneumonia, his TB flared up, and he almost died.

For the next few months my father was so ill that he was more or less confined to his bedroom, and there were endless nurses in the house, quite apart from regular visits from Dr. Rossdale (our family doctor), Dan Davies of Wimpole Street and my mother's psychiatrist Michael Davys. As for me: I spent most of my time in the Elm Park Road basement with Rita.

When my father was well enough, he managed to come downstairs for a dinner-party, and as a special treat I was allowed to sit next to him and watch light from the crystal chandeliers being reflected in fine silver on the green Connemara marble-topped table. But it was much longer before he was fit enough to return to his office. He was usually to be found in his bedroom, which was next to mine; and we sent messages to each other in code, by knocking on the wall between us. Because I wanted to be close to my father, I spent as much time as possible in my room, often having avoided school with some fictitious ailment or other.

I suppose that by this time I had come to look on Daddy as my personal property, so it made me jealous when one night at about ten o'clock I heard him going upstairs to Nigel's bedroom on the top floor. Nigel told me in the morning that he had taken a full bottle of whisky with him, and they'd played chess and drunk the night away. After that I often heard my father making his way upstairs; and sometimes I would still be lying miserably awake when he returned to his room hours later.

Still worse, a month or so after Christmas I learned that Nigel was going to Switzerland for a skiing holiday and I was to be left behind. 'Never mind, Nicola' my father told me. 'There's always next year. This time Nigel's old enough to ski, and you're not.' I was given a Cartier watch and some books with blank pages as consolation prizes; and then he and Nigel went off to St. Moritz.

By now we had given up our cottage in Fulking, and replaced it with Butterstocks, a substantial country house a few miles south of Horsham. It was a pretty house: half of it was Georgian or later, but the other half was sixteenth century; and my room was in the old part, and covered in beams. It had been decorated as I asked, with flowered wallpaper, a blue carpet, chintz curtains and a pretty chintz bed-cover; and the room was full of all the dolls my father had given me.

※

Then came a Sunday morning in May that I shall never forget. It was the worst morning of my life and would shape everything that was to happen to me for the rest of my days. My father was away on business, Nigel was at his boarding school, and my mother and I had gone down to Butterstocks for the weekend. This was always an adventure, especially if my mother was driving in her blue Hillman Imp, since she had never had to pass a test and her driving was erratic to say the least.

I had been particularly excited about going to Butterstocks on this occasion, because my father had promised me a pony for my tenth birthday. It was due to arrive very soon, so I was dying to get the stable cleaned out, and everything prepared. But when I came downstairs on the morning of Sunday 7 May 1961, I was surprised to find that the whole house was heaving with people. I assumed that my mother must have had a party the night before, because I could see so many family friends. There for example was Jennie Lee, standing at the foot of the stairs with my mother's friends the artist Roland Penrose and his photographer wife Lee Miller, and all three of them were swigging large glasses of gin. No-one talked to me, which seemed odd; but I was glad to see so many people apparently having fun – drinking at eight in the morning!

Going outside, I continued cleaning the stable; and at some stage I went to the kitchen for some breakfast. Still, no-one explained to me what was going on. Then at around 9.30 in the morning, Dr. Rossdale arrived and came out to the stable to see me.

I was thrilled, because he had become a close family friend, and I adored him. Recently I had often spent an afternoon riding with his elder daughter Sandra, and it was fun to show him the stable and all my preparations. Then he asked whether we could go for a walk together, and I suggested: 'Let's go and see all the mares from the Stud Farm next door: they're due to foal very soon!'

We walked down the road and stopped by the gate to the field with all the mares, and were feeding them carrots, when Dr. Rossdale said he had to tell me something. He was using the kind of voice which people used when they told me that my mother was ill; but I knew that she was all right, and suddenly I became very frightened.

'There is something wrong with Daddy, isn't there?' I asked. 'He is very ill again, isn't he?'

And Dr. Rossdale replied: 'Yes, I don't know how to say this.' There was a pause, and then he spoke very simply and quietly. 'I'm afraid he is dead.'

I felt deathly cold. I couldn't react. I don't even remember crying. It was like hearing of Uncle Nye's death, but far, far worse. I simply couldn't imagine life without my beloved Daddy. I couldn't think what to say, so

I asked, in a voice which didn't seem to be mine at all, would I be able to have time off school? And would Nigel be allowed to come home?

Poor Dr. Rossdale didn't know what to say either. He managed to lose his pen in the grass; and then for some obscure reason he felt that it might cheer me up if he lent me his old-fashioned pocket-watch, which he encouraged me to hold up to my ear so that I could hear it ticking. Tick, tick, tick. For the rest of my life there would be something terrible to me about the sound of a ticking watch. Tick, Daddy is dead. Tick, I shall never see him again. Tick, how on earth will we manage? And then we walked home.

CHAPTER FIVE
Drawn Curtains

B y the time we returned to Butterstocks, Arnold Goodman had arrived, and was excelling himself with the photographers and journalists. I looked round for Auntie Jennie, but she had left: I was told that she had been sent by car all the way to Nottingham to pick up Nigel from Trent College. I found that I desperately wanted to see my mother, but it wasn't allowed. Looking up at the windows of her bedroom, I had noticed that her curtains were drawn. They would stay drawn for many days to come.

*

During the months immediately before my father's death, his health had improved to the point where he was planning the take-over of Associated Book Publishers. One of the companies in the group, Eyre and Spottiswoode, were the Queen's Printers, and also published the Bible; and he joked that the takeover appealed to him because what could be better than a Socialist Jew becoming the Queen's Printer and the Publisher of the Bible?

At the same time, he was arranging to publish the autobiography of Archbishop Makarios, who since the previous year had been the first President of a newly-independent Cyprus. Unusually for him, when my father decided to go out to Cyprus to finalise the arrangements in person, he arranged to travel alone.

First he flew to Athens, where he was to rest for twenty-four hours before continuing to Cyprus. And then he went swimming in the sea, and the story is that he must have had a heart-attack soon after entering the water. But there was never an autopsy; and they only discovered his body when the tide came in, and he was found floating face-down in nine inches of water.

My father had been very excited about meeting Makarios, which in some people's eyes rules out suicide. But I'm not so sure. He knew that my mother was once again seeing Jasper, and her open infidelity must have been terribly painful for him. He had tried to take a 'modern' view, and had even invited Jasper and his wife over to Butterstocks. But I think it quite possible that he was overtaken by a fit of despair, and swam out to sea intending never to return.

※

Nigel's arrival on Sunday afternoon was a great comfort to me. That night, he and I were allowed to share the spare room, which had white wallpaper covered with bunches of violets. Nigel was devastated. Instead of finding out what had happened from Auntie Jennie, or even from his Headmaster, some boy at his school had shown him a newspaper that morning, and asked him if the Howard Samuel who had drowned was his father.

But Nigel never cried in my presence: he just looked after me as best he could. At one point he put his arm round me, and said: 'Daddy often told me that he wasn't going to live for very long. But he said that we mustn't worry, as none of us will ever have to work. Do you realise that, Nicola? He's made enough money to take care of us for the rest of our lives.'

'I expect he gave me my pony because he knew that he was going to die,' I replied. 'But then…' I fell silent.

'What is it?'

Such terrible thoughts about death and betrayal were racing through my head that I couldn't bring myself to speak.

In the meantime, everyone was very good to me. On Monday, Phil, my Dartmoor pony, was delivered; and that same day Granny Lane went out and bought me all my favourite comics, like *June* and *Princess*. It was a little like Christmas, but without any reason to celebrate.

It would be several days before I was allowed to visit my mother. I opened the door of her room, and found that it was in semi-darkness, with all the curtains closed. As soon as I went in, I was hit by that awful, slightly unwashed smell of a sick-room. My mother was lying in bed, staring up at the ceiling. I walked over, and kissed her on the forehead. She glanced in my direction, but didn't seem to see me, said nothing, and looked away. And then, after what seemed like only a few seconds, the housekeeper propelled me out again, with her hand between my shoulder-blades.

I had yearned so much to feel my mother's love and re-assurance, but after a second visit much like the first, it was obvious that she had none to give me. She was simply overwhelmed and unable to cope, and I stopped wanting to see her.

We stayed in Sussex for another ten days, during which time my mother never left her room. She had a number of visitors, including Reg Davis-Poynter, who found her 'very depressed and hopelessly confused.' Not that she was lying there altogether incapable: it didn't take her long to sell the Bentley, sack the chauffeur, and give away all my father's furniture.

In order to protect me, I wasn't even told about the cremation until later on, when Nigel informed me that he was now the head of the family, that at the cremation he had stood beside Uncle Basil, and that no women had been present apart from Jennie Lee. Afterwards, there had been a discussion in Arnold Goodman's office about what to do with my father's ashes, and according to Reg, Arnold's first rather grim suggestion was that they were scattered in the bar of the Savoy Grill, because that was the only place he had ever ever seen Howard truly at rest. In practice, they were scattered on Hampstead Heath; and later there was a Memorial Service at Langham Place, at which many of his old friends were present, including Michael Foot, Jennie Lee and Michael Davys.

※

When we returned to London, Nigel went straight on to Trent College in Nottingham. He had been a problem pupil from the time he went there; but the story is that before my father died, he had given the school a great deal of money, possibly to build a Library: so Nigel's position there was absolutely secure.

As for me, I had Rita to care for me and once again to walk behind me each day on my way to Queen's Gate. The whole school had been told about my father's death, and people were very kind to me for the rest of the term. I didn't have to do any work; and I spent a great deal of time with Annie and her family in Chelsea Park Gardens, often staying there overnight. Sometimes I also stayed at Dr. Rossdale's house in Kensington, and walked to Queen's Gate with Sandra.

Another reason why so little was expected of me, was that some months before my father's death, disenchanted with my progress at Queen's Gate. he had arranged for me to leave it at the end of the summer term and go to boarding school. This was ostensibly to make life easier for my mother; though I had been so lazy that the school authorities might well have hinted that they could happily cope without my presence.

※

When the summer holidays came, we spent most of it at Butterstocks, where we were joined by a jolly Irish girl called Lisa, whose job was partly to look after Mother and take her out in the car, partly to cook, and partly to keep Nigel and me amused. We certainly needed to be kept cheerful, because my mother was behaving very erratically, and we never knew from one day to the next whether she'd be spending any time with us or not.

Sometimes she seemed to be trying to give us a normal family life, and would even play cards or Monopoly; and very occasionally she gave me a game of table-tennis. But she was usually too pre-occupied. Despite her substantial fortune, she had come to believe that we were on the verge of bankruptcy; and so, encouraged by Jasper, she had turned her back on her painting, and bought a shop in Horsham from which to conduct an antiques business.

Arnold Goodman visited us almost every weekend. There was something about his enormous bulk which gave me a sense of security; but at first I was repelled by the hair which grew so profusely out of his nose and ears, and I was also worried that he might persuade my mother to marry him. So it was a relief when he joked about hating the country. 'Oh my God!' he would exclaim, throwing up his hands in mock panic as he looked through the drawing-room window. 'There's a cow! I've got to leave! What time is my next train back to London?'

Nigel and I were together a great deal. My father had impressed upon him that he must take care of me; and he had thrown himself into the task with gusto. Whatever I wished to do, from playing cards to bike-riding, he would do it with me. We were so close that I refused to wash unless Nigel joined me in the bath; and if I couldn't sleep at night I would go to his room, climb into his bed and listen to his Cliff Richard and Adam Faith records, which I pretended to like even though I didn't really understand them. Sometimes he teased me a little, as our father had done; but afterwards he would always kiss me and hold me very lovingly.

Sometimes I preferred to be alone: which I achieved either by hiding in my room, or by going riding; because after a long battle Nigel had persuaded Mummy that I should be allowed out riding by myself, so long as I said where I would be going, and when I would be coming back.

※

In my fantasies, Phil was no longer a little Dartmoor pony, but a wonderful thoroughbred racehorse. The groom from the next-door stud-farm had been persuaded to clip him out in suitable fashion; and when Phil and I set out alone for the first time, the parkland and farms through which I had been given permission to ride, became a faery realm. To me, it was the beautiful island that Annie Griffiths and I had once invented, an island covered in meadows and leafy woods, with bubbling streams at the side of which grew sweet-scented flowers; and on this island there was a riding-school run by Annie and me. Riding slowly through this dream-like landscape, I felt that I was in a world where all things were possible.

After the first shock of my father's death, and my subsequent conversations about him with Nigel, I had hardly let myself think about him: it was too painful. But on my rides with Phil over our magical island, I became convinced that my father was still alive, and that one day he would return. Sometimes, I truly thought I might meet him before my ride was over and, when I didn't, I told myself that he would be there the next day, or the next. He was alive, I knew that. They had all lied to me, including my mother.

Perhaps if I had been allowed to attend the cremation I might have believed in my father's death. But I had never had a chance to say a proper good-bye; and in any case, how was it possible that such a strong swimmer had drowned? Unless Daddy was still alive, then here I was, at the age of ten, with no idea at all about what my future held. My father had always promised me that the world would be at my feet, and that he would be there to look after me, come what may, and I had believed him, and I wanted to go on believing him.

Then the summer came to an end, and I had to face the prospect of boarding school. Benenden had been considered, because Annie Griffiths was going there; but it was announced that Princess Anne would be a pupil; and having his child in the same school as a member of the Royal family was too much for Daddy's socialist principles. So he found a more humble establishment, Tortington Park, a Roman Catholic school which was short of pupils and could take me in with very little notice.

CHAPTER SIX

Lonely and Abandoned

I had first visited Tortington with my father shortly before his death. Set in the bleakest part of the Sussex countryside about a mile and a half beyond Arundel (and not far from Ford Open Prison), the main building was a large white country-house set at the head of an avenue of dreary evergreens.

We were met by the Headmistress Miss Bevan, a stocky, grey-haired spinster wearing drab, ill-fitting clothes; with her hair in a bun, and a line of dark hairs along her upper lip. First she escorted us into a panelled hall, from which heavy oak doors led into a number of handsome rooms, one of which was her study. Then she showed us the grounds, and pointed out a cottage which was the home of the Principal: Miss Le Sage, an elderly Roman Catholic who had founded Tortington Park back in 1922.

Miss Bevan spoke highly of her influence as a purveyor of advanced ideas about women's education and, although he was an atheist, perhaps it pleased my father (nursed through so many bouts of TB by the Sisters of Mercy at the St. John and St. Elizabeth), to leave his daughter in an institution which had a devout Roman Catholic as its guiding light. As for Miss Le Sage: she turned out to be a thin, tiny creature who hardly ever appeared; and when I met her in one of the school corridors, there was something so sinister about her that I shrank back as she passed.

When I next saw Tortington Park, it was September 1961, my father had been dead for four months and I was about to start my first term there as a boarder. Predictably enough I didn't yet have a proper school uniform, and made a bad start by turning up wearing a purple tunic instead of the regulation fawn skirt and jersey.

Almost at once, I was taken to my dormitory by an older girl who told me that it was her job to keep an eye on me for the first few weeks until I knew my way around. It was a pink room in the main building with ten beds, ten small chests-of-drawers, and ten small cupboards. I was told that I could have one teddy-bear on my bed, and one photograph on the chest-of-drawers next to it. Luckily I found a picture of my mother; but I was the only person in the dormitory without a teddy-bear. After lights-out, this lack of a teddy-bear weighed heavily upon me. I heard the other girls crying quietly to themselves, and I began to cry too.

Soon I found things about Tortington which physically disgusted me. The smell in the loos was so revolting that I dreaded having to use them; we were only allowed baths twice a week; and I realised that our sheets were changed too infrequently to be decently clean. Worse still, I had no friends, and girls in my dormitory had soon ganged up against me and discovered my weak point: I was fanatical about tidiness. First, they teased me for folding my clothes up so carefully; and then one of them threw all my clothes on the floor, and I went completely berserk. Throwing my things around the dormitory, and hoping that I would lose my temper, immediately became their favourite game.

During the day, our life at Tortington was dominated by bells which continually rang out the hours for services or religious contemplation, just as though we were in a convent. There was certainly a measure of security in always knowing exactly what would happen during the next half an hour; but religion, far from making us kinder to each other, was utterly divisive.

Considering that it was a Catholic school, there weren't all that many Catholics, but they were given special treatment. On Sundays, they were allowed an extra half an hour in bed, and then (after going to mass in the school Chapel, which was their private preserve) they were given a breakfast of fried eggs and bacon. This was considered far too good for the rest of us, who had to be content with porridge. As for us Protestants: we weren't even allowed to visit a modest little Anglican church just beyond an iron gate at the edge of the grounds. This was considered so low-church that it was firmly out-of-bounds, and being found there carried the risk of instant expulsion. Instead, we were bussed each Sunday into Arundel to a church which, despite being Protestant, offered candles, incense, and chanting.

One break-time, talking to a very plain rather unhappy-looking girl who seemed pleased by my attention, I hoped that I had made my first friend. But then I turned to ask someone from my dormitory a question, and was completely ignored. I had made the mistake of talking to someone who was truly unpopular, and for the next three days no-one would speak to me in day-room, dining-room or dormitory. From then on, I was continually frightened that I too might become an outcast. Despite my being half-Jewish myself, and having a Jewish surname, I even distanced myself from the Jews, who were generally thought to be mean, and were much disliked.

Being teased or sent to Coventry was a horrible kind of mental torture, and I began writing home begging to be taken away. After several such missives, my mother replied:

> I have had your letters, and am very sorry you are unhappy. However, I cannot come and fetch you or anything. You must realise that girls are often difficult to get on with, and one of the reasons children are sent to boarding school is to teach them to mix with others, taking the rough with the smooth, and not getting too upset.

She never sent me the teddy-bear for which I had asked her, so I spent all my needlework lessons desperately making a black-and-white puppet-panda, until at last I had something to put on my bed, and to hug at night.

The start of my second term was even worse than the first. I felt utterly miserable until at last I was seized by the conviction that if I went in the middle of the night to the nearby graveyard, I would see my father again, and he would take me away with him. So one night I lay awake until about two in the morning, and then slipped quietly out of bed, put on my slippers and a dressing-gown, and made my way through the sleeping dormitory and down the back stairs. There I found an unlocked door which led into the gardens. It creaked a little as it opened onto a moonlit night; and I paused for a moment, terrified that Miss Bevan might have heard. But there was silence again, apart from the hooting of an owl; and I ran across the lawns, and down the path which led through a small wood to a rusting iron gate. Climbing over this gate, I found myself in the graveyard; surely now I would see Daddy again!

When nothing happened, except that the owl hooted again (closer this time), I began to shiver, partly with cold and partly with fear. I shut my eyes, and cried out silently: 'Help me Daddy! Oh, do, do help me!' And then I thought I heard a rustling noise in the grass close by, and this was so frightening that I climbed back over the gate and ran back to the school as fast as my legs would carry me. I kept that lonely vigil three more times, each time more hopeful and then more frightened than the last.

Once again, I poured my heart out to Mummy, telling her how much I missed Daddy and how much I wished that I could have my Queen's Gate friends with me again; but she only replied that my letters were rather silly. 'I will explain what I mean,' she wrote:

> How can you have your Queen's Gate form transported to Tortington? Do you remember your constant complaints about Queen's Gate School? The food, the staff, the work etc.? Now you have changed all this, and it is the girls. At any other school, how do you know that the girls would be any different? You are difficult to get on with yourself, as we have all found out at different times. Your form mates are probably trying to change your outlook, and you must be more patient, in not such a tearing hurry to make friends.

After this I turned elsewhere for affection; and in the summer I fell romantically in love with an older girl.

The object of my adoration was a lovely French girl named Marie. At first I was constantly worried about whether or not she liked me, and it was all very painful. Luckily for me, Marie was extremely kind; and at least three times she let me cry and tell her how lonely and desperate I felt. She also allowed me to buy her little bottles of perfume and other presents; and I think she was touched and flattered. Because I loved her, Tortington seemed a better place: every day, I woke up knowing that I might see her, and hoping that if I caught her eye, she would smile at me.

※

When I went home that summer, I found that Nigel, who was now sixteen, had just finished his last term at Trent College. Much to my annoyance, he told me that we had been invited to join Uncle Basil for a family holiday in Deauville. He seemed pleased by this, but I always found Uncle Basil a little too strict; I hardly knew Aunt Coral, his second wife; and I certainly didn't want to be reminded of our last visit to Deauville, when Daddy was still alive.

My foreboding was justified. The first shock was that Basil and Coral went first class, while the rest of us (including two of his children, and two of hers) had to go second. Then on arriving at the Normandy Hotel, I found that Nigel was miles away down the corridor, from where he was allowed to join Uncle Basil and Aunt Coral for dinner in the restaurant, while I was stuck in a suite of rooms where I had to eat with a nanny and the rest of the children.

And when one day I persuaded Nigel to take me to Trouville to play the slot machines, all hell broke loose on our return. Apparently, Trouville was too down-market, and we shouldn't have gone there. Nigel was shut in his room without dinner for two nights, while the rest of us were sent to bed early. I cried bitterly, but no amount of tears made any difference.

※

One good thing about Tortington was that we were allowed to have pets; and when I returned there in September 1962, for the start of my second year, I took with me a baby albino rabbit with pink eyes, which I named Arnold after Arnold Goodman who had given it to me. It seemed an appropriate choice of name: Arnold was large to begin with, and went on growing, until he had grown right out of his hutch. By now I had acquired a handful of friends, and when the rabbit seemed mature enough, we all decided that it was time for Arnold to become a father, and we tried to interest him in a doe. This was a disaster. Arnold showed no interest in his new female companion; and when the staff found out what we were doing, I lost my pet badge; and finally poor Arnold ate so much that he died of excess.

In the meantime, I had become much more fond of the real Arnold, who was doing his best to be a second father to me, and usually drove me back to school after a week-end at home. Most visitors were closely investigated to ensure that they hadn't brought any illegal substances such as corned beef or lemonade powder into the school. But because of Arnold's reputation no-one dared to lay a finger on him: and he smuggled in huge amounts of contraband on my behalf.

During the holidays, Arnold would take me to the ballet, or to a new musical; and we often had lunch together at the restaurant in London Zoo, for which he had a passion. Best of all (despite his dark, dreary Victorian flat) were the Christmases that we spent with him in Ashley Gardens. Here, my great treat was being allowed to open his Christmas presents. He received great heaps of them and, as I opened them, he separated their contents into two piles: those to be kept, and those to be given away. What he kept were perishable things like flowers or food. 'Possessions,' he would mutter gloomily as he examined yet another ashtray or vase. 'I don't want them, or need them.' Though I noticed that he liked paintings, and would sometimes break his rule if he had been sent a rather special work of art.

Amazingly, Arnold persuaded my mother to visit Tortington Park with him on sports days. I dreaded these visits. Although he looked very distinguished (and was so sporting that one year he ran in the egg-and-spoon race), he was too fat and unusual. I knew that he could never fit onto one of the tiny chairs which were put out for our guests; and I also knew that when he and my very beautiful mother had left, I would be teased about whether they might be planning to marry. And that was something I still didn't want: I loved the father I had lost, and no-one could ever take his place.

I still didn't care for either hard work or the school rules; and I shamelessly used my father's death in an attempt to evade the numerous punishments that flowed unceasingly in my direction. This made no impact upon my redoubtable thick-legged House-mistress, Miss McLaughlin. Day after day, as a punishment for my latest misdemeanour, she sent me running a set number of times around an oak tree which she could see from her bedroom window.

Fortunately for me, the Headmistress, to whom I was sent when in serious trouble, was more malleable. I didn't like Miss Bevan, because she kept confiscating my radios; but all I had to do was to burst into tears and say 'God I'm so unhappy. I haven't heard from my mother this week – and don't you realize I haven't got a father?' and instead of punishing me as she should have done, she would weakly give me a slice of chocolate cake or let me watch television.

CHAPTER SEVEN
Adolescence and a Leap from the Window

During my third year I found that my skill at games made it easier for me to be accepted: I thoroughly enjoyed netball, tennis and lacrosse, and rose to be head of junior games in my house; but I also faced a new social difficulty. All my friends were beginning to develop sexually, and I was dreadfully teased because I had no tits. So as not to be left out, I pretended that I had started my periods; and I began using a Tampax long before I needed one, after detailed instruction from a girl standing safely on the other side of the loo door.

Any more intimate help would have been out of the question: although we were all girls together, we dressed and undressed in bed; and even at bath time, partitions prevented us from seeing each other in the nude, and comparing our bodies. Ignorance was thought to be bliss; and we had to pick up the facts of life as best we could. Fortunately, Nigel had explained everything to me, because my mother said only: 'Don't worry when you start to bleed, Nicola, it will happen once a month. *My* mother never told me this, and the first time, I thought I was going to bleed to death, but kept quiet about it.'

By the beginning of the summer term, I had been teased for so long about not having any tits, that I would have done anything to make them grow and, after hearing some old wives' tales, I began buying other people's milk from them, and drinking three or four pints every day. I also started some regular swimming, which I had heard might help; and, just to be on the safe side, I prayed a great deal. And so, by the time of my 14th birthday, when after weeks of milk-drinking and swimming and praying, nature finally began to take its course, I thought that I had been tremendously successful.

Then in the autumn, as my breasts continued to enlarge, I realised that my prayers had been answered in the most extreme manner. They grew so huge, so fast, that they were covered with red stretch marks of the kind that people get when they are pregnant; and for at least a year they hurt and itched all the time. I kept them hidden, never discussed them with anyone, and was sometimes in such agony that I became frightened that I had something seriously wrong with me.

I didn't have any other growing pains; but I developed terrible rashes all over my arms and neck and, if anyone upset me, I could feel them heating up and itching and spreading further and further. There was one advantage to be gained from this. I discovered an anti-chilblain pill that I could buy in a chemist's without a prescription, and which after about fifteen minutes made my face go bright red, so that it looked as though my rash was completely out of control. This extricated me from numerous lessons (especially French ones which I hated) because as soon as I changed colour, I would be sent out.

Sexuality was now so fascinating that we began taking a great interest in the strange, intense friendships between our women teachers; and in our own lives it suddenly became important to have boy-friends who would send us letters and Valentine cards. In this respect I was very lucky having a brother like Nigel, who from the beginning of 1965 began arranging for his friends to write to me.

As for Nigel himself, he was now living in a self-contained flat in the basement of our house in Redcliffe Road; and he had fallen madly in love with Suzy, my mother's full-time nurse/companion, who had been with us since the previous spring. Suzy was an attractive girl, a few years older than Nigel, with dark-brown hair and a lovely face. She came from an artistic family (her brother was an architect), and had gone into nursing partly because she was a kind, motherly person; and partly because in those days nursing was one of the few options for an intelligent woman of her background. When she began to find hospital nursing tedious, Suzy went into private nursing, which she said suited her because of the variety of the challenges she faced; and it was as a private nurse that she had been sent down to Butterstocks by Dr. Rossdale.

My mother took to her immediately, partly because she hated nurses who wore uniforms, and Suzy arrived in a very short mini-skirt; and although at first Suzy wanted to keep her independence, she gradually became very attached to Nigel and to me, and was persuaded to look after my mother on a long-term basis.

We adored her in return. I used to call her 'nursey', and when she wrote to me at school she referred to me as 'Muffet'. And instead of being jealous of her relationship with Nigel, I felt that it was rather wonderful to have this lovely lady looking after both my mother and my brother.

※

During the Easter holidays, there was a strange interlude. My mother's latest craze was for answering advertisements in the personal column of *The Times*. In this way she acquired a brochure about a villa to rent in Teneriffe, and when she saw that on one of the walls there was a reproduction of a painting by Paul Klee, she decided that she and I must go. Through yet another advertisement, this time in *The Field*, Mother had also found a companion with a son of my age to join us.

Only two hours into our flight, Mother began panicking, and asked why we hadn't yet arrived. Told that the flight would take another two hours, she insisted on seeing the pilot. When he explained that we were flying almost as far as the coast of Africa, she looked stupefied. 'But I thought that Teneriffe was one of the Channel Islands!' No sooner had we landed on a stretch of beach, when Mother screamed: 'Take me back to London!' At which she was quietly informed her that the next scheduled flight home was not for another week.

So we disembarked: only to find that our villa was on the wrong side of the island, its furnishings were spartan, and it was so small that the companion and her son had to sleep out in a shed. In these circumstances my mother did what was, for her, the only possible thing. She went straight to bed and stayed there for the rest of the holiday.

※

A month or two later, when I was back at school, I had an alarming letter from Nigel in which he told me:

> Mummy is ill, but it is not incurable, she has not broken a leg, where the effects can be seen, but she is ill in such a way that you or I can't see the effects. This is what makes things so very difficult for everyone. But don't worry unduly, everything will soon turn out alright – believe me. I hope this makes sense as I am very serious.
>
> All that you or I can do is to show her that we love her and need her, which we both do.

Returning home for the start of the summer holidays, I found that my mother had once again retreated to her bedroom and drawn the curtains against the outside world; but no-one seemed particularly anxious. Rita was away for a short holiday with her family in Portugal; and Suzy was looking after things with her usual efficiency.

But then, one Sunday afternoon, I was coming out of a cinema hand-in-hand with one of Nigel's friends, and feeling tremendously excited by the prospect of being able to tell my schoolfriends all about it next term, when I was alarmed to see that Nigel was there waiting for us. My first thought was: 'Oh, God, Mummy's found out!' Because of course I was meant to be spending the afternoon with Nigel in his basement: not going out with a boy! But then I realized from the look on his face that it was something far worse. This came as no surprise. By this time I half-expected awful things to happen.

"Mummy has had a dreadful accident", Nigel told me. "She jumped out of her bedroom window. She's in St. Stephen's Hospital. Arnold's arranging everything and you and I and Suzy have got to stay in his flat for a while." But Arnold found it too difficult to cope with us all, so within forty-eight hours so he had booked us into Gleneagles for a week; and Nigel and Suzy and I (all three of us still in a state of shock), had set off for Scotland in the extremely fast sports car which my brother had recently acquired.

By this time, my mother was not only alive, but likely to recover. She excused herself years later, by claiming that she had been looking out of her window and had seen a drunken tramp down below; wanting to give him some money, she had simply tried to reach him by the shortest route available.

The real story was that her private life was once again in a mess. Jasper had turned out to be a playboy, who wasn't prepared to leave his wife; and in his absence she had fallen desperately in love with a good-looking ex-army major called Basil Brooke, who sold his portraits at holiday camps for the grand sum of £5 with frame. He had a kind heart, but he also had a family; and although he was separated from his wife, it seemed uncertain whether he would divorce her. It was probably this fresh anxiety that drove my mother to her suicide attempt.

What had saved her, was that she was as relaxed as a baby, having swallowed almost a complete bottle of sleeping pills before she jumped. Even so, she broke practically every bone in her body; and on 21 August 1965 (while Arnold spent his 50th birthday waiting loyally close by) she had to be operated on for seven hours.

Unfortunately, Sunday wasn't the best of days for jumping out of windows, because whichever junior surgeon happened to be on duty made a very bad job of patching her up. Numerous operations followed in which bones had to be re-broken, so that they could be stuck back together more effectively. Her arms were always an odd shape after this; and her hands had an abstract look to them, as if they had come straight out of one of her paintings. This was especially curious to me, because she had always been mildly obsessed by hands, painting them, collecting china hands, and even wearing little gold and enamel hands as costume jewellery.

Nigel and Suzy and I, (spending a week of storms at remote Gleneagles, which seemed enormously dark, dull and dreary) knew little or nothing about what was happening down in London. Nigel felt very guilty, because he had lured Suzy downstairs and so was entirely responsible for her absence at the critical moment; and I noticed that from this time on, he began to hide his real feelings beneath layer after layer of charm and good manners.

As for me: I felt confused. By this time my mother was so distant that although I was amused when she was high, in general I disliked her, and felt sorry for myself for having such a mother. After her fall, I didn't experience any of the normal emotions which might have been expected from a daughter. Instead of praying: 'Oh, God, please make Mummy live!' I simply felt a little colder and lonelier, as though the Snow Queen had captured me, and there was a crystal of ice embedded in my heart.

CHAPTER EIGHT
Sexual Assault and Becoming a Superstar

Soon after our return from Gleneagles to Redcliffe Road, Rita came back from Portugal. Normally so calm, she was in a deeply emotional state, and kept repeating: 'Nigel, Nicky, I shouldn't have left your mother alone. I knew she was ill, and I couldn't stand it. Oh, why did I go? Why? Why?'

We all went to visit my mother in St. Stephen's. It was a gloomy Victorian pile, and we found my mother with her legs hanging in the air and drips everywhere. She was in a crowded public ward in which sick people were mingled with geriatrics; and while I was sitting by my mother's bedside, one old woman came up saying: 'Gosh you look comfortable, Mrs. Samuel. It must be so nice having your legs in the air!' A few minutes later another one sidled up and asked: 'Can I build you a nice fire to keep you warm?' 'Yes, please!' answered my mother; To which the old lady replied: 'Well then, I'll just go and fetch the coal!'

This surreal conversation appealed to my mother's sense of humour, and a rare smile crossed her face; but most of the time she was so depressed that she didn't even want to eat. This alarmed Rita so much that she began going to St. Stephen's three times a day to tempt her with home-made soup and other delicacies.

When I returned to Tortington Park that autumn, my mother was still at St. Stephen's; and towards the end of September, after her third operation, she wrote in her undeveloped child-like hand to tell me that:

the operation was awful when I came round & for three days I nearly felt finished. However yesterday I started on cigarettes and claret & haven't looked back since! Everything is otherwise the same. Basil stayed in Redcliffe Road last week & was up for 2 nights. Arnold has been to visit me, Reg Poynter, Sue Gordon [the wife of her partner in the antiques business]. Also Rita, Jorge is home and he is coming in one afternoon soon... Also, Michael Foot. Nigel sent me a lovely flower arrangement.

This was the curious kind of communication that she sent me: something about herself, a great deal about her visitors, little or nothing about the two of us. At the start of October she was moved to the London Clinic in Devonshire Place, from where she continued to bombard me with news of her attentive minions; and once she told me that she wanted to borrow my record-player in order to learn French.

By this time, I had begun to attract some quite attentive minions myself. One of these was Suzy's brother Jonathan, who was studying architecture at the London Polytechnic, and had written to me towards the end of the previous term to compliment me on, the 'warm delicate lustre' of my complexion. For a while I encouraged him. He wrote to me three times a week, impressed me by knowing members of leading pop groups like *The Pink Floyd*, and was always there to take me out when I came home. But he was so gentle and respectful that eventually I found him boring.

One of Nigel's friends wrote to me for the first time that October, in a letter which began 'Darling Nicola, I hope you don't feel you're demoralised by the opening. I hear from a close friend of mine that you feel desolate and in need of company – here it is!' He had dreadful acne, but became so besotted by me that although I never had any strong feelings for him, I was intrigued, and allowed him to give me French kisses, and to let his hands wander over my body while we cuddled.

In my unhappiness I had begun to take religion seriously, and often prayed in secret. This was so unfashionable that when I arranged to be confirmed into the Church of England, I pretended to my friends that it was simply because it meant a day off school. Nigel and Suzy came down to Arundel for the confirmation service on 6 December, and I wore a very short white dress with crocheted sleeves, which Suzy and I had bought in 'Countdown', a fashionable Chelsea boutique.

The most difficult part of confirmation was talking privately to the priest immediately beforehand. We had to confess our sins, and I was terrified by this; because although I was still a virgin I had done a certain amount of 'heavy petting', and I wasn't sure whether this had been sinful or not. In the end I didn't mention it, telling myself that I had only been searching for affection: so it didn't really count; and immediately afterwards Nigel and Suzy took me to see Rita Tushingham in *The Knack*, my first X-rated movie.

I liked my life to be full of contrasts, and nothing could have been more different from my down-trodden existence at Tortington, than the reception I was given when that Christmas holidays I went to Coutts to open a bank account. They had become my Trustees after my father's death; and now I was given lunch, taken on a grand tour of their headquarters, and treated with extreme deference.

※

The following summer, when I was fifteen, Mani and Luba d'Astier offered to have me to stay; and soon after term was over, Nigel escorted me to Paris, where we found our way to their grand but somewhat decayed apartment in Les Invalides. We had arrived on 14 July, Bastille Day, and that evening there were fireworks and dancing in the streets.

The next morning Nigel returned to England; and I travelled down to an hotel on a remote part of the Brittany coast with Mani, Luba, and their third son Jérôme, who was only a year younger than me, and seemed very attracted to me. However, it was his father who gave me trouble. It all began one afternoon when it was siesta time, and I was lying on my bed reading. Mani came into my bedroom, closed the door, and sat down on my bed. At first I felt honoured that this good-looking man, who had won the respect of world leaders, should want to come and talk to me alone.

But this hero of the Resistance wanted to do more than talk. After a few minutes he started telling me how wonderful I was, and then his hands were down my cleavage and undoing my shirt, and taking it off, and undoing my bra. 'Let me touch you,' he said, 'Let me feel you: you're so lovely.' His hands moved onto my breasts, stroking my nipples; and then suddenly they were down inside my jeans and under my pants. I was being loved and desired, so I let it continue; but I was also very confused, because I had always liked and trusted Mani, who was a father-figure in my life and I could not understand how he could think that what he was doing was acceptable; and I was very scared, because Mani was far too powerful for me to resist him.

By this time he had slipped down his trousers and pants, as he had a large erection which he could no longer keep to himself. I was amazed by its size. He didn't want to come inside me, but he wanted me to put my hands on this large purple cock with the blood pulsating up and down, and play with it. Then he pushed it towards my mouth, and asked me to suck it. I didn't dare to argue. His prick was certainly fascinating, and although I didn't enjoy the sucking, I must admit that as I rubbed my lips up and down on his manhood it gave me a sense of power, and I wanted to find out what would happen next. The reality was that he groaned, and the sperm just oozed out and his powerful tool became flaccid and ugly, and I had to look an old man in the face and pretend that it had all been wonderful.

Dread was my constant companion for the rest of the holiday. I was sure that Luba would find out, and be angry with me. And every day, as two o'clock approached, I lay terrified in my bed, waiting for the door-handle to turn, and for the predator that lurked between Mani's legs to find its way once again into my mouth. I had been hoping for affection, and I had found chiefly fear and abuse. But this terrifying experience had also taught me that men would go on wanting to be with me, as Mani did day after day, so long as I could give them something sexually.

When I returned to England, my mother told me that she had commissioned some photographs of me from David Armitage, a handsome photographer who was friendly with Patrick Lichfield.

I was soon besotted by David, because at 26 or 30 he seemed to be a complete man of the world; and where Mani D'Astier had simply called me 'lovely', David Armitage said that I was stunningly attractive. As he adjusted his lights, and then came over and used his hands to move my body into new attitudes, and touched my cheeks, and smoothed down my fashionable Vidal Sassoon-style haircut (very short at the back, but with long sides and a fringe), the atmosphere in the studio became more and more highly charged. 'You're so beautiful,' he told me again and again. 'You could make money as a model. Do you realise that?' What I did realise, from the way he looked at me, was that he was fascinated by my tits; and sure enough his next tentative question was: 'You've got such a wonderful figure. Would you mind very much if I photographed you stripped to the waist?'

Already hypnotized by his flattering comments, I was excited by this request, and finally stood there bare-breasted under the arc-lamps, hoping that it might be the prelude to his making a pass at me. It wasn't; but at least he sent me a lovely letter which I could show my girlfriends, telling me how beautiful I was, and enclosing one of his more respectable photographs.

※

By the autumn of 1966 living in Chelsea, and having lots of boyfriends who wrote to me was turning me into a superstar at school. I was now so popular that some of the younger girls began getting crushes on me: two in particular. I was flattered, and tried to be as nice to them as Marie had been to me, but it wasn't easy. It helped, having a very good-looking brother who broke all the rules. Nigel would turn up outside visiting hours in an Alfa Romeo or a Lotus Elan, wander into the school with a pretty girl on his arm, and give me the latest records, copies of subversive newspapers, and even (on one occasion) some hash to smoke.

Nigel's twenty-first birthday was in March 1967, and he immediately came into a substantial inheritance. To celebrate the occasion, he gave a family dinner-party at the Cafe' Royal and afterwards Nigel and Suzy, who were now planning to get married in May or June, took me on to Ronnie Scott's Jazz Club, at that time Nigel's favourite haunt.

'So, what are you going to do now?' I asked Nigel over a glass of champagne.

'I want to continue our father's work,' Nigel told me very earnestly. 'That's the most important thing for me now.'

It made me think seriously about my own future.

My chief interests were artistic, and I began to wonder whether I might study fashion design. Then during the Easter holidays, a casual date who was also a student at the Royal College of Art persuaded me that I might be given a place there if I passed enough O-levels.

So, I returned to Tortington at the start of the summer term of 1966, with O-levels less than two months away, determined to do my best. Whatever happened, this would be my last term there: Nigel had persuaded my mother that I should be allowed to leave in August, and Dr. Rossdale was negotiating for my re-entry to Queen's Gate. This would put me with Annie Griffiths, who was planning to return to Queen's Gate for her A-levels; and it would also mean that I could live in London full-time.

Luckily, I had a good memory, but however hard I worked, I soon realised that in most subjects I had left it too late. I felt under tremendous pressure. My rash grew worse again, and I was unable to sleep.

On top of this came dreadful news from home: something had gone badly wrong between Nigel and Suzy, their wedding had been called off, and Nigel, who had become involved with a girl from Amnesty International, had gone abroad for an indefinite period. Things seemed to be going from bad to worse; and I became so nervous that Dr. Rossdale suggested a course of tranquillisers. 'They tell me you've become a communist?' he queried sympathetically while writing out his prescription for Valium.

'Not quite,' I said, smiling for the first time for several days. 'It's because I always insist that I'm going to vote Labour – and to them that's the same thing.'

※

Half-way through the exams I had a very narrow escape. Nigel, who had returned from the USA, was driving me back to school in his Lotus Elan Sports Car. It was a two-seater, and his Amnesty International girlfriend was in the other seat, so I was lying on the ledge at the back of the car. Nigel was not only drunk, but also high on hash; and just before Arundel, on the corner at the top of Bury Hill, he drove straight into a tree.

The car turned upside down, and then righted itself. Amazingly, all three of us came through this terrifying experience without even a scratch. A passing driver helped us out. 'We're all right, thank you, but very shaken up,' said Nigel in a very controlled voice. 'Do you think you could possibly take us to the nearest pub?' As soon as we arrived there, he ordered a treble whisky; and by the time the police came to question him, they couldn't tell whether he had been drunk at the time of the accident, or had become drunk since. Later we went by taxi to a small house near Billingshurst which our mother had recently bought as a substitute for Butterstocks, and we spent the night there.

The next morning Nigel took me back to Tortington, and we walked into the school when everyone was on the move between lessons. After a night's sleep Nigel was looking like every girl's dream; while instead of my school uniform, I was wearing a short pink mini-dress and matching coat, which I had hidden in my luggage to wear at the end of term. Everyone crowded round excitedly, with a storm of questions.

✻

Reality soon intervened; and the exams continued. As I struggled with my papers in the near-silence of the examination hall, I felt immense desperation about my prospects. The only agreeable feature of those weeks was that the roses were in bloom, and I comforted myself by placing their petals against my skin.

At last, the exams were over: the next day was my sixteenth birthday; and in three weeks term would end.

I began to look forward to my new life. During my occasional forays into the King's Road, I had been excited by all the young people with their shoulder-length hair and their flared velvet trousers. There were so many of them now, wandering about the face of the earth proclaiming love and peace, and I desperately wanted to join them. Nigel, I knew, was already mixing with some of their kind; and towards the end of the term, he sent me 'A very hurried note to tell you of my activities.'

One of his ventures was to be 'backing Jim Haynes's theatre', which soon achieved fame as the 'Arts Lab.' 'It will be fun,' he told me; 'also we will be able to promote / buy plays etc…' More immediately, he was setting off that evening for Venice, 'with Yoko Ono, Anthony Cox, child and one other… to make a film! I am going to be second cameraman.' The vision of Nigel as a cameraman made me smile. I couldn't help thinking that perhaps his real role in the project was to provide funds.

※

During the last few weeks of term there was one noticeable improvement. The staff, knowing that I was leaving, began treating me in such a friendly manner that I even began to like the previously hated Miss McLaughlin. The only one I couldn't forgive was the Headmistress.

The very last day of term found me waiting with some other girls outside Miss Bevan's study door for our special farewell interviews. 'Ah, Nicola,' she began when I was called in, 'May I wish you every success for the future? Your career here has been…' She looked down at the papers on her desk, and shuffled some of them about, sighing heavily as though she was finding it difficult to think of anything complimentary to say. 'I know you've had a difficult time; but I hope that… that some of the values you've learned here, loyalty, hard work…' She was on safer ground now, and was fairly launched into her standard hymn of praise for the private school system, when I intervened.

'I'm sorry, Miss Bevan, but I can only thank God that I'm getting out of this dump,' I told her. 'I've stuck it for one hell of a long time. You've given me a lousy education, and I've learnt almost nothing the entire time I've been here. I haven't even been taught to want to know anything – and please may I have back the ten radios that you've confiscated from me over the years?'

She went to a cupboard and found them for me in absolute silence, piling them into a large cardboard box which she placed on the edge of her desk.

For a while I too was lost for words, and then I made a defiant gesture, somewhere between 'Fuck you!' and a genuine attempt to hit her.

She flinched; and then I found my voice, and prophesied that the school would be bankrupt within two years. It actually lasted another three. Then

I picked up my box of broken radios, turned on my heel, and had soon left Tortington Park behind me, resolved never to set foot in it again.

※

Later that Saturday I was back in London where my mother, who was in a slightly better state of health, had recently moved us from Redcliffe Road to one of her houses in Henniker Mews. It was thrilling to wake up on Sunday morning and face what I hoped, what I knew would be an entirely fresh phase of my existence.

Indeed, before the day was out, I had visited the Arts Lab (then just about to open); I had been offered my first job by Yoko Ono; I was sitting at a large kitchen table in her flat near Regent's Park, with Yoko and Miles and Jim Haynes and Allen Ginsberg; and the air was heavy with the sweet, slightly sickly smell of marijuana.

CHAPTER NINE

Working for Yoko Ono

Lingering over breakfast in Henniker Mews, I savoured my newly-found freedom. It was as tangible to me as the toast I was biting, as sweet and darkly mysterious as the aroma of freshly-ground coffee which filled my nostrils. I would never have to return to Tortington Park, and it made the morning glorious. No more of those terrible nightmares in which I suddenly had to admit to one of my boyfriends that I was too young for him, that I had to get back to boarding-school and put on a uniform again, that I wasn't really twenty (as I had pretended), but only sixteen… Still more wonderful, my brother had promised to drive me over to the Arts Lab in Drury Lane to meet some of his new friends.

I wanted to make a good impression; and before leaving the house, I checked my appearance in the hall mirror. Above that slightly anxious but excited face, my hair was growing out of its formal Vidal Sassoon cut; while below, I wore a dress and trousers which I had made myself out of an Indian table-cloth. The trousers were bell-bottoms, and the dress (which came almost to my knees) had bell-bottom sleeves.

Closing the door gently behind me in case my mother was still sleeping, I cut down through Chelsea Park Gardens, and began walking along the King's Road. Apart from having no bells and beads, I looked in my new outfit just like any of the other flower children who thronged these pavements, even on a Sunday morning. It was hot and sunny, and I didn't have a care in the world.

There was no answer to my first few rings on the bell of Number 203, Pavilion Road; and then Suzy opened the door in her dressing-gown, looking slightly flushed, and made me another cup of coffee while Nigel got dressed. I could hear him singing tunelessly but cheerfully in the distance. 'Suzy,' I said, laying a hand on her bare fore-arm, 'I'm so glad you're back together.'

"Isn't it wonderful, Muffet? I feel as if I've come home again. And you know that we're going to be married very soon; and afterwards we're moving to a house Nigel's bought in Portman Square.' She flashed a radiant smile at me; and then, when Nigel came into the kitchen, jumped up and began fussing round him, straightening his hand-painted silk tie (which he wore over a hand-painted silk shirt); and helping him into the jacket of his velvet suit.

'What do you think, Nicola?' Nigel gently detached Suzy, and presented himself for inspection. 'The suit's from Savile Row; and I bought the shirt and tie yesterday from 'Mr. Fish' in Cale Street.'

At a time when hippies had made it fashionable for everyone to be scruffy, I had to admit that my brother looked superb; and later that morning, when he had parked his Alfa Romeo, and the two of us were walking down Drury Lane towards the Arts Lab, I could see people turning their heads and wondering who he was.

※

On the way over, Nigel had been telling me about his involvement with International Times. 'It was crazy,' he said very quietly. 'It's the most important publication in the country; but Miles and Hoppy and Jim Haynes were running it from the basement of Indica Books.'

'How on earth did you get to know them all?'

'Quite simple, really. It was just a few months ago. I turned up at Indica Books, and asked if there was any way I could help. I said I'd gladly start out by selling copies of IT on the street. Miles seemed rather surprised at first; but he soon realised I meant what I said. And I've been able to do a little more than any of them guessed.'

We had almost reached our destination, when Nigel slowed to a crawl and stopped the car in Betterton Street. I was just about to ask why we hadn't parked a little closer to the Arts Lab, when he motioned me out of the car, and showed me an attractive three-storey house on the other side of the road, with a SOLD notice on the front. 'That's it! The new IT building. I bought it last month. I'll take you inside another day, to show you my office. Not that it's really mine of course: things are all going to be shared in future. It's just lucky that having so much money means that I can help things along.'

'I hope you can help me along, too,' I said, taking his arm affectionately. 'Mummy's giving me £25 a month, but I've got to buy all my clothes out of it. What I really need is a job.'

'I remember: it was in your last letter; and I've got some ideas,' said Nigel mysteriously. 'No, don't ask: just wait and see.'

※

The Arts Lab was being set up in an empty warehouse; and when Nigel and I went in through the main entrance, we found ourselves in a large, white, rather dirty room, where a woman and several men were standing around a trestle table on which some building plans had been spread out. I recognised one of the group as Miles, whom I had met casually at Pavilion Road. They stopped talking when we entered, and one of them came over immediately. Not Miles, though he smiled and waved; but a tall man with long black hair, a round face and a small moustache, who was introduced to me as Jim Haynes.

As he took my hand, Jim gave me a very direct look. He was casually dressed, but very clean, and he smelled as if he had just stepped out of a bath. I guessed that he must be in his mid-thirties (almost old enough to be my father); but I liked the firm pressure of his hand on mine, and just being close to him made my heart beat faster. Then he leaned forward and kissed me on the cheek. The whole of his energy and masculinity seemed to be concentrated in that kiss. From that outwardly insignificant touch of his lips, and the slightly ticklish feeling of his moustache on my skin, something spread out through the whole of my body, until (much to my surprise) I was gripped by a feeling of desire so powerful that I made an immediate decision. Mani d'Astier had stolen my innocence;

but my heart and my virginity were still intact; and Jim Haynes should have them both.

From that moment everything felt completely different; and it seemed strange when Jim went on talking to me in his soft American drawl as though nothing had happened. I began to listen to what he was saying about how much he appreciated my brother's help, and what he was hoping to do at the Arts Lab, and I realised that he was not only the most desirable but also the most interesting person I had ever met.

After a while we were joined by the woman, who was small and Japanese, with a serious face and long black hair which stretched down beyond her waist. Eying me shrewdly, she told me that she was Yoko Ono, and she expected that I had heard of her?

'Yes of course!' As an artist, Yoko was already a cult figure, well-known in the newspapers for her habit of putting people into paper bags. I remembered Susie writing to tell me how she and Nigel and Yoko had gone to the Dorchester with some other friends. First the men had nearly been refused entry for not wearing ties; and then they had all got into the lift, where they had climbed into a paper bag. So, on the spur of the moment, I asked Yoko: 'Have you got any large paper bags with you?'

She smiled. 'No, but they're screening my new film in the cinema just through there: come and see – oh, but first you must say hello to my husband, Tony Cox!'

There was something in Tony's expression which made me take an instant dislike to the man; but I agreed to go and watch some of Yoko's film with her. Soon I wished I hadn't. The film was called Bottoms. It hadn't yet had its official premiere, and it was as boring as its title suggests: just one bottom after another, so meaningless that after a while I felt as though I was looking at cuts of meat. I was relieved when Tony came in, and said that Nigel was going to drive us round to the flat he shared with Yoko.

It was a handsome flat: six large rooms with high ceilings and elaborate plaster-work, in an Edwardian apartment block whose wrought-iron balconies overlooked Regent's Park. It was also quite unlike any other place I had ever seen, because although there were masses of cushions everywhere, there was almost no furniture (except for a large pine table in the kitchen), and Yoko had painted everything white, and even put a white carpet in the sitting-room. It must have been dazzling at one time; but now it was all very grubby; and when I asked to visit the bathroom, I found dirty clothes strewn everywhere.

Soon after we arrived, we were joined by Allen Ginsberg, with his distinctive long dark hair, straggly beard and large glasses. I hadn't been to the poetry reading at the Albert Hall where he had stirred up the audience by taking all his clothes off; but I had read HOWL, his fashionable book of beat poems, and I could hardly believe my luck when a few minutes later I found myself sitting next to him at Yoko's kitchen table. Even the dreary brown rice which she offered us with a few nondescript vegetables seemed magically transformed by the surrounding company. Here I was, the day after leaving school, sitting down to table with some of the high priests of the alternative culture, most of whom were smoking joints. 'You've done it!' I said to myself. 'You've made it into the real world!'

Nobody seemed to speak very much. In fact, there were long silences; and it seemed surprising when one of these was broken by Yoko leaning across the table towards me, and saying rather diffidently: 'I hear you're looking for a holiday job?' I nodded eagerly. 'Then would you like to come and look after Kyoko,' – here she gestured to her four-year-old daughter, who was busy pouring salt onto the floor – 'and maybe help me with my art?'

I accepted at once. Nigel looked on approvingly. I wasn't very keen on looking after Kyoko, but I would do my best; and it would be exciting to work alongside such an important artist.

※

When I reported for duty soon after nine the next morning, I thought that my first job would be to get Kyoko dressed, and perhaps make her some breakfast; but when I asked Yoko about Kyoko's clothes, she looked quite shocked.

'Oh, no! If she wants her clothes on, she'll tell you."

"Shall I get her some breakfast, then?"

"Don't worry! If she's hungry, she'll let us know."

A moment later, and Kyoko began pulling out some knives and forks, and dropping them all over the place. I was about to gather them up again, when Yoko smiled and said: 'Just look – isn't that good? She really wants to find out about cutlery.'

"I expect this all comes as a surprise to you,' Yoko explained to me later that morning; 'but if we really want to change the world, the most important thing we can do is to bring up our children in complete freedom. They can learn from us or not, as they wish; but we must never try to teach them anything.'

This was a long speech from Yoko, who was usually very quiet. I observed that her philosophy of child-care certainly gave Kyoko a great deal of freedom. It also left me with a somewhat limited rôle to play. I could only look on, while Kyoko led a curiously self-absorbed life on the fringe of the adult world. She took very little notice of what anyone said; and she had such a strong will, and sometimes stared at me with such intensity, that there were times when I felt uncomfortable being in the same room.

There was no daily routine of any kind, though occasionally I was sent out shopping; and much to my disappointment I was never asked to help with any of Yoko's artistic projects. In the mornings, if we were alone, she simply wandered around talking vaguely about her future plans, none of which seemed to make much sense.

But we weren't usually alone: people constantly drifted in and out; and as they were all much older than me, and I had nothing very definite to do, I found their presence in the apartment unnerving. Walking into the sitting-room, I would see Yoko and half a dozen of them sitting on her cushions in almost complete silence, smoking joints and occasionally making some enigmatic remark which gave them an air of enormous intelligence.

Occasionally some of us would sit down to eat together. Two large saucepans were kept permanently on the stove: one of them full of brown rice which was stuck to the sides, and had gone gluey like porridge; and the other (with mould growing round it) full of vegetables: mostly rather discoloured beans. I soon found that generous helpings of Soya sauce were the only way of making it at all palatable.

I felt happier when Nigel was one of the visitors. Everyone seemed to like him, and to become more talkative in his presence. Not surprisingly. 'You really shouldn't have all this money,' I heard one of them say to Nigel, shaking his head sadly. 'You should be using it to help the cause.' 'Yes, of course, I know that,' Nigel replied with a smile. 'I know I shouldn't have all this money. Tell me what your project is, and how much you need!'

I found nothing sinister about any of this: both Miles and Jim Haynes, in particular, were genuinely fond of my brother, even when he was difficult to work with.

※

I had only been part of Yoko's household for a few days, when Nigel and Suzy were married. The wedding took place in a tiny medieval church with thick stone walls in the middle of a cornfield just outside the village of Ingleton. Suzy had decided not to wear white, the first wedding having been postponed; but when she walked down the aisle on her father's arm, she looked ravishing in a long pink printed dress by Annacat, with a sash and a high lace collar, and sleeves with white lace over the cuffs. Nigel, who was waiting for her and looking very happy and contented, wore a maroon velvet suit.

There was only room inside the church for thirty people, and there were balloons and flowers everywhere. The atmosphere was wonderfully cheerful; the service was in that wonderful seventeenth-century English; and at an appropriate moment the poet Adrian Hill read out a number of metaphysical poems.

Afterwards Nigel and Suzy came out into the August sunshine, and walked alone through the golden corn. As I watched them, I felt with a thrill of alarm that it was almost too perfect, like a dream sequence in a film. But the feeling passed; and we went back to her parents' home, a pretty Georgian house, where we ate lobsters and drank champagne in their panelled drawing-room.

※

Back in London, I felt that I must try to make something out of my difficult situation in Hanover Gate Mansions. So, I found some handmade Japanese paper in Soho, and suggested to Yoko that we should try making throw-away paper dresses. She was always open to new ideas, and this appealed to her. For a few mornings she became keen and enthusiastic, and we completed a number of dresses which we hoped to sell for large sums of money.

In the afternoons, however, she usually disappeared: probably to see John Lennon, with whom (though I knew nothing about it at the time) she had been having an affair since the previous November. That left me alone with Kyoko, who continued to be difficult; and Tony Cox. I didn't enjoy this much, and one day I simply failed to turn up. Yoko didn't seem to mind, and we remained friends. The great advantage of this separation was that it gave me far more time to spend at the Arts Lab, where I could be close to the man I really wanted.

CHAPTER TEN

The Arts Lab and Queen's Gate

Now that I was no longer working for Yoko Ono, I made myself useful to Jim Haynes by wandering up and down the King's Road, calling in on shops and boutiques, trying to sell the weird photographic posters which he had imported from Amsterdam.

One afternoon I took some posters into Hung On You, where the extremely handsome proprietor introduced himself to me as Michael Rainey, and invited me to have tea with him next door at the Flying Dragon Tea House. He asked me so charmingly that I accepted. Over tea I gathered that he was one of the smarter set of hippies. The friends whom he mentioned included many celebrities, from the musician Eric Clapton, to Nigel Waymouth, who ran Granny Takes a Trip, the most fashionable boutique in the King's Road.

'You know,' Michael said, bending his head forward, and looking down at his tea with a furrowed brow, 'I hardly like to say this.' He paused, and then looked me straight in the eyes. 'But I find you tremendously attractive. I think you're much too young and beautiful to be selling posters. You could be in real danger.' He put a hand protectively on mine. 'I shan't really be happy unless you allow me to walk you home. May I?'

When I nodded, he released my hand at once, said 'Good' in a very business-like manner, and then summoned the waitress (with an air of tremendous sophistication) so that he could pay the bill. I hadn't been able to resist his flattery; and I felt tremendously proud walking along the street with him beside me. For the first time in my life, I was being escorted by a man who was just as elegant as my brother.

When we reached Henniker Mews, I asked him in. We went up to my bedroom, where I put on one of my Stones records. Then we both sat down on the bed, and he put an arm round me, and kissed me on the lips. It was a gentle and affectionate kiss. I liked it; but it didn't thrill me in the way that Jim's kisses on my cheek thrilled me, and I drew back a little. Michael did the same; and when I moved back towards him, he broke away, and left.

I felt very confused about this until the next day, when he rang to apologise, explaining that he was under emotional strain because his wife Jane (Lord Harlech's daughter) was pregnant with their second child.

※

In the meantime, my 0-level results had arrived at Henniker Mews. The self-addressed envelope from Tortington Park was waiting for me one morning when I came down for a late breakfast. My mother was on one of her 'highs' and had gone out for the day with Basil; and Rita was shopping. I made myself some toast and coffee, and toyed with the envelope for a while. When I plucked up the courage to open it, I discovered that I had only passed in three subjects: History, Geography and English Literature.

To begin with I felt very upset, especially by my failure in Art. But then, what did any of it really matter? That very same day, I was away in Covent Garden, trying to attract Jim Haynes's attention at the Arts Lab, which was still not officially open. Jim usually kissed me on the cheek when I arrived; but to-day he was in a very cheerful mood, and gave me a friendly hug, which sent my spirits soaring into the stratosphere.

I had been finding out everything I could about Jim, and was slowly amassing a collection of newspaper and magazine cuttings. From these, I learned that he had been born in Haynesville Louisiana (a town apparently founded by his grandfather), had been sent to Scotland on military service, and decided to stay there after his discharge; that the first highlight of his career had come in 1963 when he had helped to found Edinburgh's Traverse Theatre; that three years later he had come down to

London, where his presentation of a series of experimental, late-night and lunch-time plays, concerts and readings at the Jeannette Cochrane Theatre in Holborn, had won him the prestigious Whitbread Prize; and that his major talent was considered to be the ability to inspire. I would lay these cuttings out on my bed at Henniker Mews, put on a Rolling Stones record, and read them over again and again while I hugged myself and fantasized not just about going to bed with Jim, but about him and me spending the rest of our lives together.

Yes, I was completely besotted; and by now I was following his advice in everything. 'You should try Dorothy Parker,' he told me once, when I'd been joking rather unkindly about one of my mother's friends. 'You and she have something in common.' Another time he recommended Lawrence Durrell's *Alexandria Quartet*. 'It's one of my personal favourites,' he told me; and before the day was over, I was several pages into *Justine*, entranced by Durrell's description of: 'Melissa, washed up like a half-drowned bird, on the dreary littorals of Alexandria, with her sex broken.' I was also busily absorbing his revolutionary beliefs.

"Freedom: freedom and love, that's what matters,' Jim used to say to anyone who was listening, especially if it happened to be a woman.

'Talking about free love is too simple. But we can love people, while remaining essentially free. That's what matters. As for keeping love and sexuality within the confines of a single legal relationship – it's an obscene form of theft.'

So far as I could make out, Jim's basic belief was that we should all be going to bed with each other as often as possible, and I was hopeful that one day he might look in my direction. But sadly, his theories never seemed to apply to me. Sometimes this apparent lack of interest on his part was extremely depressing, but it only seemed to make me love him more.

※

In September the holidays came to an end. The Arts Lab officially opened its doors to the public; and I was due to return to Queen's Gate to re-take my O-levels, and begin some A-level work. I was no longer the slightest interested, and without Jim's encouragement, I might well have stayed away.

However, here I am on my first day back at Queen's Gate. As I walk onto the school site, it feels uncomfortably as though the prison gates are once again clanging shut behind me. I notice that most of the sixth-formers are wearing a kind of uniform which makes my Granny Takes a Trip mini-skirt look positively outrageous. 'Annie!' I call out, catching a glimpse of her, deep in conversation. 'Still in tartan skirts and twin-sets?'

'Hello!' She makes her way towards me with her friend, a bright-looking girl who is wearing a black-and-white dog-tooth suit. 'You haven't met Eleanor, have you? We were at Benenden together. Good heavens, Nicky, is that make-up you're wearing?'

Annie and Eleanor and I had soon formed a little group of our own, with another friend known as Podoff. Together we went to Dinos, a nearby Italian restaurant where we drank Expresso coffee and smoked cigarettes; and sometimes, in the lunch-hours, I would go there to meet Michael Rainey's sister-in-law, Alice Ormsby-Gore, a girl of my age who went to school at a catholic convent just round the corner.

After the excitements of the summer, a combination of Queen's Gate and Dino's was no longer enough to satisfy me; but at first I was intrigued by the sixth-formers. Many of them were only there, it seemed, because their parents thought it was a convenient way of keeping them occupied during the day, while at night they were 'coming-out' as débutantes and doing the season.

Had I been allowed to join them, my life would have turned out very differently. Queen's Gate was an excellent school and, after only a few weeks of term, I had been pleased and flattered when a teacher had taken me to one side, and told me (for the first time in my life) that I had a good brain, and should certainly stay on to do A-levels. But my mother was totally opposed to my becoming a débutante and, in any case, Arnold said that we couldn't afford it. So my name appeared on none of the social lists, and the only special tea-party to which I was invited turned out to be a complete humiliation. As soon as it was discovered that my mother wasn't giving a dance, or even a cocktail party, pencils were put down, notebooks were closed, and I was completely shunned.

And since I could clearly never compete in the society to which most of the leading lights of the school belonged, I left the tea-party then and there; and I promised myself that I would leave Queen's Gate at the end of the term, and find a place for myself in the world of the Arts Lab and the swinging sixties, a world in which my brother could guide and protect me.

It was probably the worst decision that I ever made in my life.

※

I still had to turn up to Queen's Gate in the mornings; but I discovered that I could disappear in the afternoons without anyone noticing: and I spent most evenings and weekends at the Arts Lab. When my friends heard where I was going, they were intrigued; and I persuaded Annie, Eleanor and Podoff to meet me there one Saturday lunchtime.

Once inside, we found ourselves in the large white room that had been intended to be bright and clean, but was already becoming dim and dirty. Near the front, there was a counter where everyone was supposed to check in to prove that they were members. In practice few people bothered: except when I was on duty on a Saturday or Sunday afternoon. I made a great many people pay for their year's membership before allowing them in.

"Now we have to take off our shoes," I explained to the others. "No-one's allowed to wear them beyond this point." Podoff took hers off and handed them carelessly across the counter as though she had been coming to the Arts Lab ever since it opened. The others followed her example, and then began looking round. They seemed amazed by what they saw.

There was an art exhibition in progress; but in between the paintings, there were dozens of posters advertising pop concerts and unusual 'happenings'; and in between the posters there were messages written straight onto the walls (in the name of the New Freedom) by people who were looking for somewhere to stay.

"Have you noticed the smell?" I asked Annie, who was admiring a poster for a concert by Tyrannosaurus Rex at the Roundhouse. "The whole place stinks of hash and smelly socks!"

I led them over to the cinema, which instead of traditional seats had foam rubber pieces cut into mattresses on the floor. "There's nothing showing this morning," I explained. "But this afternoon it'll be packed out. They're starting a twenty-four-hour session – a complete season of Ingmar Bergman, starting with *The Seventh Seal*... have you ever seen it?"

Later on, we made our way to the front of the Arts Lab, went upstairs, and sat down at one of the pine trestle-tables in the restaurant. This was presided over by Sue Miles: a tall, handsome woman with blond hair, whom we could see bustling about in the distance, directing operations with enormous energy. She was not only a very good cook; but had her food served up on decent china – even if one sometimes had to wait a long time for it to arrive.

※

When my three guests had left, I wandered over to the workshop and began climbing up the ladder which led to Jim's inner sanctum. I had been up there many times before: it was a kind of roof-studio, but had no windows, and almost no furniture: just a few cushions, and a large foam mattress made up with dirty sheets, and strewn with books, magazines, play-scripts, and even a typewriter. As I climbed, I began to hear Jim's voice. I found him sitting cross-legged on his mattress, dictating a letter to Lindsay, his secretary. On another part of the mattress sat a girl who was busy rolling a joint. Jim looked up as I came in and sat down beside him, nodded amiably, and finished dictating his letter. 'Address it to Lord Goodman at the Arts Council,' he concluded, 'with a copy for information for Jennie Lee.'

Then he turned to me and kissed me on the cheek. I felt filled with happiness. "They're not too pleased about you and Nigel being so involved," he said quietly. "Remind them that I'm looking after you, will you?" While he was still speaking, another girl had come up the ladder and joined us. At that moment, the lit joint was passed to me, and Jim took it from my hand. "Nicky doesn't use this stuff," he said calmly.

"Boring!" said the newcomer, sitting down close to us. She was beautiful, with dark brown eyes and high aristocratic cheek-bones. "You're Nicky Samuel, aren't you?" I nodded, flattered that she had heard of me; but then she spoiled it by turning to Jim and asking: "Why don't you encourage her to loosen up a little?" She turned back to me. "If you'd like to really turn on and have fun, I've got some high-quality coke."

Strangely exciting sensations were running through me; but before I could reply, Jim had intervened. "Fun? Do you call it fun to screw up someone's life?" He puffed on the joint, and passed it on to Lindsey. "Sexual freedom", he said very quietly, "that's a kind of liberation. But hard drugs – it puts one right back in prison again." Then he raised his voice just a little. "Nicky, you and I are going out for a coffee. All right?"

As if he needed to ask! I just wished that he would stop looking at me as though I was a nice little girl who needed protecting. After a while I began to believe that Jim's continuing lack of sexual interest in me, must have something to do with an unspoken fear that I wanted him as my exclusive property. So I laid some false trails in the hope that if he saw me going out with other men, it would make me appear less threatening.

Re-kindling Jonathan's interest in me didn't take long; and we began going out together at week-ends. One of our favourite haunts was UFO, in the Tottenham Court Road, where Jack Henry Moore's psychedelic light-show had transformed a large unprepossessing cellar full of drugged-out hippies, into something quite magical.

Jonathan appeared to be intoxicated by me (as I danced in my tie-dyed T-shirt and crushed velvet bell-bottoms); and I was intoxicated by the swirling lights, the glimpses of old silent movies which were projected onto the walls, the smell of incense, and the loud insistent beat of the music from groups like Soft Machine or The Pink Floyd.

When the cellar became too crowded for comfort, we followed UFO to their new home at the Roundhouse in Chalk Farm, an enormous building which had once housed railway steam-engines. With its shell of iron girders, its brick walls and its broad concrete floor, the acoustics were better, and it could hold far more people; but the atmosphere was never quite the same.

We also visited The Speak-easy, just off Oxford Street, which was frequented by a much smarter set of people; but although Jonathan was intrigued, I preferred Middle Earth. Located in a basement in Covent Garden, Middle Earth was filled with the sound of all the latest music; and somehow the combination of records and live groups, of showmen like Jeff Dexter and the disc-jockey John Peel, of the scent of incense and the smell of hash, made it an invigorating experience.

But by the time I had begun going regularly to Middle Earth, I had left Queen's Gate; I had some new friends; I had found myself a proper job; and at home there had been a major change for the worse.

CHAPTER ELEVEN
Monty Berman and Making New Friends

My leaving Queen's Gate at Christmas very much annoyed the Headmistress, as it drove a coach and horses through her rule that no-one was allowed to go there simply to do re-takes; and she compelled my mother to pay the fees for the rest of the academic year. However, I had made my decision, and that was that. My mother didn't try to oppose me; but she said rather desperately: 'If you're going to leave school, you must do something, Nicola. Go and talk to Arnold about it.'

So, I went to have breakfast with Lord Goodman; and over a plateful of kedgeree I told him that, subject to interview, I hoped to go to Hornsey College of Art in September to study fashion. He studied his empty plate thoughtfully before re-filling it with a generous second helping. 'The problem is, Nicola, that in the meantime you're going to get very bored and very lonely.' I opened my mouth to reply, but he waved a forkful of kedgeree at me, and went on: 'It's no good, Nicola. I insist. Your mother insists. If you're going to leave school you've got to do something. So what shall it be?'

I answered vaguely that I was interested in the theatrical world; and within a few days, Goody had arranged for me to be interviewed by someone at Shepperton film studios. The interview was not a success. It was made abundantly clear that if I wanted work, it would be making cups of tea and being a general dogsbody. So I made my excuses and left. I had begun to realize that I was never going to be poor, so what was the point of doing anything unless it really appealed to me?

However, Arnold was unyielding; and his next step was to contact Monty Berman, a friend of his who ran a theatrical agency in the West End. Bermans supplied costumes not only for all the big movies, but also for whatever was being produced at Covent Garden or Sadlers Wells, so working for them sounded interesting, and it would be useful experience before going on to Hornsey in the autumn. Monty Berman himself interviewed me, eying me so closely that I almost wondered whether the front of my blouse had suddenly become transparent. Presumably he liked what he saw, because he offered me a job straight away in his production department at a salary of £15 per week.

I accepted and, on the day that I was to begin, I woke up feeling very smug about having a job while all my friends were still at school. I had set my alarm for 7.30, dressed in a very conventional short black skirt with a Shetland sweater, and caught an eight o'clock bus which took me almost all the way to Bermans' production department in West Street, just off Cambridge Circus.

Going in, I found myself in a very smart ground floor, well-carpeted, with comfortable chairs, and a counter to one side, by which stood a glamorous woman with long painted nails, false eyelashes, and a voice so soft and low that she seemed to purr as she spoke, and from then on I thought of her as Pussy. I was just explaining who I was, when the door opened behind me, and I turned to see a famous film-star walking in. Pussy glanced at an appointments diary on the counter.

'Miss Gardner,' she purred, for this was indeed the legendary film actress Ava Gardner. 'You wanted to choose the colours for your new costume. Excuse me just one moment.' Then she turned back to me. 'Just run downstairs, Nicky, and introduce yourself to the others. They'll explain what you have to do. You can go through there.' I nodded, and walked through an office where an old dragon was hunched over a desk examining what looked like a pile of receipts. I slipped past, muttering my apologies for having disturbed her, found the stairs, and was soon down in the basement.

There I met my new colleagues: one girl about my age, who had only recently started work; and another who was seven or eight years older, and had been put in charge of us.

'You'll enjoy it here,' the older one said cheerfully. (The younger one, who was standing beyond her, made a face at this, and it was all I could do not to laugh.) 'The stock-taking's fairly routine, of course. But most of the time you'll be out and about. Come and look at this map, and I'll show you where you can find our main suppliers.'

The time raced by, and suddenly it was eleven o'clock, and time for a coffee-break. The girl of my age brought me a cup, and I tasted it and made a horrible face. Just then Pussy (who was in overall charge of the three of us) came slinking through the doorway carrying fifty yards of chiffon, and murmured that she needed it pleated that afternoon. She was looking shrewdly at me as she spoke; and she suddenly asked me: 'Is there something the matter?'

'It's only this coffee – I think it's been made with boiled milk.'

This was the moment for Pussy to show her claws. She reached out with her long painted nails, grabbed me by the arm, and began pulling me towards the door. 'Nicky,' she said very quietly. 'Just come upstairs for ten minutes.'

There I found dozens of girls, many of them no older than me, cutting and sewing, cutting and sewing, making hats and dresses to levels of almost unattainable perfection. Pussy picked up a long Elizabethan gown from some-one's work-table. 'Look at this: it's only going to be on screen for a minute and a half, but it's all hand-stitched and beautifully made, and the materials are exactly right for the period. But that wasn't why I brought you up here. Have a good look round, talk to some of the girls, and then (if you still feel badly about the coffee) report to my office.'

It was exactly the eye-opening experience that Pussy had intended. The top three floors were nothing more than a sweat-shop. The girls worked from 8.30 in the morning till six at night; if there was a rush order they came in on Saturdays and Sundays as well; they were being paid far less than me; and most of them had to hand the bulk of their wages straight over to their families. I never again complained about the boiled milk in my coffee (though I didn't like it any better); and I returned to the basement determined to fit in as best I could.

The chiffon that Pussy had wanted pleated was dealt with by taking it to another sweat-shop in Soho; and then there was a break for lunch. I had been given a two-shilling luncheon voucher; but the three of us in the basement weren't allowed to go out to lunch at the same time, so I bought a sandwich, ate it in the street, and then wandered aimlessly round the shops. After lunch, Pussy wanted five hundred red beads; and then another two hundred in blue, and then, and then…

That night, as I lay in bed, I felt tired but satisfied, and with much to think about. For one thing, I was suddenly very conscious of sounding too much like a deb. For another, I felt very pleased that I had managed to do everything that had been asked of me.

During the next few weeks, I came to relish the fact that I was being paid for doing a proper job – and doing it well. I had soon learned where in London to get any material that was wanted, from silks and satins to french pleating velvets, in whatever quantity and in whatever colours were required; and I loved getting my pay-packet at the end of each week.

Gradually I added silk or lace scarves from the Chelsea Antiques Market to my wardrobe, and bought long leather boots which were made-to-order in Islington. I took a special pride in turning up to work in clothes which I had paid for out of my earnings; and if ever I wanted to appear particularly dashing, I could always wear one of my Granny Takes a Trip dresses: of which my favourite was the one made of crepe, its billowing satin sleeves covered with stars and moons.

I had only been there a few weeks when I was unexpectedly given a raise. Monty Berman met me in the street; and as he greeted me he took my arm, squeezing it just as if he were testing a piece of fruit for ripeness. 'You feel… that is to say, you look hungry, Miss Samuel,' he told me; and he increased my wages on the spot from £15 to £20.

My success at Bermans pleased me all the more, because when I went to be interviewed at Hornsea Art College, they took only one brief look at my portfolio of dress designs, abstract drawings and oils, before deciding that I was definitely surplus to requirements.

After a few weeks at Bermans, I had even solved the problem of what to do in my lunch-hour. It only took me ten minutes to walk to the Arts Lab, which left forty minutes to eat lunch with some of my new friends before walking back again.

These included a lovely tall girl with long red hair down to her waist; a short ugly creature who lived in Brixton, and used to write me long mad letters; and my favourite girl-friend, Hazel, an actress whom I had deliberately cultivated in the first place chiefly because she had a pronounced cockney accent which I wanted to copy. But she was also unbelievably ravishing: the sexiest creature I had ever come across. So far as I could gather, she lived in Islington with a drunken father and a host of brothers and sisters; and she seemed to change her boyfriends almost as often as she changed her rôles. She was always returning from an audition with some new part to play; but within a very short time she would grow bored and want to move on elsewhere.

I had also acquired several new men friends, the most respectable of whom, curiously enough, was a friend of a friend of my mother's, Nicky Ryman, then in his first or second year at Cambridge. Then there were two Jewish boys in their twenties whom I met in the Betterton Street basement, where Joe Boyd was in charge of an operation producing and selling posters for International Times. They stood out from most of the people I knew in the Arts Lab/IT world, because they were elegantly dressed in smart leather jackets, good quality shirts and tailor-made trousers; and aftershave was the only thing of which they stank.

'We've heard of you,' the dark, curly-haired, more good-looking one told me. 'Have you heard of us? This is Ian,' he said, indicating his long-haired companion, 'and I'm Peter. We call ourselves The Firm.'

'Haven't I seen you up at the Roundhouse?'

They smiled at each other. 'That's right,' said Ian. 'We're the heavies. We make sure everyone stays in line.'

This was the start of a friendship which lasted for several months. We would have lunch or supper together; they would talk to me for hours on the telephone whenever I was feeling miserable about Jim, or worried about Nigel; and sometimes I would ride on the back of one of their motor-bikes to the Roundhouse. I hadn't believed that they were heavies; but there was no doubt that other people became very quiet and restrained in their presence, and I didn't have to endure the usual string of people asking me to put in a good word with Nigel on their behalf.

They were very loving and affectionate, and Peter even took me over to his parents' house in Deptford to meet his family. We sat in their front room eating sandwiches and drinking tea; and (as always in his company) I was very much aware of my Jewishness. At first this felt strange. I had spent so many years at school denying my origins; and now I found myself with people to whom the name Samuel, taken in tandem with a Coutts cheque-book, meant something very positive.

Before long they had involved me in a seemingly endless round of parties and happenings; and inevitably the moment came when I started taking drugs. Nothing hard: just hash and grass, which I took mostly out of politeness, because I never really liked them. I certainly didn't need hash to relax me, because I had been taking valium ever since my last term at Tortington Park; and, more recently, when I had complained that I was finding it difficult to get to sleep at nights, Dr. Rossdale had prescribed Mandrax, a relatively new and very popular sedative drug which was only later discovered to be addictive.

After evenings out with Peter and Ian, I often came home at three or four in the morning; and I was disappointed when my mother didn't take the slightest notice. But then, she was heavily pre-occupied with her relationship with Basil Brooke who, much to my fury, had moved into Henniker Mews early in the New Year of 1968.

✻

Basil was good-looking, kind, loyal, and everything that my mother needed; in fact, he looked after her tirelessly. However, he was not my father; and I am sorry to say that I behaved very badly towards him. Despite all I had learned from Jim about the new permissive society, I was deeply shocked by the fact that he and my mother were sharing a bedroom, and making no secret of the fact. I particularly hated going into her room to say good-morning before I left for Bermans, and seeing him eating breakfast in bed, prepared for him by Rita exactly as she had once prepared my father's breakfasts.

At least I still had a brother; and I spent many evenings with Nigel and Suzy in the large penthouse apartment which they shared in Portland Place, Portland Square. Their furniture, which was mostly modern, came from places like Habitat, and I didn't much like it; but Suzy had decorated the apartment in a pleasingly eccentric style, with lots of cushions on the floor, and a stage at one end of the enormous sitting-room in which we sat and talked.

I usually met Nigel beforehand in his offices in Betterton Street. This meant negotiating the stairs past the first floor most of which, with Nigel's permission, had been taken over by a group of ten or twelve men, women and children belonging to the Hare Krishna, a Hindu sect founded only two years previously in New York City. Shaven-headed, wearing orange Hindu garments, and constantly chanting, they lived, cooked, ate and slept with only primitive rush mats between them and the floor. During the day they wandered up and down Oxford Street seeking converts; and in the evenings they somehow overcame a complete lack of any proper facilities, and cooked exotic vegetarian dishes.

In the early days Nigel and I had eaten with them several times: this involved sitting cross-legged on the floor, and listening to a great deal of chanting before we were allowed to begin helping ourselves to morsels of food wrapped in betel-nut leaves, washed down with nothing stronger than water, and followed by little cubes of marzipan cake. However, by now the first floor had become so squalid that it was easy to resist the robed figures who beckoned me to eat, and I would climb past them up to the third floor.

This was Nigel's domain, and everything here was perfect. Indeed, it was so much like being back in our father's Library at Chuffs that I half expected to see a little Indian on top of the book-shelves. The carpet had a comfortable deep pile; there were leather armchairs everywhere; also a television set, and some stereo equipment; and Nigel was sitting at a partners desk with his whisky and half-a-dozen telephones.

The only problem (from Nigel's point of view) was that the telephones hardly ever rang, which he found frustrating. However, he amused himself by managing a pop group called Tintern Abbey; and he was also taking a serious interest in Black Power. Once when I knocked on his office door, and walked straight in as usual, I found him deep in conversation with a black man in a very sober suit, who seemed to defer to him in everything. They both stood up as I approached, and Nigel, beaming with pleasure, said:

"Michael – this is my sister. Nicky – This is Michael X. I've been wanting you two to meet for a long time.'

Michael X held out a hand in a self-effacing kind of manner. I shook it, but didn't look closely at him. 'It's a pleasure to meet you, Miss Samuel. Your brother's such a good friend to me!' Then he turned to Nigel. 'This is all peace and love, man! We'll talk again another day.'

After Nigel had seen him out, he came back to his desk and poured himself a small whiskey. 'A very important man,' he said, nodding in the direction of the door. 'He wants to do everything he can to look after the black people of this country. We're discussing how I can be of use. You know, of course, that Daddy always wanted to go into politics? But I can't say any more at present. And in any case, Michael says that perhaps what I'm doing here is the most important thing I could be doing.' He sipped reflectively on his whisky, and added: 'I'm having supper with him and his wife in Islington this evening. It makes such a change to talk to someone who cares about what's right for me, and isn't just after my money!'

'It seems a strange name. What do you know about him?'

'I don't know the whole story,' Nigel replied, 'but I gather he was poor when he started – very poor. He began by doing whatever he could to stay alive: collecting rents, that kind of thing. I think he was mixed up with Rachman, and a great many bad people. But then he began reading all about Malcolm X, and what Malcolm had achieved for black people in America, and that changed him completely.'

At this time, Nigel was full of optimism; but as the weeks went by, and the telephones on his desk remained silent, his mood changed. He tried presiding over International Times board meetings. 'But what's the point?' he said to me despairingly one April afternoon, pouring out the last of the whisky, draining his tumbler, and then reaching for his second bottle of the day. 'All the important decisions have always been taken before the meetings begin. D'you know, I've just had lunch with Miles and Jim at the Cafe Royal. I told them what I feel.'

'And what did they say?'

'Nothing. Sometimes I think that Michael's the only one who really understands what I'm trying to do.'

'Perhaps you shouldn't be giving them so much support, if they don't listen to you?' My intervention had a much more dramatic effect than I had intended.

'You're right.' He drained another half-tumbler of whisky in a single gulp, and lurched angrily to his feet. 'You're right, Nicola, that's it. I'm Nigel Samuel, and I'm going to close this building down. I'm going to close this newspaper down. The whole thing. Now. Down. That's it.' And he stormed out of the room, his angers and frustrations swirling around him like a flock of attendant demons.

From downstairs I heard raised voices. I stood up, feeling terribly sad, and left the building. Not that I was surprised by what was happening: I had lunched with a very unhappy Suzy the previous day, and she had told me that Nigel wasn't well, and that she was worried about him. We had both cried, and hugged each other. We were both so dependent upon him; and these violent mood-swings were making Suzy's life especially difficult. As for me: I looked still more fervently in Jim's direction.

※

The day after Nigel had threatened to close down IT, I ran into Hazel in the restaurant at the Arts Lab. She was drinking a coffee, and as soon as she saw me, she called me over. 'Hi, Nicky! How are you doin'?' As soon as I was within range, she seized my hand, and I could see that her large dark eyes were dancing with excitement. 'Guess what! I've been talkin' to Jim 'Aynes.' She smiled so warmly that I felt a stab of jealousy. I looked down at her breasts, gorgeously full and seductive above that tiny waist. She was so lovely. How could Jim resist her? 'Nah, nah! Nothin' like that!' She must have been reading my mind, and I blushed deeply. 'The point is, 'e knows you love him; but listen, darlin', 'e says 'e don't want to 'urt you.'

'So what does he mean by that?'

But she was already getting up. 'No more to say, darlin'. You'll 'ave to ask 'im yerself. I'm on stage in 'alf an hour. Another ruddy audition! Be seein' you!'

As soon as I could, I found some pretext for going to Jim's room; and then summoned up the courage to repeat my question to him in person.

He flushed a little, before saying abruptly: 'Sit down a moment, and listen. I'm very fond of you, Nicola, you know that; but because of Nigel you're a problem. You know that he's been threatening to withdraw all his support?'

I nodded. 'I was in his office yesterday.'

'It's not just the money… I like Nigel. If I didn't…' He sighed, and for once seemed almost at a loss for words. 'Lord Goodman… we're all… everyone's worried about him. If they thought that you and I… it's just impossible.'

I began crying, and he lent me a grubby handkerchief and gave me a hug. I wanted so much more, but this was good, and I felt happy again. Jim got up rather suddenly, and said: 'Let's spend time together next week, shall we? I'll meet you at Guys and Dolls, and we'll have lunch.'

It was incredibly painful to me that Jim persisted in treating me like a child; and then I thought of a way to make him take me seriously. I had showed him a newspaper article once about flower-power on the U.S.A. campus; and he had told me how backward our students were compared to those in America, where the new ways of looking at things had already improved so many lives. What better way of impressing Jim than by going over there to experience those new ways for myself?

※

My first step was to go round to Portland Place, where I discussed my plans with Nigel and Suzy. 'I've saved £100,' I told them. 'I can live on that for a few weeks; but I shall need help with the air fare.'

'Nigel will take care of that, won't you?' said Suzy, taking his arm. 'Did I tell you that we're off to Paris next weekend? It'll be like another honeymoon…'

'Yes, I'll do that,' said Nigel. He stood up, and was soon pacing thoughtfully up and down on the stage. 'And I'll ask Mike Henshaw what he can do to help. He's got friends over there.'

'Who's Mike Henshaw?'

'My accountant: he's doing a lot of work for me at the moment. I'm buying a castle down in Cornwall: there'll be enough room for Tintern Abbey to have a proper recording studio. Look,' he said, pulling a wallet out of his pocket, and coming down to re-join us, 'I've got some photographs here. It's more like a French chateau, really...'

My next step was to give two weeks' notice to Bermans. I did this all the more easily because, having learned the ropes so well, I was now bored to tears. Most days I had done all that was required of me by two in the afternoon, there were three hours to kill until we went home, and I hated sitting there twiddling my thumbs with nothing sensible to do.

Next, I had to explain what I was doing to Mother and Basil. I was nervous about this; but Nigel sent Mike Henshaw round, and he told them about his relatives in Boston, and that made them happy for me to go, especially as Jane had begun to think that I was spending far too much of my time at the Arts Lab. For once, everything seemed to be working out well; and when Jim learned of my plans he told me that, of the two of us, he thought that I was the truly strong one: which mystified me completely.

At last my ticket was bought, my passport was in order, and it was the eve of my departure. I lunched with Mother and Arnold; and then in the afternoon Nicky Ryman came round, and invited me out. I had already done all my packing, so I agreed; and that evening I put on my stars and moons dress; and he introduced me to a completely different side of the alternative culture.

※

It began when Nicky knocked on the door of Sarah Skinner's house in Redcliff Gardens; and we were invited in by Sarah herself. She was tall and elegant, with large brown eyes, and long brown hair whose reddish tints caught the light. She was wearing expensive jewellery, a beautiful snakeskin jacket, and snake-skin boots; and her house was full of beautiful antique furniture.

Suddenly I had found all the traditional wealth and good breeding of the Queens' Gate debutantes, combined with all the revolutionary ideas of the Arts Lab. It was a mind-blowing combination. Within a few moments, I was seated on a large comfortable sofa, with Nicky Ryman's thigh against mine, pretending to be hip and eying some strange exotic creature who was offering me a drink. 'Is it a man or a woman?' I asked Nicky, slightly too loudly.

'Shut up!' he said, kicking me in the shins. And when the person moved on, he explained: 'That's Amanda Lear. Haven't you read about her?'

Then the door-bell rang again, and in came a very handsome and clearly quite genuine man wearing a flowery shirt and velvet trousers: another celebrity, but this time I recognized him instantly. It was Nigel Waymouth, owner of Granny Takes a Trip on the King's Road, one of whose dresses I was wearing at that moment. I had seen him several times in his shop, but noticed nothing except that he had a kindly face.

Now I decided that I wanted him to like me; and we were both part of a group which stayed together when the rest of the company had broken up. First we went to see a movie version of D.H. Lawrence's *The Fox*; and then on to my first smart dinner, at a restaurant on the Fulham Road called the Baghdad House. Upstairs it all seemed quite conventional; but we were ushered downstairs to an area full of glamorous-looking people smoking joints and eating humus. We found a table (though most of the people were sitting on cushions on the floor), and Nigel Waymouth sat next to me.

In one corner there was an Indian who was playing lush, sentimental music which seemed to go with the Indian food and the smoke in the air; and after a while, a young girl in an eastern costume began belly-dancing. Immediately there was a slight hush. With her generous swaying hips and her large thrusting breasts she seemed to be inviting men's desire; and they evidently loved it.

'Do you know about this place?' Nigel asked me, when people had begun talking again. I shook my head, and he continued quietly: 'That's the owner, in the corner over there next to the Oudh player. He's a very sweet man. Abas. The dancer's his girlfriend.'

Abas must have guessed that Nigel was talking about him, because he came over to our table, and bowed. 'And who is being the lovely lady?' he asked Nigel.

'Nicky Samuel,' he answered obligingly. 'Remember her, Abas. She's all right.'

'I am most pleased to hear it. By the bye, you know that upstairs tonight we have Detective-Sergeant Grimes – a coming-up man in the C.I.D. So we must all be a bit careful tonight!' And he smiled and left us; and clapped his hands, and the belly-dancer stopped her gyrations and went to sit on his lap.

And the next day, which was Sunday 2 June 1968, Suzy and my brother Nigel came with me to London airport, and I flew to New York.

CHAPTER TWELVE
Reaching San Francisco

Soon after the plane touched down at La Guardia airport (with a few terrifying lurches which no-one else seemed to notice), I began to feel panic-stricken. New York was still some distance away from Boston; so tonight, I must find a taxi and an hotel... but supposing something happened to me? I had seen films about New York. As I went through customs and immigration, I began picturing the headlines: **SIXTEEN-YEAR-OLD RAPED IN TAXI** or even **HEIRESS IN CEMENT OVERCOAT**. But then as I walked out into the arrivals area, I saw a large placard with my name on it, being held up by a kindly-looking Jewish couple who both wore enormous fur coats.

I thought for a moment that there must have been another Nicola Samuel on the flight. But when I walked over to ask whether it was *me* they were looking for, the lady gave me an enormous hug, and said: 'Nicola, my dear! I am Mrs. Hoffmann! This is Mr. Hoffmann! Arnold Goodman called us.' I felt amazed and yet terribly relieved.

Apparently (while I was flying at 30,000 feet over the Atlantic), my brother, becoming nervous about me, had telephoned Arnold and explained that in a few hours' time I would be arriving completely alone in New York, with no-one to meet my plane. So Arnold had contacted the Hoffmanns (he was a fancy solicitor, and she ran a nursery school); and they whisked me away to their home in Riverdale, a wealthy community on the northern edge of New York City, and just south of Yonkers.

As we drove up to their large, smart house, with its large, smart swimming-pool, in a neighbourhood which exuded an atmosphere of discreet wealth, I felt very strange; and when we went in through the front door, and a maid curtseyed to me, I felt stranger still. The Hoffmanns sat me down in a plush sofa, held my hand lovingly, enquired after my family (whom they had never met), pressed me with all kinds of food (strictly kosher), introduced me to their daughter when she came home from work (she was only a few years older than me but wearing a suit) and sent me to bed. As I nodded off to sleep, I kept thinking that meeting a truly Jewish family was like straying into a pack of over-affectionate St. Bernards.

The next day, Mrs. Hoffmann begged me to stay with them another night, to give them time to arrange my flight to Boston; and Mr. Hoffmann gave me money, and promised to send me an allowance every week while I was in America; while their daughter found a friend for me called Steve. He also wore a suit, drove me round New York, gave me lunch in a cheerful down-town area called 'the Village', took me to see *The Prime of Miss Jean Brodie*, and never even tried to kiss me.

Then on Tuesday the Hoffmanns drove me to the airport. Mrs. Hoffmann blew her nose on a large handkerchief and told me to take care, Mr. Hoffmann slipped another few twenty-dollar bills into my hand, and I flew to Boston.

※

When I walked into the arrivals lounge at Boston, I was longing to see Mike Henshaw's friends. I knew that they would be the type of people I wanted to meet: lovely laid-back relaxed hippies; and at first I walked right past the tired, perspiring gentleman in a plain suit, carrying a briefcase, who said right in my ear: 'Are you Nicky Samuel from England?'

Mr. Kramer, who unsurprisingly turned out to be not a hippy but a chartered accountant, led me to his car, an enormous battered-looking vehicle which looked as if it had seen a good deal of stock-car racing and come off worse every time. Then he drove me through miles and miles of suburban sprawl, depressing and seemingly endless because Boston was now only one part of a megalopolis which had swallowed up the city of

Cambridge and half a dozen small towns. As he drove, Mr. Kramer told me it was very fortunate that I had arrived today, because tomorrow his daughter Roz was graduating from High School, which would be a great occasion; and when eventually we reached a particularly dreary-looking house in a particularly dreary-looking street, he parked the car and pressed two or three times on the horn, looking quite cheerful for the first time since I had met him. 'We're in Newton Highlands now,' he said. 'We're Home!'

Then he took me in to meet Mrs. Kramer, who greeted me very kindly, took me up to a hot and humid room at the very top of the house, and explained that she was very sorry that there was no air-conditioning. All the heat seemed to rise right up through the house, but guests who had stayed there had said it was all right if you kept the windows wide open all night. I unpacked my bags and sat on the bed. I looked through some copies of IT I had brought with me. Then I started crying.

When I came downstairs again, I heard the sound of laughter coming from the living-room. I walked in and there, sitting on a sofa watching *The Lucy Show*, was an overweight girl with long brown hair, a darker skin than mine, and a featureless face. This was Roz, and when I came closer, she jumped up and extended a pudgy hand in my direction.

"Gee, so you're the English girl! It's so great that you're here! You're just in time for graduation day!"

The following afternoon found me sitting outside under a roasting sun watching Roz and dozens of her fellow-students (wearing scruffy gowns over their everyday clothes) going up one by one to have their names called out and receive a certificate saying that they had graduated from High School. Everyone was taking photographs, Mrs. Kramer was crying, a band was playing, and suddenly everyone got to their feet and started fervently singing 'God Bless America!'

'Now that's over,' said Roz kindly, 'I'm gonna introduce you to all my friends.' And so she did. I found them rather alarming: bright young women called Alice and Katie, who were so much more in charge of their own lives than any young woman I had ever met before; and brash young men called Bruce or Joe, who were so out-going compared to English boys of their age, that I felt they would swarm all over me if I gave them half a chance. They all seemed to be driving cars from the age of fifteen, and distance meant nothing. If they said we were going to the beach, it could easily mean a drive of thirty miles up to Rockport or even (on one occasion) the seventy-miles down to Martha's Vineyard.

However, they were all deeply conventional; and when we came back home in the evenings, there was usually nothing more exciting to do than to sit next to Roz in front of the television set while she giggled her way through yet another episode of *The Lucy Show*. I began fidgeting after a while, and said I was tired and must go to my room; where I thought of the Arts Lab and going out to the Roundhouse, and wept tears of frustration.

Fortunately, before I left London an American girl called Betsy had given me the name and address of her sister, Ginger, who lived in Boston; and five or six days after arriving at the Kramers I telephoned her and arranged to meet her in Cambridge. Arriving there by taxi, I saw with delight that it was quite unlike Newton: we were travelling into a ravishingly pretty area with good clean roads, long avenues of trees, and whole streets of eighteenth-century town houses, looking as beautifully manicured as if they had been built for dolls.

I found Ginger ('Call me Gingie!') waiting for me on the doorstep of the German restaurant where we had arranged to meet. She was a shapely girl, with long wavy auburn hair, a lovely expression, and a personality to match. For the first time since I had come to America, I had found a real friend. I almost cried again, this time with relief.

After lunch, Gingie took me to what she called 'the Indian shop' on Newbury Street. This was a genuine hippy shop, just like those on the King's Road in London. It was very small, the air was heavy with incense, and it was crowded with bells, bracelets, odd bits of pottery, and all the alternative culture books that you could think of.

'I thought you'd cotton to this place,' said Gingie, taking my arm. Over lunch I had told her how terrible it was living out at Newton, and she added: 'Listen, kid – you know Betsy's on her way home? Well, I guess any time you care to spend with us, you're more than welcome. And now – let's go join the Love-In!'

The 'Love-in' turned out to be a huge gathering of people just over the road from the Indian shop on Cambridge Common. This was the place,

Gingie told me, where an American army had gathered to fight the War of Independence against England back in 1776. 'Not so good for you guys, huh?' she smiled. And now a new army had gathered here, fighting another war of independence, this time from worn-out traditional values.

As soon as we had stepped onto the common, we were among a mass of people. Close to the road there were whole families who had come prepared to camp out for weeks if need be, with tents and barbecues, and dirty barefoot children running around like savages. Further on, we passed someone quietly singing a Bob Dylan ballad, and accompanying himself on a guitar, surrounded by a semi-circle of listeners sitting cross-legged on the grass. Most of them looked stoned out of their minds, and there was a strong smell of hash.

Much further on, there was a makeshift stage where a full-scale band was preparing to play. The atmosphere was very peaceable. Even a large group of Hells Angels seemed entirely un-threatening; and although the police were in evidence (and I still hadn't got used to the fact that they carried guns, and that their gun-belts had real live rounds of ammunition in them) they seemed more bemused than anything.

I tried taking Roz to the Indian shop one day, but she seemed ill-at-ease among the beads and beards, and after that I escaped into Cambridge on my own whenever I could. Usually I met Gingie; but the first time I went back to the Indian shop alone, I took some copies of International Times with me, and the effect was magical: the people who ran the shop immediately drew me into their inner circle, and they even suggested somewhere in Boston where I could sell some of Jim's posters.

By this time, I had begun to hate returning to conventional Newton Highlands; but how could I get away from the Kramers without appearing rude? Then I had a stroke of luck. It was getting close to my seventeenth birthday; and the Hoffmanns rang up from New York to ask me if I would like to get away for a few days.

'Oh, do you think I could?'

'Why not come back here for your birthday?'

It was almost too good to be true. I accepted at once. Roz drove me to the airport, and I flew back to New York, where I spent four glorious days.

Not only was it lovely to be back in such palatial surroundings with such sweet people, but I had another glimpse of the Village; and I spent a memorable day walking around the Museum of Modern Art, where I particularly admired some works by Andy Warhol. I also took the opportunity of telephoning London to ask my mother whether I could stay with Gingie and her parents for a while, and to my delight she agreed.

So there I was, right in the centre of Cambridge. Some days I went to the museums and art galleries, and looked at pictures all day long; others, I spent as much time as possible soaking up the atmosphere on Cambridge Common. Quite apart from the love-in, and the occasional free concert, I once found myself in the middle of an anti-Vietnam War demonstration, caught up in a procession of people carrying placards and banners, and chanting 'L.B.J., L.B.J., How many kids did you kill today?'

I would have happily stayed in Cambridge for the rest of my time in the USA; but one evening I was invited out to supper by friends of the Hoffmanns, David and Cynthia Sears. It was Cynthia who opened the door to me. She was tall and thin and extremely pretty, with blonde hair, and a warm smile, and she was smoking a cigarette. She led me across a hall-way which was crammed with packing-cases.

'You know we're on our way back to L.A.?' As we went into the living-room, I could see two small children playing with some building blocks; and then a slightly-built bookish but good-looking man wearing glasses, who put down a newspaper and stood up to shake my hand. 'This is David – David this is Nicky Samuel.' I had already heard from the Hoffmanns that David normally taught psychology at UCLA in California, but had just spent a year as a visiting professor at Harvard, whose campus was just on the edge of Cambridge.

Although David and Cynthia were both conventionally dressed, they were lively and good-humoured; and half-way through the meal David looked across at his wife, and she nodded, and he smiled at me and said: 'Nicky, while you're over in this great country of ours – how about coming to the West Coast for a few weeks? We've got a great little place in L.A. – and we'd like you to join us there. What do you say?'

I jumped at the offer; and eleven days later (after I had made one last solitary tour of the love-in on Cambridge Common) I set off, ticket-in-hand, to meet them at the airport. Somehow there was a terrible muddle over my ticket, and I missed my plane; but the upshot was that some hours later the airline admitted that they had been in the wrong, and flew me to Los Angeles first class.

This was wonderful: we were treated like royalty. We boarded first, and then, instead of being squashed into a tiny seat, I found myself with room to stretch out; there were several free gifts; and instead of warding off starvation with a tasteless tray of mass-produced food, I revelled in a plate of lobster thermidor in a delicious white wine sauce. It was the first time I had travelled in such style, and I was hooked for life.

David Sears met me at the airport and drove me to his home out in Westwood, the home of the University of California. He and his wife owned a simple, comfortable house with a plain garden in an avenue of houses all looking very much the same. What struck me chiefly was the enormous fridge and freezer, both of which were always bulging with food, and quite unlike anything I had ever seen in England.

The day after my arrival, there was a ring on the door-bell just as we were finishing breakfast. 'I'll get it,' said David, exchanging a secretive smile with Cynthia. 'I think I know who it's going to be.' A few moments later he returned with a large bearded, long-haired man in his early twenties, wearing jeans and a T-shirt. 'Nicky,' said David. 'I want you to meet Dick Whitney. One of my finest students.'

Dick came over and held out a large hand, which I took shyly. During the next few minutes, I learned that he had just finished his UCLA course and was beginning a PhD in psychology. He wasn't good-looking, but he struck me as kind and protective, and when he offered to help Cynthia and David show me round L.A. I was glad to accept.

The next few days were a happy time. David showed me the University campus, and even talked of my enrolling at UCLA and studying English; I had long conversations with Cynthia; there was swimming in the day and parties at night; and Dick was such a frequent visitor that I began to be disappointed if a day went by without him arriving to take me out in his car for an hour or two: sometimes to see the sights, sometimes just to go to the beach to watch him surf-boarding. He was so good at riding those Pacific rollers that I began wondering what he would be like in bed.

However, before that could happen, he was driving me to the airport for the next stage of my American adventure. David and Cynthia were passing me on to some lawyer friends of theirs in San Francisco: the Waldmans, with whom I could stay for almost two weeks before starting the long journey back to England.

※

The Waldmans were something else. They had the most wonderful house in the whole of San Francisco. Right at the top of one of the hills on which the city is built, they owned a magnificent building: so modern that the whole of the front of it was a massive unbroken sheet of glass. And they seemed to give dinner-parties almost every evening.

One of their friends, Dede Brinton (Dick would have called her 'a sweet thing'), was a cheerful girl of about my own age, who had sparkling eyes and a smile as wide as the Pacific. The day after my arrival, she drove me over the Golden Gate Bridge into an extraordinary world of great beauty and great excitement and zeal. Berkeley College was one of the hot-beds of the alternative culture; and although it was the summer holidays none of the students seemed to be away on holiday. Instead, in that lovely setting, there were angry demonstrations against the war in Vietnam, and riot-police on every corner. Everyone smoked pot; and for the first time I met people who were also taking hard drugs like LSD.

Another day, Dede took me to Haight Ashbury in down-town San Francisco. For what was billed as the centre of a hippy universe dedicated to the ideals of flower-power and free love, Haight Ashbury was unbelievably seedy and squalid. The dirty streets were full of homeless draft-dodgers. Junkies wandered around in a kind of daze. Filthy, smelly people clutched at our clothes and begged for money.

I was both horrified and fascinated; and when Mr. Waldman kept producing smart young men from his office for me, I often insisted on them taking me down to Haight Ashbury. With one of them, I went to an enormous open-air concert given by The Grateful Dead; another took me to Chinatown; and the Waldmans themselves gave me lunch on a very beautiful island out in the Bay.

Then, sadly, it was the end of July, and time to leave. Dede drove me to the airport, and saw me off with a hug and one of her most enchanting smiles. I spent two or three days in New York with the Hoffmanns, and then flew back to England, where Nigel and Suzy were waiting for me at London Airport. They seemed to be quite unchanged: which was strange, because I felt so very different. The only thing that remained exactly the same was my longing for Jim Haynes. Or perhaps not quite the same. I was still determined to seduce him, but this time I would be more circumspect in my approach.

CHAPTER THIRTEEN
Seducing Jim Haynes

While I was away in the U.S.A., the silence from Jim Haynes had been so profound that on my return it seemed important to show him how independent I had become. Instead of haunting the Arts Lab, I now spent most of my time in a round of frenetic activity. This included visiting my friends, spending evenings out at all kinds of places, from Ronnie Scott's to the Roundhouse, starting a course of driving lessons, and flat-hunting. If I saw Jim at all, it was only briefly, on my way somewhere else, with other people. Sometimes, to my great delight, I noticed him following me with his eyes, looking surprised, as though he no longer understood me.

One weekend I even gave myself another holiday from London, and joined Nigel and Suzy at their Cornish castle. The three of us went out riding one afternoon through a most beautiful forest. There was almost no sound but the thudding of the horses' hooves, and the sighing of the wind in the trees; and for a little while I felt obscurely, darkly, secretly happy.

As for Mummy: after another spell in a Nursing Home, she was now sleeping without pills and feeling perfectly calm; Basil's divorce had come through, and the two of them were planning to get married. Although the thought of Basil becoming a permanent feature of Henniker Mews was still disagreeable, I found that I was mainly relieved to find Mummy so much happier and so much more normal than she had been ever since Daddy's death.

It was at the very end of August, when I was passing through the Arts Lab, and pretending to take a keen interest in a poster advertising 'The Doors' at The Roundhouse, that Jim finally laid a hand on my shoulder. 'Hello, Jim,' I said, continuing to look at the poster, though my heart was beating a little faster. 'We're just off to the Baghdad House. Would you like to join us?'

'No, not really. Why not stay here? You can have a sandwich, and I'll read you some poetry.'

Naturally I accepted; though as soon as the poetry-reading began to flag I thanked him and said good-bye and hurried back to Henniker Mews.

Then a week later I visited Jim again. We sat on the floor of his bedroom, where we talked for hours and by giving him a heavily-edited version of my American travels I believe that I finally made him a little jealous. 'Dick was so sweet,' I reminisced. 'So protective. A strong person, but gentle.' I could see Jim wondering whether or not we had been to bed together. I sighed as though recalling some particularly passionate embrace, and went on:

'We used to go to the beach late at night. It was so romantic with the surf pounding the beach... You know that I'm thinking of going back? I liked the University there so much, and David Sears – Did I tell you about him? A lovely man – so mature –'

I sighed again. 'He thought I could study English Literature; and I'm sure he wouldn't mind if I went on staying in his house...'

'Nicky,' Jim broke in rather sharply for once. 'It's a great idea to study. But why go all the way to the West Coast? You've proved you can do your own thing. Once you've found your flat, you'll be all right. You know I can always help you with your reading.' He leaned past me to pick up a book from a large pile which was gathering dust on the floor next to me.

For a moment we were very close, and I wondered whether he was going to kiss me. But this still wasn't the right moment. Hiding my disappointment, I glanced coolly at my watch. 'Thanks for your advice, Jim. I'll take the book. But I can't stay any longer. I've got to be up early in the morning. I'm seeing David Armitage. He's talking of some more photographs.'

David was now living in a little flat in Argyll mansions. It was a typical bachelor pad, with dirty sheets, books, papers and clothes all over the place, and filthy china everywhere; but I had remained a little in love with him ever since he had told me that I was a great beauty. I always secretly wondered what he had done with those bare-breasted pictures of me, and whether he would ever want to take any more; and I would have visited him anytime, anywhere.

This time, when I told him that I was looking for a flat, he became quite excited, and explained that 'right here in Argyll mansions' there was another ground-floor flat to rent, because its tenant was going away for six months. It was very tiny, with a small orange kitchen/sitting-room, a bathroom, and a brown bedroom at the back where a flight of stairs led up to a large double bed; but it opened onto the garden and I jumped at the idea. My mother agreed, provided that I could find another girl to share it with me. Which seemed like a major problem, until Jonathan introduced me to Clement Freud's daughter Nicky, who was also seventeen, and also wanted to move out of her parental home.

I found Nicky Freud clever and amusing, but she hardly stayed with me at all. One Sunday lunch-time she invited me to her family home; and we sat round the supper table while Clement told jokes in the lugubrious, slightly nasal tones which had already made him a popular television celebrity. Towards the end of the meal, he asked me one or two questions about his daughter; and then said: 'Well, I'm *so* glad you're such *very* good friends,' but he said it in such a way, and gave such an inscrutable smile, that I couldn't help suspecting that he knew the real situation perfectly well.

I felt very lonely in my little flat that night; and the following afternoon, when the lovely Hazel told me that she was having problems finding somewhere to stay with her boyfriend (Steve Took of Tyrannosaurus Rex), I rather stupidly suggested that the two of them should move in with me.

'Are you sure, Nicky?' She looked very searchingly at me. 'Won't it be difficult for you?'

'No, I should love to have some company!'

I meant this at the time; but it didn't turn out at all well. It wasn't too bad during the day, but at night it seemed only fair that they should take over my large double bed while I made do with the much smaller bed down below. And then I had to listen to them making love, which they seemed to do all night long, with great relish and abandon.

Being in a room where two other people are joyously making love (and taking no notice of you) is one of the loneliest experiences in the world. I never talked about this to Hazel, because I felt that my proper reaction should have been to feel happy for them. But I began taking more and more sleeping-pills, and I felt even more isolated than I had done when I was completely alone.

My sense of isolation was increased towards the end of October when Mummy and Basil were married at a Registry Office. The result was that I came to depend more and more upon Nigel and Suzy; and when (a week or two after Mummy's wedding) they set off very happily together for a holiday in Russia, I felt even more depressed. However, they say that the darkest hour is always before the dawn, and now at long last came the event for which I had been waiting for almost a year and a half.

※

It was 11 November, the day after Jim Haynes's birthday. He invited me out to dinner with him. I accepted, and afterwards we went back to the Arts Lab and climbed up to his room and made love.

In one sense it was very unromantic. There were no crisp Irish linen sheets, no lovely puffed-up pillows, no subdued lighting, no scent of exotic essences. His room was the same as ever: a complete slum with a dirty old mattress, greying sheets, pillows with the feathers coming out of them, and grey blankets which looked as though they belonged in Wormwood Scrubs.

But none of that mattered to me at all.

Jim was very gentle. First he undressed me, and I lay down on the bed, waiting for him. Then he undressed himself, and I watched eagerly but also nervously as he slid his pants down and I saw for the first time the male weapon (still limp and un-threatening) which I had so long wanted to penetrate me. Then he lay down on the bed beside me, and kissed me gently on the lips. I would have held him there, though I felt curiously tense; but he moved my arm aside, and began kissing me all over my naked body: on my throat, on my upper arms, on my belly, on my legs.

All this was so affectionate, that I began to relax. His kisses hardly seemed lustful. I felt so delicate and yet cherished beneath them, like a china doll that might break, but was in safe hands. Sometimes the kissing stopped for a moment, and he stroked my skin instead, while he told me how lovely I was. I felt completely secure, and happy. Then he moved back up my body, and for the first time began kissing my breasts. As he moved across my body, I could feel his prick growing longer and harder; and for a moment I thought of Mani d'Astier and shivered.

But then I felt a surge of pleasure so outrageous that my nipples began hardening beneath his tongue. The pleasure had permeated through my entire body, and I felt a great longing and readiness. From moment to moment, Jim seemed to know what I needed. He moved his head down, and kissed my inner thighs; and then when I was almost crying out for him to fasten his lips on my most private parts, he began.

Each suck of his lips, each lick of his tongue made me want him more; and then suddenly he was into me, his prick as firm as a rock, pumping up and down inside me. It was just what I had longed for. I wished to be battered, to be broken by his lust. I felt overwhelmed; and then my back arched, and I was moaning and shuddering in delicious orgasm. I wanted it to go on and on forever – and then, all too soon, he gave a little cry, and disengaged himself. Because he had taken what he wanted, or perhaps for some other reason, I loved him more than ever, and put an arm round him and stroked his head tenderly and watched him drift into sleep.

※

During the next few weeks, everything but my hours with Jim seemed shadowy and insubstantial. I was only real when I lay with him in bed: though not ever again in the Arts Lab. I had decided that Jim's bedroom was too squalid a place for our love-making; and since (shortly after their return from Russia) Nigel and Suzy had set out for a month in Jamaica, I moved into their flat in Portman Square. That was where I lay with Jim, damp with lust, learning every fold of his flesh, every movement of my body that could give him pleasure.

In between times my ghost-self wandered about in the everyday world: took a driving test, and failed it; visited Yoko Ono in hospital, where she was recovering after having miscarried a child of John Lennon's; ate and slept (often alone, because Jim only came to visit me every four or five days) and talked to friends. The only time that the outer world swam into sharper focus was on my visits to a remarkable shop in Eccleston Street off Chelsea Green.

※

It was Judith who suggested that I should go there: Judith, a beautiful Hungarian lady. She was a friend of Jim's, but with her long black perfectly groomed hair, and her exotic clothes, she was quite unlike the other girls at the Arts Lab. I was talking to her one day over a cup of coffee, admiring her embroidered Hungarian waistcoat (which had sparkling beads sewn into it), and telling her that I was tired of living in a flat that wasn't mine, and contained nothing of mine.

'In that case, Nicky, you must start at once thinking about how you would like this flat of yours to look. I have told you about Christopher Gibbs's shop, have I not? It is quite simply the best.'

'But isn't that where people like Talitha Getty go shopping?' I felt quite alarmed. Judith only smiled, drained her coffee, and stood up.

'Come. We are going now, I think! It will be an education.' I followed without another word.

When we reached the shop, an early Victorian building, I paused and looked at the window display. Most of the space was taken up with a beautifully carved Moroccan table. Above it, hung a Dutch brass chandelier; and the walls were lined with fabrics of every kind: including Greek, Moroccan and Victorian embroideries. It was superbly stylish and elegant. When we walked in through the door, an old-fashioned bell tinkled. It was dark inside; and then as my eyes grew accustomed to the subdued light, I began to realise that I was in an Aladdin's cave. Antique treasures were piled high on every side: exotic cushions of every size and colour; wonderful candle-sticks; gleaming chandeliers; tables made from darkly-coloured wood taken from ancient Moroccan ceilings; mirrors with two wooden doors made from the same wood, richly carved into mosaic patterns.

I noticed that Judith was calling me over to the desk at the back. She introduced me to the large Turk who sat behind it, and who rose to his feet as I approached.

'Nicky, this is Bouclant. He's in charge when Christopher's away. Bouclant, this is Nicky. In a month or two, she's going to be a good customer of yours. But first she needs to get to know what she likes.'

Bouclant bowed. 'That is wise: very wise in one so young and, if I may be permitted, one so beautiful.' He was very charming, and I felt myself blushing. 'And now, before you begin your inspection, I may offer you some tea, I hope. Will mint be satisfactory?' As if by magic he produced a tea-pot and three tiny tea-cups into which he poured a deliciously aromatic and refreshing mint tea.

It was on my next visit that I first met Christopher Gibbs himself: a thin, lean, very good-looking man, with rings on his fingers, and long blond curly hair. What was especially striking was the fact that he was wearing a Djellaba, a long white garment like a night-shirt with Moroccan embroidery all over it. I had seen hippies on the King's Road wearing similar garments; but where their clothes looked filthy dirty, Christopher's were freshly-laundered.

I hardly talked to Christopher Gibbs at first; but it was clear that he was a man of enormous taste and discrimination; and I felt that (in due course) I could learn from him much that was lacking in my knowledge of how life should be lived. In the meantime, I soon realised that he was quite unpredictable: one day he would be sailing down Oxford Street in his Djellaba, apparently quite oblivious to strange looks; the next he'd be in a tweed suit, or even in plus fours; and at one point, not long after I first met him, I noticed that he had shaved all his hair off. But whatever he did, and whatever he wore, he carried it off with such style that it always looked exactly right.

It was not until Jim and I had been making love to each other for some weeks that I told him for the first time how much I loved him. I remember that it was three or four in the morning, and I was very happily lying in his arms. But instead of responding in the way that I had hoped, a strange rather weary expression crossed his face; and he kissed me lightly on the forehead, and got out of bed and began getting dressed. Then he left. He had promised that he would come round again in a few days' time; but as the door closed behind him, I felt terribly lonely, having begun to realize, with a desperate sadness, that Jim could never accept the kind of love which I wanted to give him.

And then, late one evening, came the last moment of unalloyed happiness that I ever had with him. The door-bell had rung. Slipping on my dressing-gown, I raced to the door and opened it. There was Jim: but as I put my arms around him to welcome him (my dressing gown falling open so that my naked body was pressed closely up against him) I looked over his shoulder and saw that he had two girls with him.

'Hello, Nicky,' said Jim in his usual kindly voice. I disengaged myself from him, gathering my dressing-gown together as I did so. 'This is Iris, and this is Josie. They've just arrived in London. May we come in?'

'Yes, of course.' Looking at them properly for the first time, I noted with a feeling of extreme jealousy that they were both very beautiful. 'Would you all like some coffee?'

'I don't think we want any coffee,' said Jim, as they came in. 'I think we'd just like to go to bed.'

The two girls giggled. My heart sank still further; but I so much wanted to please Jim that I led the way into the large bedroom. The others followed, and immediately started getting undressed. Josie, who was slim and fair, undid her blouse and took off her bra, and then she turned and began hugging Jim from behind, pressing her breasts into his bare back. Jim had taken off his shirt already, and she slipped her hand down and found the zip of his trousers, and unzipped them and slid her fingers in and began stroking him through his Y-fronts.

By this time Iris, who had long dark hair, and an hour-glass figure, had slipped out of her skirt. She was wearing stockings and suspenders but no pants, and she came over to where I sat on the edge of the bed, feeling terrible and not knowing which way to look.

'Listen. Don't be shy!' She straddled my knees and opened my dressing-gown. 'Why, you've great boobs. Mine aren't bad, either.' She pulled a T-shirt over her head. Her breasts were even larger than mine, and she leaned forward and rubbed them against me. It was a curious sensation, rather exciting. 'Nicky, they're gorgeous. Do you mind?' She put her head down and began sucking on my nipples. Over her shoulder I could see that Josie had slid to her knees, and Jim had turned round, and she was caressing his balls and he had the biggest erection I had ever seen, and as I watched she began taking it into her mouth, just as I had dreamed of doing only a few minutes before.

Iris was still sucking at my nipples, and I could feel my body beginning to respond to her caresses, but it was all wrong. Everything was terribly wrong. Iris stroked her fingers down my thigh, and began moaning a little, and then her fingers wandered a little further, and her lips began looking for mine, and it was unendurable. I pushed her off me and got up from the bed and ran into the kitchen.

It was a narrow room with blue tiles round the surfaces and stools at a counter of white Formica, and I leaned on the counter and looked at the blue tiles and thought of the sea. I thought for a moment I could hear the waves breaking on the beach: there was a rasping sound, like the sea on the shingle, or perhaps it was someone drowning; and then I realised that I was sobbing.

I staggered away from there into the narrow spare room, which Suzy had decorated for me with flowered wallpaper covered in anemones. I lay on the bed and looked at the anemones. And then I looked at the bottle of sleeping-pills by my bedside and imagined being found dead in the morning. I could see Jim's face watching the ambulance carry me away; and there was my coffin being lowered into a narrow trench in the ground, and Nigel and Jim were throwing earth in on top; and I was beginning a long peaceful sleep...

I was just reaching for the pills when I heard one of the girls crying out in pleasure. That brought me to my senses. I realised that I was being just as old-fashioned as all the bourgeois people Jim had taught me to despise. By wanting to own him, I had failed him. But perhaps it wasn't too late to make amends.

I made my way back to the main bedroom, where I found the three of them lying very peacefully in bed. Iris and Josie had their arms around each other, and Jim was lying with his head in the small of Josie's back. They all looked very happy, and they were passing around a joint.

'I'm sorry,' I said. 'I'm afraid I've behaved rather badly.'

As I spoke, I began crying; and they made room for me in the bed, and Iris and Josie hugged me and kissed me and dried my tears, and Jim said soothing things to me, until I felt wrapped in a wonderfully loving cocoon. After a while, we tried again, until we reached a moment when Iris, no longer content with sucking at my nipples, had taken my left hand and placed it between her legs. 'Help me,' she whispered, 'Please, please help me...'

Suddenly I went cold, and that affected everyone. We all moved apart, and they began getting dressed. I tried to pretend that everything had been all right, but it wasn't any good. 'Jim,' I said, as they were leaving, 'I'm sorry I've been so difficult. Will you call me tomorrow?'

He turned and kissed me gently on my forehead. 'I'll come round,' he said kindly; and then he and Iris and Josie went away. I shut the door after them. I could hear them laughing and joking as they walked away into the distance.

It was just five days before Christmas; and I felt lonelier and emptier than I had ever felt since my father died. The person I loved most in the world had just walked out of my door probably imagining that he had given me a wonderful experience which would enhance my life, when all he had proved was that he could never give me the undivided love I needed.

This didn't stop me loving him. The very next day I waited and waited for him to come round, or telephone; and when he did neither, life seemed unendurable. Once again, I looked at my bottle of sleeping pills, and thought seriously about killing myself.

CHAPTER FOURTEEN
Chesil Court and a Bunch of Violets

In the morning I thought of a better way forward. I went down to the Arts Lab. Jim was there, and he looked anxious. 'Nicky, I'm sorry about not coming round yesterday. Arnold was on the telephone. There's a crisis in funding. Join me for a coffee, and I'll tell you about it.'

'That's all right, Jim,' I said, flashing him a smile. 'I haven't got time to stop. I just wanted to leave you a message. Look, here it is. 'Bye now!' And I turned on my heel, and walked back towards the door; where (in full view of Jim) I astonished some particularly scruffy hippy I hardly knew by kissing him warmly on the mouth. He tasted rather unpleasantly as though he hadn't brushed his teeth for a week.

※

However, Jim never replied to my message; and on Christmas Eve I heard that he had gone away to Cornwall. Nigel and Suzy were also away, so I went to Henniker Mews to see my mother, who was there with Basil. She told me that they were hoping to move down to Devon and, after listening to their plans for a few minutes, I went to collect a few things from my room. Finding that it was my room no longer, but had been completely taken over by one of Basil's daughters, I freaked out completely and ran out of the house gasping for breath.

A few minutes later I found myself at Chesil Court, in Chelsea Manor Street. This is a strange Victorian institution with porters on the entrance, and a glassed-in central area from which floors lead north, west, south and east, just as in many Victorian prisons. I was looking for my mother's psychiatrist Michael Davys who owned a flat on the third floor of the northern wing, and I was very relieved when he answered the door and welcomed me in. Michael had been a family friend for years; but as I sat down on his sofa, telling him about how I no longer had a home, I realized that he was treating me far more attentively than in the past and began flirting with him.

'Nicky,' Michael said to me eventually, 'I think I can see a possible solution to at least one of your problems.'

'Are you going to ask me to move in with you?' I teased him.

'Not exactly', he replied; and then suggested that if my mother really was moving to Devon, he could take over her house in Henniker Mews, which would free up his Chesil Court flat for me. 'Have another look round!' he went on. 'There's even a balcony, though it needs a coat of paint. In any case, I'm sure that Jane and I could come to some kind of arrangement.'

I thought it over. The sitting-room and bedroom were both a good size. It would all need redoing, but I could make it as elegant as Sarah Skinner's flat. 'Yes,' I said. 'Why not?'

※

While Michael and my mother were coming to terms, I escaped to Paris for a few days with Hazel. While we were there, I rang Luba d'Astier's son, Jean-Francois Bergery, and he and his girl-friend Katrine took me out to lunch. He looked at me hungrily, and I suddenly realized how handsome he was. A day or two later, on New Year's Eve, there was dinner at a Chinese restaurant with Jean-Francois, Katrine, Mani d'Astier & Luba. Strange company: Mani, whose prick I had been forced to suck when I was a girl of fifteen; and his step-son, whose prick I found myself hoping to suck at some time in the not-too-distant future. When we saw in the New Year of 1969, I was off-hand with the hero of the Resistance almost to the point of rudeness; but I hugged Jean-Francois very warmly. I wanted him to feel the imprint of my body against his for a long time to come.

Back in England, knowing that my only hope of regaining Jim's interest lay in pretending that I was no longer obsessed by him, I decided to find myself a plausible boy-friend. This didn't take long. His name was Henry: a dark, good-looking boy with medium-length hair who looked a little like the actor James Coburn, specialized in psychedelic lighting and occasionally worked at the Arts Lab. He was unexciting in bed, but very sweet. I installed him in my brother's house in Pavilion Road; and sometimes I wished that I could love Henry half as much as I loved Jim.

This deceptive romance led nowhere. The only major development was that my brother Nigel came round unexpectedly to Pavilion Road one morning, and announced that Suzy was pregnant. I was about to congratulate him, and was already pouring him a large celebration whisky, when I realized that he was not at all happy.

'I need cheering up,' he said, oddly. 'No, don't ask any questions. I expect things will be all right.' He drank his whisky in silence for a while, and then changed tack. 'You know, of course, that the Arts Lab is dying on its feet? Just as Michael X predicted.' He reached for the bottle, which he had been eyeing nervously, and poured himself another glass. 'He's the only one who's never lied to me. I'm off to see him now.' As I was helping him on with his overcoat, he asked whether Henry and I would join him for dinner at the Café Royal the next evening.

'Will Suzy be coming?' I asked. He shook his head. 'Then may I bring along my beautiful cockney friend?'

Unfortunately, as it turned out, he agreed. That evening at the Café Royal Nigel was the perfect English gentleman: refined, knowledgeable, courteous and utterly charming. Hazel, who had recently broken up with Steve Took, was overwhelmed. Over the soup, she and Nigel exchanged a few salient features of each other's lives, such as where they had been born, whether or not they were frightened of spiders, what their favourite films were, and so on. By the time we had reached the main course, the two of them were already staring into each other's eyes with a slightly dazed expression; and over coffee they were holding hands and murmuring little private jokes, as though they had been close friends for half their lives. Henry and I might just as well not have been there at all.

I had expected Nigel to be cheered up by Hazel, but not quite so dramatically. Within three days, he had booked an entire carriage on a night sleeper to Cornwall, so that he could take Hazel and Henry and me down to his Cornish castle for a long weekend; and within three weeks, he had asked Henry and me to move out of Pavilion Road, so that Hazel could move in.

By this time, I was so bored by Henry's constant devotion that I didn't at all mind leaving Pavilion Road. I couldn't move straight into the flat in Chesil Court, because it still needed a great deal of work; but Nigel had offered to settle me temporarily (at his expense) in the Cadogan Hotel, which was just round the corner in Sloane Street. Ah! The Cadogan! So wonderfully old-fashioned. My bedroom had an extremely comfortable Victorian bed; there was also an elegant sitting-room; and day-and-night room-service. It gave me a taste for hotel life which has never left me.

Nigel now had Hazel living in Pavilion Road, while Suzy remained in Portman Square. I felt sorry for Suzy, but what had happened between Nigel and Hazel was so much my fault, that I guiltily avoided her company and we became estranged. I was also on the verge of becoming jealous of Hazel, who was being showered with presents, when one morning, as she was showing me some exquisite new silk shirts, she noticed that I was rather quiet and guessed the reason. 'Come on,' she said, linking arms with me. 'It's all on Nigel's account – let's go and get something for you as well. No, of course he won't mind!' Soon we were in Piero de Monzi in the Fulham Road, buying more silk shirts, and some beautifully tailored Italian trousers. Hazel signed for them with a flourish; and after that we used to go there almost every day.

As for Nigel himself: even a wife and a mistress didn't wholly satisfy him, because they were both white, and he had developed a fondness for going to bed with beautiful young black women. This had been encouraged by Michael X with whom, having quarrelled with most of his former associates, Nigel was spending more and more of his time.

Soon after I had moved into the Cadogan, I was enjoying a late breakfast in bed, when reception rang to tell me that Nigel was on the way up. When he came in, he looked round with an air of satisfaction, and rubbed his hands together. 'I hope they're looking after you properly, Nicola?' Before I could reply, he sat down on the side of my bed, and said very enthusiastically: 'He'll be with us in about half-an-hour, you know. Michael X! We're going to be working very closely together from now on. Have you got anything to drink up here, by the way?'

I poured myself some more orange juice, rang down to room-service for a bottle of whisky; and a little later Michael X made a dramatic entrance, dressed in long white robes. He swirled up to Nigel and clapped him on the shoulders. 'Hey, Nigel! It's great to be here, man. Truly great.' Then he turned a very kindly face towards me, said 'Nicola, how rude of me!' and held out a hand. When I held out mine, he seized it, and carried it to his lips 'It's truly wonderful to see you again. Such beauty.'

He was so charming and enthusiastic that I couldn't help being attracted to him, although I had just heard from Nigel that he already had not only a wife but also three or four mistresses. Retrieving my hand, I found myself wondering whether it was true what they said about black people being enormously well-endowed. Fortunately, I had the presence of mind not to ask him; and instead, I mentioned that my Father had been proud of having published Colin MacInnes, whose 1957 novel *City of Spades* had been a celebration of black immigrant culture.

'Colin! Oh, yes, indeed,' said Michael X. 'A great man; and one of my closest friends.' He went on to talk about his plans for a black 'urban village' somewhere in London which would be a centre of Black Power and Black Culture. But I hardly heard what he was saying: because as he talked to me, I was looking him straight in the eyes for the first time; and it gave me a terrible shock. There was no life in them whatever. I could hear a voice talking; I could feel a hand briefly touching my arm. But I felt as though I was looking into the eyes of a dead man.

※

Towards the end of February, The Arts Lab staged a remarkable mini-musical, *Vagina Rex and the Gas Oven*. Written by Jane Arden, a convinced feminist, it starred Victor Spinetti, playing a traditional, oppressive husband; and Sheila Allan, as his much put-upon wife. Watching it, I began to understand why it was that my mother had never wanted children. By starting a family, the Sheila Allen character had become a slave; and now, at long last, she was demanding the return of her freedom.

Members of the audience who wanted to show their support for Women's Liberation could dance naked around the stage; and a highlight came when the entire company tumbled through the paper loins of a moaning mother-goddess, almost into the laps of the audience. Full frontal nudity under swirling psychedelic lights, with everyone and everything bobbing around to rock music, made *Vagina Rex* by far the most popular play the Arts Lab had ever put on.

Every night at nine, when the performance was over, Victor Spinetti and Sheila Allen would descend on a pub just over the road. 'What are you having to drink, love?' Sheila asked me, when I joined them after the second night. 'You don't know? Well, it's bloody cold outside. Join me in a port-and-lemon – that'll warm you!'

I gulped it down, loving its soft velvety texture. I bought another, then another; and before the evening was over, I was roaring drunk. It was a wonderful experience. In recent months, I had been relying on Mandrax to relax me in public, doubling and tripling the normal dose, and buying supplies on the Black Market when I felt that I couldn't ask Dr. Rossdale for another prescription just yet.

But Mandrax didn't produce anything quite like this warmth, this comradeship: Victor Spinetti raising his eyebrows and telling amusing stories about other actors and actresses; someone asking when I was going to join the revellers on-stage: 'Darling Nicky' – followed by a suggestive droop of the eyelids – 'we should so much like to see more of you!' And then laughter, and another round of drinks, and a taxi home to bed, and a curious dream which somehow involved the owner of Granny Takes a Trip, Nigel Waymouth, dancing with me on a sinking ship (though I seemed to be the only one who had noticed that it was sinking) and offering me a glass of port as the water crept up around my thighs.

When I woke up, the dancing seemed to be the most important part of my dream, and I realized that I had been given the perfect way of showing Jim that I was truly liberated and worthy of him. On the last night of

Vagina Rex, when I knew that he would be in the audience, I would impress him by joining the others on stage.

When the moment came for me to unhook my bra, pull down my pants, and then tumble onto the stage utterly naked with a full house looking on, I felt panic-stricken. But then, as we all surged into the glare of the lights, there was a cheer; and we were dancing together so happily, and the audience was giving us so much warmth, that for the first time in my life I felt happy about my body. It seemed weird that I had ever been ashamed about the size of my breasts. They were perfect. I flaunted them as I danced. I was perfect. Through the power of love, we were all perfect! Was this the start of a new age? Under those whirling lights, it seemed so.

Drunk again (but this time only with excitement) I found Jim talking to Victor at the bar of the pub over the road, and took him by the arm. 'Well?' I asked. Catching a glimpse of myself in the mirror which ran behind the bar, I could see that my eyes were shining. I looked like a wild thing, as alive and dangerous as a fire-storm, and as sexy as hell. But Jim looked at me very coolly and I suddenly felt as though a cold tap was dripping away in the centre of my stomach. It was too late to stop myself, and I was already saying: 'Didn't you think I was great?'

'You joined the others on stage, did you?' He looked at me for another second, said nothing more, and then turned back to Victor. I couldn't believe it. Instead of being pleased, he seemed cold and distant. Suddenly I felt that I must have cheapened myself in his eyes; and I took a taxi back to the Cadogan, rang room service, and knocked myself out for a few hours with a dangerous cocktail of port and Mandrax.

※

My life seemed to make less sense than ever. Nigel was so caught up with Michael X that he was no help to me. He was in the process of acquiring a block of property in the Holloway Road, and all he could talk about was the 'Black House' into which it would be converted. Even Hazel felt excluded sometimes. She and Nigel began quarrelling, and sometimes she would be very tearful when she came to see me: first at the Cadogan, and then at my newly-renovated flat in Chesil Court.

Moving in had been strange. On the surface, it seemed that I now had everything I wanted: a flat of my own; a large allowance (not to mention friendly Trustees who had paid for all the work at Chesil Court without a murmur); and a few good friends. I also had help in the flat. Rita, who had lost her job when Basil and my mother moved to the country) was now working for the film-star Peter Lawford; but she came round to clean for me twice a week; and I had another woman who came in every day. So I was free to do exactly as I pleased. But what was that? In practice I spent many mornings alone in bed, and many afternoons alone in the cinema, my only constant companion being anxiety about whether or not I had a future with Jim Haynes.

Perhaps there was a way to find out. Hazel was convinced that our lives are governed by the stars, and persuaded me to begin weekly visits to an astrologer at a spiritualist centre in Belgrave Square. It cost a great deal of money: £10 for a private sitting of half an hour; but it was something to cling onto, until the day came when Jim listened with complete indifference to the news that Henry and I had broken up.

That afternoon, feeling utterly hopeless, I made my weekly visit to Belgrave Square. My usual old lady looked into a crystal ball for a while, and then shivered as though the air round her had suddenly become extremely cold, and told me that I was giving her such bad vibrations that she wanted me to leave her room and never return. 'Don't worry', she said, 'You won't be charged!' But she looked shaken and couldn't meet my eye.

Feeling horribly frightened, I returned to the main desk, where they found someone else for me to see. Soon I was in another darkened room, and sitting down opposite another lady, who seemed even older, her face a mass of lines, and so thin and shrunken that it was like talking to a death's-head. At least she had no crystal ball on the table in front of her. She just looked me steadily in the eyes. She didn't speak for a while, and then her voice was so thin and reedy that it seemed to come from far away. 'It's very hard... very hard to talk to you,' she whistled rather than spoke, 'because I know what's going on in your head.'

'What can you see?' I asked; although in my heart I already knew the answer.

'You've got a bottle of pills at home. There they are, in your bathroom cabinet; and you're thinking of taking them.' And then she paused again, seeming surprised, and looked over my shoulder. At the same time, I felt a strangely comfortable feeling – yet not so much a feeling as the memory of a feeling; but it gave me some relief, I wasn't sure why; and there was a sweet scent in the air. I began to cry; and when the old lady spoke again her voice was a little softer. 'All I can say, child, is that your Daddy is here. He is asking you not to take the pills. He is offering you, instead, a bunch of sweet-smelling violets.' Encouraged by the feeling that my father was still there for me, even beyond the grave, and not wanting to let him down, I fought against the depression that had threatened to overwhelm me, and carried on.

※

I was soon glad that I had done so, because only a few days later Jim knocked on the door of my flat in Chesil Court. He was alone. When I asked him in, he explained that he had been heavily pre-occupied by worries about the future of the Arts Lab. It seemed impossible to raise enough money to keep it going, and after two years of working twenty-four hours a day he was thinking that it might be time for him to move on to a quieter life in Paris or Amsterdam. Then he asked if he could have a bath. A few minutes later, I was undressed and waiting for him in bed; and he came in from the bathroom, and towelled himself down, and joined me beneath the sheets. It was wonderful to have him back; and, knowing what he liked, I lay back and opened my legs and let him slide down my body and begin gently sucking my cunt.

Later on, when we were resting, and he was lying peacefully by my side, I took things a stage further. Remembering how much he had been aroused by Josie taking him in her mouth, I went down on him, held his prick in my hand, and began licking the tip with my tongue. As he grew longer and harder, I took him into my mouth, using a gentle pressure from my lips to stimulate him further. He was groaning with pleasure, and telling me how beautiful I was; and now, caressing his balls gently with one hand, I began sucking his prick as though it was a huge lollipop, up and down, up and down, until his erection had become truly magnificent.

Afterwards we slept; and when I woke again, light was just beginning to filter in through the curtains. Jim was still beside me, lying on his back with just a sheet over him; and as I looked down the bed, I saw from a hump in the sheet that he had a huge early-morning erection. Sliding my head down under the sheets, I began sucking once again on his prick. And then, with a thrill of delight, I realized that he was awake; and he clasped me round the thighs, and pulled me towards him; and I felt his tongue entering me, and suddenly I was both sucking and being sucked. It was a delicious experience.

However, we were soon back into the old pattern. However good the sex had been, he would always leave me in the early hours. At long last I understood that he would never make a total commitment to me, and I began looking round for a more satisfactory partner.

Before long, my choice had settled (ambitiously) upon Nigel Waymouth, the most fashionable hippy in the King's Road, clean, good-looking, elegant, and the friend of people like Mick Jagger and Brian Gibbs. I remembered dancing with him in my dream; and he seemed to have been somewhere in the background of my life for a long time. My very first Coutts cheque had been written out to Nigel's Granny Takes a Trip in payment for a mini-dress in Indian cotton; and I had developed a slight crush on him ever since meeting him at Sarah Skinner's house just before my flight to America. But although I sometimes saw Nigel in his shop, looking stylish in his flowered shirts and velvet trousers, I was too much in awe to make a direct approach. Within the King's Road set, Nigel was a super-star. While I was still wondering how to engineer another meeting, I found help from a totally unexpected quarter.

CHAPTER FIFTEEN
David Litvinoff and Nigel Waymouth

One of my favourite haunts was the Picasso, a cafe on the corner of Chelsea Manor Street not far from Chesil Court; and I was having lunch there one day, feeling lost, lonely and unhappy, when a complete stranger walked up to my table. He was stocky, with heavy, powerful features and the scar of a razor-slash across his face. He wore an old tweed jacket which looked as if it needed some attention at the elbows; and round his neck, instead of a tie, he sported an enormous red and white handkerchief. As soon as he reached me, he bowed his head a little and began talking in a quiet, but curiously insistent voice. His clipped accent was like an echo of Noel Coward; and as he spoke, he made elaborate gestures with his hands.

'Hello! Nicola Samuel! You're Howard's daughter, of course. A great man. I say that reverently and in all sincerity. From a fine Jewish family, too. We Jews should look after each other, I think, don't you? I'm so sorry, how rude of me not to introduce myself. My name is David Litvinoff, and I'm a homosexual. May I sit down?'

I nodded, amazed to be recognized.

'You are a Jew,' he went on; 'but not a practising one, I think? Your mother, I know, is a Protestant. Ah, well.'

He sighed as though the Protestant religion was a distasteful subject; but then brightened almost immediately, and went on:

'A painter I believe? But so sad for you to have abandoned the Jewish faith. Such a rock in an uncertain world. Should you not study it? Go back to your roots? Perhaps, as a first step, a visit to Israel?'

I soon realised that there was no need to answer any of his questions; and as this curious monologue proceeded, I grew steadily more and more fascinated.

Had I known anything about David Litvinoff's background, I might also have been alarmed. The black sheep of a remarkable Jewish family which had fled from Russia and begun life again in the slums of London's East End, he had developed a taste for danger, and living on his wits. Where his half-brothers, both of them writers, had used legitimate means to work their way out of the East End, David had found work as a Rachman rent-collector, before becoming closely involved with those notorious gangsters, the Kray Twins.

Litvinoff had been lucky to survive his association with the Krays. At one point they discovered that he had siphoned off a large sum of their money; but because they liked him so much, they decided not to kill him outright. Instead, they shaved his head, scarred his face, and hung him upside down from a top-floor window in Kensington High Street. Fortunately, the driver of a milk truck spotted him early in the morning, and he lived to tell the tale. Somehow, he even talked his way back into the Krays' confidence, and acted unofficially as their book-keeper long after they were sent to jail.

When I met him, 41-year-old Litvinoff was still living by his wits. His chief source of funds was providing William Hickey (the *Daily Express* gossip column) with anecdotes about the rich and famous and, in the curious mélange of late Sixties society, he was one of the 'fixers' who brought together pop-stars, poets and peers of the realm. 'And what do you think of the current political situation?' he was asking me.

'No particular opinion? Too busy, I expect, though I should welcome your views. In the film world, of course, we hear very little about politics. Donald Cammell was saying to me only the other day – you know we've been shooting a film with Mick Jagger, we're calling it *Performance*...'

His voice tailed off for a moment as a new idea struck him.

'Nicola, do you believe that you look after yourself properly? Have you a butler, for example? Ah, I thought not. In your father's time, of course...'

He smiled sadly at me (as though my lack of a butler marked a fatal stage in the social decline of the Samuel family); and then he discreetly changed the subject.

'I have a young associate, Gerry Goldstein, a man of great talent. A friend of Clare Peake – Mervyn's daughter. I'm sure you've read *Gormenghast*? And Eric Clapton thinks highly of him – gives him guitar lessons at the Pheasantry. I think you would be good for each other. Perhaps you should meet?'

'Yes,' I said, trying to hide the excitement in my voice. 'Yes, I should very much like to meet Gerry. I'm sure I've heard of him… Isn't he a friend of Nigel Waymouth?'

Gerry Goldstein turned out to be another rather affectionate very sweet boy rather like Henry, and I allowed him to visit me. David Litvinoff was delighted. He had been trying to find Gerry a rich young girl, so I fitted perfectly into his scheme of things. But Gerry remained more a part of David's life than he was of mine. I asked Gerry about this one day. We were in my flat, and he was stretched out lazily on the sofa. 'So why do you let David go on running your life?'

He shifted his position slightly.

'Sometimes it's awkward, I know. But I owe him everything – he found me when I had nothing. He's been like the most wonderful elder brother. Nothing's ever too much trouble for him. And he knows everyone. He's even promised to introduce me to Bob Dylan.' He sighed happily. 'Can you imagine meeting Bob Dylan?'

And then he left, promising to telephone me early the next day.

There was no telephone call, and when the door-bell rang I thought it would be Gerry, but when I opened the door I found instead a drink-sodden tramp on my doorstep. On one arm he had an umbrella of the British flag; at his feet were about a dozen carrier bags; and he stank to high heaven. I was appalled, and I was just about to slam the door on him, when he announced in a strange sing-song voice:

'It's all right, now don't you worry. It was David's idea. He sent me. I'm John Ivor Golding. I make a very good chicken stew, and I've come to be your butler!'

I was so much in awe of David that I let him in. Later, I learned that Litvinoff had found John Ivor Golding at Victoria Station; and it was his practical joke on Chelsea Society to inflict him on various of his friends just to see their reaction. Rather like Litvinoff, the tramp talked endlessly, hardly pausing to draw breath. At first what he said was interesting, but after a while it tailed away into complete alcoholic madness. 'Do you have any books here?' he began.

'Plays are my favourite of course. Plays and poems. Have you ever seen *The Caretaker* by Harold Pinter? I was the original for the tramp, you know; and if you have his poems, you can read a dedication to J.I.G.: John Ivor Golding. Yes, Harold has made me famous.'

He sighed and sat down heavily in an armchair. From one of his carrier bags, he extracted a brown paper bag; and from the bag he extracted a brown snake, which slithered onto his lap.

'I suppose I have been a big reader in my day, a reader of solitude and melancholy. Mr. Pinter I believe found me very sagacious and psychometric in mind; but you know I find so many are like leeches on my confidence…'

Misinterpreting my horrified gaze at his snake, he broke off for a moment.

'Now don't you worry. I was better garbed once than what you see me in. I was a master of ceremonies at holiday camps, for Old English and Modern Ballroom, do you see? And I wore a proper top hat and tails. But I don't trust the law. I have to be quite frank about that.'

By now I was desperate to get him out of my flat. I asked if he would like a drink; and when he said that he would, I took him to the pub opposite, which had two doors. We went in through one into the Public Bar, and I bought him a pint of Guinness. While he was happily drinking it, and telling me that it would take him more than two dozen cases of brandy and whisky before he would give the police a thought, I told him that I was going to the loo, and went instead into the Lounge Bar and escaped through the other door.

※

The next day, Litvinoff rang up. He said nothing about John Ivor Golding, but told me that he had arranged for Gerry and me to stay with Bob Dylan. I completely believed him, and was already packing a suitcase, when he rang a second time to tell me that Bob Dylan had had to cancel because he was wanted in New York.

When Gerry came round, we decided to have lunch together at the Picasso; and there at long last my hopes were answered. Just as we were leaving, we ran into Nigel Waymouth. He and Gerry greeted each other like the old friends they were; and then Gerry began introducing me. But Nigel, who had begun looking at me so hungrily that I felt quite weak at the knees, cut him short. 'That's all right, Gerry. I remember Nicky. We met at Sarah Skinner's, and went on to The Baghdad House. Where are you living now, Nicky? I've been hoping I'd run into you again.'

I could hardly believe what I was hearing; but I summoned up the presence of mind to scribble my address and telephone number on a scrap of paper. 'There you are – come and visit me anytime!'

He took me at my word, and a few days later he telephoned me at one o'clock in the morning. He asked whether he could come over to see me. I agreed. As soon as he walked in through the door, and I saw this slim, handsome man I felt incredibly sexually turned-on. We began kissing almost at once, and within a few minutes we were in bed together, having the most wonderful time.

※

The next few weeks were very weird and confusing. Nigel Waymouth came round from time to time, but I couldn't be sure how he felt about me; and one night, when he hadn't visited me for a day or two, I swallowed so much Mandrax that when he did unexpectedly turn up I had absolutely no memory the next morning of anything that had happened. Jim Haynes spent a night with me; Michael Davys took me out to a dinner-party, and David Armitage photographed me again. And then Nicky Ryman reappeared on the scene. He still seemed very fond of me, and once we even went to bed together; but he had changed a great deal: religion, not sex, was now at the centre of his life. He talked endlessly about his Indian guru, and about meditation and preserving one's Karma, so when during the second week in June he invited me to join him for a holiday in Spain, his invitation was so casual and un-threatening that I happily accepted.

It was after this that Nigel Waymouth suddenly became far more attentive; and this was what I wanted, more than anything. Although Granny Takes a Trip appeared to be in financial trouble, Nigel still seemed to know all the most interesting people in London, and talked amusingly about them. When he heard about John Ivor Golding being sent round to be my butler, he laughed and told me that was typical of Litvinoff. 'I'm glad you took John Ivor to the pub, at any rate. David uses him as a kind of cruel measure of people. He'd have called you a cold-ass if you'd simply slammed the door in John's face.'

'You don't think I'm a cold-ass, do you?'

'Just come here and find out.'

Over breakfast the following morning, I told Nigel that I was going to Spain with Nicky Ryman. 'Would you like to come too?' I tried to make it casual, but I had to cough to cover the fact that my voice was trembling with emotion. When he said 'Yes,' I couldn't really believe it, and I spilled the orange-juice I was pouring.

I don't know whether Nicky Ryman's nose was put a little out of joint by this, but I was too excited to care. I just said to him: 'Nicky, I'm bringing Nigel along with me.' No doubt he accepted it as part of his destiny. A week later, when Nigel and I flew out to Marbella, Nicky was waiting for us at the airport. I noticed that (in deference, perhaps, to his new religious beliefs) he was wearing an embroidered Indian top.

✢

Marbella was clean and beautiful. A small sea-side town with cobbled streets, her white-washed houses all seemed to have brightly-coloured Bougainvillea or Morning Glory growing up their sides. Nicky drove us to a little hotel called the Fonda, where Nigel and I shared one of the rooms which surrounded a central courtyard. In the evening Nicky joined us for dinner, bringing with him Sarah Skinner, and a few other local friends. Once again, I noticed how pretty Sarah looked, and how the red in her hair caught the light so attractively. 'Nigel, it's silly you and Nicky staying here,' she told him over coffee. 'Why not come up to my place? The house is full; but no-one's using the cottage, and the two of you could share it for a few days.'

So the following day – which was also my eighteenth birthday – we moved up into the hills above Marbella, where Sarah lived in a traditional stone villa, simply and elegantly furnished, beside a large swimming-pool. That evening, to celebrate my birthday, Nigel and Nicky had dinner with me at a restaurant in Marbella. It should have been the perfect end to a perfect day; but I was feeling uneasy about my relationship with Nigel. Was he genuinely with me, was I his girlfriend, or had he just come along for the holiday?

That question would soon become still more relevant. One afternoon we were sunbathing by Sarah's pool when I heard the noise of a car arriving. Then there was something of a stir by the house. When I opened my eyes and looked up, I could see that a group of women had arrived and the most beautiful of them, who had oriental looks and long black hair, was being greeted by Nigel with the warmest of embraces. 'This is José Fonseca,' he told me when he had disengaged himself. 'I forgot to tell you that I'm one of her English Boys!'

'That's the name of José's model agency,' explained Sarah. 'Mark Palmer began it three years ago.'

'He included all his friends,' said Nigel.

'All the handsome ones,' said José, squeezing his arm.

'A very mixed bunch,' said Nigel, ignoring her. 'Everyone from antique dealers to aristocrats. Christopher Gibbs, Julian Ormsby-Gore. Then he started English Girls.'

'Among them the famous Christine Keeler,' said José. She was now looking at me so closely that I was horribly conscious of the fact that I was wearing nothing better than one of my tie-dyed T-shirts from the Chelsea Antique Market, while José wore a marvellous fashion-setting chiffon dress which I later discovered was an Ossie Clark original.

'And then Mark simply took to the road,' said Sarah, 'in a horse and cart, can you believe it, to spread the word.' They all laughed heartily. I did my best to join in, but I wasn't really listening. I had realised that José was fashionably flat-chested. Had she been staring at my enormous breasts? I flushed; and then (as if plucking the thought from my mind) the others began teasing me about their size.

I pretended to take it in good part; but it was like being back at school again, and the comments from these jet-setting friends of Sarah's were cruel. After one of them said in mock sympathy: 'It must be terrible for you walking past building-sites!' Nigel made a gentle protest: 'Now then, give her some space!' To which came the inevitable reply: 'Sorry Nigel, of course we will.' (Pause for effect.) 'She needs it!' Followed by more laughter. Once again, I did my best to join in; but I felt excluded and miserable.

Nigel could see how upset I had been and that night, when we were getting undressed, he suggested that we should move on to Morocco. It was a romantic proposal. There was a moon in the sky outside, and our room was full of the scent of orange-blossom. I was so delighted with him that I flung myself into his arms, hugged him, and whirled him all the way round the room and onto the bed.

※

We went by boat from Malaga; and as we approached the coast of North Africa, I began to feel intensely excited. Tangier harbour became visible. Behind it, above two-hundred-foot cliffs, I could make out the crumbling walls and minarets of the Kasbah; and as we approached our landing-place, I could hear that from one of the minarets a muezzin was calling the Faithful to prayer.

Soon we were on dry land; and hundreds of Arabs (many of them children) pressed in on every side, crying out 'Baksheesh, Baksheesh!' and trying to sell us everything under the sun, from silver bracelets to their sisters. Just when I thought we were going to be overwhelmed, they scattered as a huge lorry drove past, decorated in silver and jewels. 'That's a water-lorry!' explained Nigel, who in the midst of all this confusion was calmly arranging a taxi and an hotel. Now that the crowd had thinned for a few seconds, I was chiefly aware of a rich odour, an unforgettable mixture of incense and mule-droppings, of herbs and spices, and bad drains.

Our hotel was depressingly traditional, but that afternoon Nigel walked with me along a series of cobbled alley-ways to the souk (or market-place) at the centre of Tangier. 'Here we are,' he said. 'The Cafe Central. This is where all the expatriate hippies hang out. They say if you wait here long enough, you'll see all your friends sooner or later! Let's go in.' We sat down at a little table, where Nigel ordered mint tea; and before long people were coming up and greeting him, and eying me curiously, and telling him about their latest amours.

'Come on', said Nigel after a while, 'I think it's time for us to go and call on Suki.' He had told me about Suki Potier. She was an old friend of his who had lived for years with Brian Jones of the Rolling Stones, and had borne his child. 'She came out here to lick her wounds after she'd broken up with Brian,' Nigel reminded me. 'She's a lovely girl, and I think you'll like her.'

Lovely was an understatement. Suki was ravishingly beautiful. When she opened the door of her flat to us, the first thing I noticed was the mane of black hair which (helped by a touch of henna) gleamed in the sunlight. Beneath that hair was a gentle, dreamy pre-Raphaelite face; beneath that again, a silver choker dangled at her neck; and she wore a velvet dress, with a dark-green top embroidered with gold, and heavy silver bracelets on each wrist. When I asked where she had found such wonderful clothes, she smiled, and fingered her velvet dress. 'This is a Moroccan wedding-dress – it's lovely, isn't it. Would you like to borrow one while you're here? You must stay to supper, and I'll show you my collection. I buy them from Ahmet. Has Nigel told you about him?'

'Not yet,' said Nigel. 'But I certainly think we should all pay him a visit. Why don't we have a session with him tomorrow, Suki? In the meantime, I'll just tell Nicky that Ahmet's the source of the best dope in London (ask Suki's ex.); and the best material too. Christopher Gibbs swears by him.'

The following evening, Suki came round with a Spanish girl-friend of hers, and the four of us went to Ahmet's shop in the souk. Here we saw bundles of material piled high from floor to ceiling; and then Ahmet walked in, and for a moment I wanted to laugh. We Europeans were all wearing ethnic Moroccan clothes; while Ahmet, a strange little man who can't have been more than four foot five, was impeccably attired in a Savile Row silk suit by which even my brother Nigel would have been impressed.

Ahmet bowed when he saw Suki (invested with an extra glamour in his eyes by virtue of being the mother of Brian Jones's child), and immediately ushered us through into a small lamp-lit room at the back of the shop, saying that he would join us shortly with some refreshment. The room was filled with Moroccan divans, on which we made ourselves comfortable;

and the walls were covered with pictures of the Rolling Stones. The largest picture was of Brian Jones; but you could only see his head, as the rest of the print was covered with pictures of flowers. 'It looks as though he's cut them out of seed catalogues,' said Nigel when I pointed this out to him. The Spanish girl (to whom I was taking a dislike) shivered, and clutched Nigel's arm, and said: 'Oh, I don't like that: it makes this room look like a funeral parlour.'

For a moment or two the atmosphere became very sinister; but then Ahmet returned with mint tea, and hash cake. At some stage, Ahmet put on a record by Jimi Hendrix. After a while the needle became stuck, and the endless repetition of a few bars of rock music added to my sense of alienation.

Ahmet went out for a while. When he reappeared, he had changed into a long Moroccan robe; and he began declaiming more and more wildly: 'I am the man of hashish! Later, I will give you the best, and you will buy a quantity, and I shall seal it safely for you and send it to England. This is what you must do… So says the man of hashish! Will you buy from me?'

Suddenly I felt frightened. Nigel had the presence of mind to say that we were going to be in town for several days, and that he would return and order something in the morning. Ahmet didn't answer this directly. Instead he groaned, and then waved an arm dramatically towards a pile of cushions in the corner of the lamp-lit room, and said in a strangled voice: 'There's a coffin underneath one of those cushions: someone's dead!'

He had made it sound like a threat; and in the morning we moved to another hotel, which made us feel safer. But Ahmet had been right: someone was dead. Down on the beach that morning, we met one of Nigel's friends, who told us that the news was already on the radio, and would soon be in all the papers. Brian Jones had died in the night. After that shock, we decided to move on to Fez, most ancient of Morocco's four imperial cities.

※

We boarded the train in baking heat. The last part of the journey took us through an idyllic countryside of low hills covered with olive-groves and orchards; and in the cool of the evening we arrived at Fez. There we booked ourselves into the Palais Jamais, an old Moorish Palace which had become a magnificent hotel. High up above the ancient city, and surrounded by lovely gardens, much of it was exactly as it had been for the past two or three hundred years. Because it was midsummer, there were hardly any other guests, and it was easy to imagine that the whole hotel was our private palace.

We climbed up onto the roof, and spent a long time hand-in-hand looking out over Fez as dusk fell, pointing out to each other the beauty of the ancient battlements, of the stone towers, of the thirteenth-century minaret of the Great Mosque; and then just hugging each other, alone but together under that vast North African sky. I felt very happy and at peace; and I began to hope and believe that what had begun as another of my school-girl crushes on an older man, had the potential of becoming my first truly complete adult relationship.

During the day we wandered through the souk, the whole of which was completely under cover. Not a trace of sky anywhere; and very few landmarks. We became happily lost, and spent the day wandering among the shops of the potters and the leather-makers, the goldsmiths and the silver-smiths. I especially enjoyed visiting a scent-maker, who had oils of every description which he mixed up for me into an exotic scent so strong that it lingered on me for days.

※

The homeward journey was an anti-climax, especially when we returned to Marbella and once again there was an evening when I felt horribly excluded by Sarah Skinner's friends. Much to my surprise (especially after those wonderful days in Fez), when I told Nigel the next morning that I wanted to return to England, he simply wished me a good journey, and said that he intended to stay on in Marbella for a while. I felt very confused by this show of independence, but tried not to show it, and flew straight home.

There, for the next ten days, I felt very much alone. It wasn't that I was languishing in my flat in Chesil Court: far from it, I ate out at the Picasso and the Baghdad House with my brother Nigel and Hazel; I had lunch with Mother and Basil, who were briefly in town; I went to visit Suzie in hospital, where on 14 July 1969 she gave birth to Nigel's son Howard; and I caught up with numerous old friends. But as the days went by and I heard nothing from Nigel Waymouth, I grew more and more depressed. And then on 20 July Nigel suddenly reappeared.

I had spent most of the day in bed, getting up only to go out and lunch at the Picasso, and then returning to my flat to watch the moon landing on television. Then Nigel rang on the door. One look at the love in his eyes told me that he had spent much time thinking, and had finally decided that his home was with me. I welcomed him with open arms, feeling tremendously happy; and we spent the rest of the night alternately making love, and watching the moon landing unfold. Soon after eight o'clock in the evening came the news that the *Eagle* had landed; and in the early hours of the following day we watched as Neil Armstrong became the first person to step onto the lunar surface.

CHAPTER SIXTEEN
The Black House and Modelling

That evening, we went out to supper at the Baghdad House. We reclined on cushions downstairs; and the hashish fumes and the eastern music reminded me of our happy days in Fez. The impression of being back in Morocco was heightened when Christopher Gibbs came in, wearing his djellaba. Nigel waved to him, and he came over. 'Christopher, have you met..?'

'Yes indeed. The beautiful Miss Samuel!' He made a kind of bow in my direction, and then swirled away to join a group of his friends.

Nigel turned to me in some surprise. 'You didn't tell me you knew Christopher?'

'We're not – he only knows me as a customer.'

'He's a very sweet man,' Nigel observed.

'You're not jealous, are you?' I laid a hand on his thigh. 'Tell me about some of the others. Who were all those people who waved to you when we came in?'

Nigel looked round thoughtfully. 'Isn't that Litvinoff at the table in the corner? And d'you see the man in brightly-coloured clothes, sitting next to him? That's the Australian artist Martin Sharp.' Nigel had already told me that before the days of Granny Takes a Trip, the centre of his world had been The Pheasantry in the King's Road. This was a building full of artists and musicians, and Nigel had shared studio space with Martin, who owned the whole of the top floor. 'He's not only wealthy, but incredibly talented. Have you seen his pictures for OZ magazine? They're curious, totally surreal, like a mixture of Van Gogh and Mickey Mouse…'

Nigel's voice tailed away as the belly-dancers began dancing, and then as I watched their swaying hips I heard a voice in my ear.

'A most interesting spectacle, don't you think Miss Samuel?' It was Litvinoff, who was sliding down onto the cushion next to mine. 'I see you are more than usually intent,' he continued. 'The religious element, no doubt? Have you given any more thought to the possibilities we mentioned? A return to the faith? But you're right,' (I had said nothing), 'this is neither the time nor the place. Do you know my friend Mr. Sharp?'

Martin Sharp was already deep in conversation with Nigel, and I could see that he was a well-built, good-looking man, who managed to look impressive despite wearing a multi-coloured T-shirt covered with cartoon characters. When he saw that Litvinoff was trying to attract his attention, he grinned and nudged Nigel. His Australian accent, which had previously been a gentle drawl, suddenly became extreme.

'Fair dinkum, cobber! So, this is the tasty little Sheila you've shacked up with! Why, she's got bigger…'

'I apologise for my friend's colonial crudity,' Litvinoff cut in. 'Too much meat, too much sun, that's the problem. Allied to a mercurial artistic temperament. Isn't that right, Martin?'

Martin laughed and held out a hand to me. 'I'm sorry – just teasing you a little.'

'What we came over to suggest,' said Litvinoff, 'was a little excursion next month. The open-air concert on the Isle of Wight. Dylan's going to be there of course. Keith Richards. Donald Cammell. Shall we make up what one might very loosely term a party?'

※

A few days later, Nigel was in my drawing-room at Chesil Court, screwing a lens into his camera. He wasn't quite living with me; but I'd noticed that he now kept a blue toothbrush on the rack above the hand-basin in my bathroom; and a couple of men's shirts had appeared in my wardrobe. 'Did

I tell you?' he said. 'We've been invited to a party this evening. It'll be a chance for you to meet some more of my friends.'

I so much wanted the evening to be a success that it took several Mandrax to calm my nerves before we set out. When we arrived at the party, it was full of extremes of light and shade. Here and there, brilliantly-lit groups gossiped elegantly under chandeliers: I noticed Michael Rainey talking to two very beautiful women, both with long well-shaped necks and large eyes and high cheekbones. 'The one on the left is his wife Jane,' Nigel told me softly; 'and the other one's her sister, Victoria Ormsby-Gore.'

Also in the light, we came across a tall, lean man with a wonderful face and a still more wonderful voice, talking to a well-endowed blonde with curly hair and glasses. Nigel introduced me; and a moment later the legendary Sir Mark Palmer was kissing my hand. From what I had heard of his epic wanderings around Britain, I had expected a rough diamond. Instead, I found a pure-bred English aristocrat.

'I hear you live in a caravan,' I said cheekily. 'Have you got the ponies tethered outside?'

'Sweet of you to ask,' he said, his eyes smiling. 'They're not here. I've put them out to grass up in North Wales.' Then we heard a woman protesting, and a voice being raised in anger. Mark's eyes stopped smiling and became quite steely. 'Excuse me,' he said. 'I do hope we meet again. May I just introduce you to Catherine Tennant?' And then he was gone. The blonde peered at me for a moment and then attempted a smile. 'Such a gallant knight, don't you think? And such a friend to Jane.' And then she too slipped away.

Nigel and I looked at each other, shrugged our shoulders, and passed on into the near-darkness of the next room, where junked-out hippies smoked joints and only very occasionally broke the silence with some enigmatic pronouncement. Nigel seemed quite at home, but these were not my friends and I felt curiously isolated.

※

Fortunately, I had remained close to Hazel, my beautiful Cockney friend. We spent many happy hours in our leather shoes and bells, going to films or just 'hanging out' in the King's Road; and one morning I noticed that a window was open at the back of Vidal Sassoon's.

'Why're yer stoppin'?' Hazel asked.

'Suzy goes here,' I answered. 'But I'm tired of paying their high prices. Let's sneak in!'

Hazel looked intrigued. 'Garn, Nicky, they'll find us aht, There'll be a helluva row!'

'They won't – it's all done on tickets. Once we're inside, no-one'll ever know!'

So we climbed in through the window, and went into the salon as though we had just come back from the loo. Then we approached Ricci Burns, the Jewish hairdresser who had been cutting my hair since I was sixteen. I had become very fond of Ricci. He had a warm heart, and hid a passion for women beneath an amusingly camp exterior. His long blond hair was always very elaborately done up; and his talk was highly theatrical. Somehow it made me feel very safe with him; and we sometimes compared notes about our mothers: he was devoted to his, which seemed to me a trifle eccentric.

'Darling!' he said, giving me a hug, and kissing me on the cheek, as he always did. 'Darling! You look sensational. And who's the lovely friend?' He was already toying with Hazel's hair. 'Oh yes, oh, my, how gorgeous! We can really do something with this.' He steered her into a chair, reached for his scissors, and began cutting with his usual speed.

On the way out, we helped ourselves to some cigarettes. Hazel was nervously fingering her hair. 'I should have warned you,' I told her. 'If he decides you're going to have short hair this week, that's it! But it looks wonderful: he's a real artist.'

※

That evening, I rang Jim Haynes. I had meant to tell him all about my relationship with Nigel; but he seemed to know already; and instead, I heard myself inviting him round. Soon after he arrived, we found ourselves in my bedroom, and he was sucking me off just as slowly and deliciously as ever. The feel of his tongue licking me was so very sweet – almost as sweet as it had been that very first time at the Arts Lab.

When he finally thickened up and slid into me, I grasped him with my cunt walls. The sensation of being so closely sheathed drove him wild, and he plunged his teeth into my neck and shoulders and breasts. I felt controlled, but out-of-control, writhing and twisting under him, welcoming each thrust, each bite, clasping his buttocks as he rode me and rode me. When at last it was over, and he had slipped out of me, I wanted the sex to go on. I pulled his hand towards me. He understood and I felt the delicate touch of his fingers, and then delight after delight.

Afterwards, smoking a cigarette, I said to him: 'It's strange, isn't it, that we should be lying here like this when everything's changed.'

'Changed?' He sounded surprised. 'How has it changed? Except that you're even better in bed.'

'I was thinking of Nigel.'

'Does that alter anything?' He looked at me shrewdly. 'I respect Nigel: he's a damn fine artist. But your relationship with him has got absolutely nothing to do with your relationship with me.' And with that he leaned over, and kissed me lightly on the forehead before slipping out of bed and reaching for his clothes. 'Everything's finished for me in London,' he said, as he pulled on his jeans. 'If you don't hear from me for a while, send a Poste Restante to me in Paris or Amsterdam.'

And then he was gone; and instead of feeling deserted, I began to feel strangely comfortable and secure. Whatever happened, Jim would always be there for me. He had become closer to me than my own quarrelsome family, who were united only in being deeply suspicious of my relationship with Nigel Waymouth.

One weekend, for example, I was having lunch with my brother Nigel and Hazel. Over several large whiskies, Nigel had talked about his recent foreign expeditions with Michael X: one of them by chartered aeroplane to Timbuktu, where he claimed to have become a Muslim.

'A grand ceremony,' he had told us. 'I had to wear special robes – oh, blast!'

He had spilled some of his whiskey; and I was just about to pour him some more, when Hazel said reproachfully: 'If yer reely a Muslim, 'ow come yer still drink?'

Nigel's good mood had evaporated faster than the spilled whiskey; and once Hazel had rushed off in tears, Nigel had turned on me.

'Who is this Waymouth person? Has he ever asked you for money?'

'No, of course not!'

'Just tell me one thing. Who paid the hotel bills when you were on holiday?'

I got to my feet, choking back tears, and fled from the room. Nigel must have stood up too, because I heard a crash as his glass of whisky hit the floor. He was cruelly calling after me: 'You can't answer that, can you? And when you next see him, ask him how his business is doing, why don't you?'

Arnold Goodman wasn't much better. He couldn't resist making fun of the fact that my boy-friend's surname was pronounced in the same way as Weymouth, a pretty little town on the south coast; and the next time we had one of our breakfasts together, he put down his copy of The Times, peered owlishly at me, and declared: 'I hear from brother Nigel that you've – um – taken up with a seaside resort!'

I smiled, walked round the table and ruffled his hair. 'Goody, you're being mean about him. He's very nice, truly!' I bent down and kissed Arnold on the cheek before wandering over to the sideboard to find some toast and coffee. 'But we needn't talk about him to-day. It's my brother I'm worried about. I don't see how anyone can cope with him these days. And have you any idea how much money he's sunk in the Black House?'

Arnold looked terribly glum, and pushed his plateful of ham and eggs to one side. 'I know, Nicola. It's a bad business, I'm afraid.' Then he brightened a little. 'Why don't you take your sea-side resort to investigate?'

※

So one afternoon Nigel Waymouth and I set off together for the Black House. It had been hot and sticky all day, and now there was that yellowish light and heavily-charged atmosphere which means that a thunderstorm is on the way. In the taxi Nigel told me something he had learned about Michael X. 'I was talking to Litvinoff. You know he worked for the Krays? Apparently so did Michael. Heaven knows what he did. But if you mention him to David, he just goes very quiet, and says: "He was a dreadful, dreadful man."'

We were both silent for a while. And then there was a rumble of thunder, and a flash of lightning, and a moment later rain began drumming on the roof of the cab. By the time we reached the Holloway Road, a depressing place at the best of times, the storm was at its height; and I had to shout to the cab-driver: 'Just up there on the left! Do you see those three empty shops?' We pulled up alongside the first of the three, and Nigel and I made a dash through drenching rain into the doorway. This semi-derelict block of property was the Black House. We pushed the door open and stepped inside.

'What you want?' A large black man, stripped to the waist and holding a crow-bar, blocked our way. The storm had darkened the sky, and there was no electric light; but beyond him I could make out more black workers sitting on packing cases and looking suspiciously in our direction.

'I've come to see Nigel Samuel – he's my brother.'

'Oh, Ni-gel!' He drawled over the word, and grinned, and stepped to one side. 'Hey everyone, this is Ni-gel's sis-tuh!' Everyone relaxed, and went back to their coffee and cards. And then a flash of lightning briefly lit up the room, and another figure emerged from the shadows.

'Hello there, little sister!' It was Michael X, dressed in his long robes. He spoke kindly, but his eyes were still dead, and it seemed to me that his whole head radiated evil. I tried not to show that I was scared.

'Don't call me that! I'm not your little sister! Where's Nigel?'

He beckoned us to follow him. A large hole had been smashed through the wall into the next-door building. We stepped through it, over a pile of rubble, to see a still larger hole into the ground-floor of the third house. We stepped through that, and saw a flight of stairs, down which my brother was walking unsteadily, glass in hand. Helping to support him was an attractive black girl. When he saw me, Nigel beamed with pleasure.

'Nicola!' And then (rather less enthusiastically) 'Nigel!'

'I see they've begun the great work,' I said.

'It's wonderful, isn't it? All thanks to Michael, of course. This floor is going to be the supermarket, running right through all three shops. When we've got the shelves up, it'll be tremendous. Oh, have you met…?' But the black girl, after a dismissive nod from Michael X, had made a rapid exit.

'And the other floors?' asked Nigel Waymouth, to fill an awkward silence.

'I'm glad you asked that,' said Michael X, 'because that's the heart of the project, man. It's going to be so great. A supermarket catering for black people, run by black people; and on the floors above the first two shops, lots of rooms for the workers, who will each have a share in the profits – that's right, Nigel?'

'And above the third shop,' said my brother, smiling indulgently at Michael X, 'there's going to be a Black Museum; and above that, my office. That's almost ready: come and have a look.'

It was very like being in his former office in Betterton Street, with the same furniture standing on a similarly thick carpet, and the same endless supply of whisky. There was one major difference, which explained exactly why the workmen had been so happy to see a sister of Nigel's. On a huge blackboard someone had chalked the word: 'WAGES'. Beneath that, in smaller writing, was a list of names and sums of money; and below that again there was another notice in larger letters: 'TO BE PAID BY NIGEL SAMUEL.'

When I reported this visit to Arnold, he gave me a rare and unexpected hug, and then let go of me rather quickly and stood with his back to me and looked out of the window for a while. At last, he spoke. 'I'm sorry, Nicola,' he said slowly, in a voice full of sadness. 'But there's nothing to be done. What a shame he was given his money all at once. If only your dear mother…' Then he turned back to me, and said more briskly: 'You know that your own inheritance is due?' I nodded, and he went on: 'I've got some ideas which I think will make things easier for you in the long run. It'll take a few months to sort out. In the meantime, I'm sure your Bank won't mind very much if you want a few little extravagances. A new dress? A holiday perhaps? But don't, whatever you do, put any of it in your brother's direction.'

From time to time, I returned to the Black House, but signs of progress were few. What I did notice was a collection of sleeping-bags, portable stoves and the like. Michael X's henchmen were not only being paid good wages for doing virtually nothing, but were also squatting in the unfinished building. Nigel seemed blind to what was happening. 'This is only the start!' he told me, brushing aside my objections. 'We've got important business in Trinidad.'

'But when do you think the supermarket will be open?'

'They've got the shelves up, haven't they? And we're opening the museum next week. Why don't you come along? Did you know that John and Yoko are going to be there?'

So Nigel Waymouth and I attended the grand opening of the Black Museum. What we found, when we walked into a room crowded with free-loaders getting quietly smashed, was a single exhibit: a shrunken black head in a glass case. Beside it, looking very pleased with himself, and superbly elegant, stood my brother Nigel, with a black girl on his arm: not the one I had seen before, but just as pretty. He told us where to find John Lennon and Yoko Ono: 'They're up on the roof. I think they're enjoying themselves.'

I recognized John at once from his photographs. 'It's a great day, isn't it,' he enthused when Yoko told him who I was. 'Your brother's brilliant. Absolutely brilliant. He and Michael are really doing something. Have you got the scissors, Yoko?' She fished in a carrier-bag, found two large pairs of dress-making scissors, and passed him one.

'It's such an occasion,' Yoko said to me quietly, putting the other pair of scissors up to the back of her head, and gathering a great tress in one hand. Then, to my horror, there was a loud snip. 'We're cutting off our hair to celebrate. Will you join us?' When I declined, muttering something about Ricci Burns being the only person I allowed to touch my hair, she made a slight face, shrugged her shoulders, and turned away to continue the good work.

We left soon afterwards, passing a camera team from the BBC on the way up. The Black Museum (so far as I know) acquired no more exhibits, and the supermarket was never opened; yet Michael X's sinister power over my brother grew greater from week to week.

Towards the end of July, Nigel Waymouth and I went to London airport to see the two of them leave for a visit to Trinidad. Michael was surrounded by bodyguards, wives and mistresses. He looked unexpectedly sombre. 'It's been great, little sister,' he said when he shook my hand. 'But now we're doing man's work. It's time for my black brothers and black sisters to be set free!' Nigel was smashed out of his skull, and they had considerable trouble getting him on the plane.

✻

In the meantime, I had begun to think about being married to Nigel Waymouth: but how precisely (I wondered) would we live? My brother had been right about one thing: Granny Takes a Trip was definitely failing. In a way that didn't matter, because I knew that I would soon be coming into my inheritance; and Nigel had made it clear that whatever happened between us, he would still want to work.

'The business may be going wrong,' I told Nigel Waymouth, 'but it's on a good site. Do you think there's any hope of our buying the lease? We could easily find something else to deal in – rare books, perhaps?'

When this idea came to nothing, Nigel remembered that a few years ago he had been encouraged by Joe Boyd, an American production and tour manager, to collaborate with the artist Mike English on posters and record covers which were then printed and distributed by Osiris Visions. This had been a successful venture; and one of Nigel's better ideas was to expand the business by seeking fresh work in the U.S.A.

I liked the idea of another journey to America. "But what shall I do? I asked Nigel one morning over breakfast, "While you're making your first million?"

"With a body like yours," he said, "there's only one option!" He meant of course that I should think of becoming a model. And although I knew that I didn't need to work, the idea of earning money in my own right remained appealing.

A telephone call and a taxi-ride later, and I was being shown into José Fonseca's office in Models 1, the new agency which she had started up in Redcliffe Road after leaving English Boys. Above a pair of chunky platform shoes, I was wearing a red printed cotton Afghan dress from David Lindall's shop in the World's End. It had a full red skirt with flowers on it, below an embroidered top; and it was gathered in at the waist by a silver Afghan belt. At the last moment I had added a Moroccan choker necklace. As for José: she looked even more beautiful in London than she had done in Marbella. I guessed she was wearing another Ossie Clark original.

'Nicky darling,' she said, coming out from behind a large modern desk covered with photographs and telephones. She kissed me lightly on the cheek, and then stepped back to cast a professional eye over me, 'You look absolutely ravishing,' she said. Several of the telephones were ringing, and a man was doing his best to answer them. José seemed unconcerned. 'That's my partner Adrian. I'd introduce you, but as you can see, he's rather tied up at the moment. How tall are you, by the way? Nigel seems terribly happy. Just turn round, will you? And the other way? None of us realized how serious it was. Now, standing still, look over towards the window – and back to the door again. Oh, and show me your hands.'

While she was examining me, I noticed that the wall opposite her desk was completely covered in sets of small black-and-white photographs of each of the models on her books, together with their details. I wondered whether I would soon be on that wall. Then José sat me down, and came and knelt on the floor beside me.

'Nicky, you're a lovely girl, and I think we should definitely have some photographs taken. But you know…' She paused for a moment, and looked rather troubled, as if she wasn't at all sure how best to proceed.

I made a slight face. 'Go on: tell me the worst!'

She smiled and the tension went out of that lovely oriental-looking face. 'The fact is, you're not tall enough. Also, you've got wonderful boobs – but they're just not fashionable. For God's sake, Nicky, don't be depressed about it. Do you know what a model's life is like?'

I shook my head.

'Bloody hard work with very little glamour. Dieting all the time; looking good all the time; trudging round like cattle in a market-place looking for work.'

'So there's not much hope for me?'

'Show me your hands again. They're lovely.' As she held them, I examined them myself, curiously, as if I was seeing them for the first time. 'And when you give that enigmatic look, it's something quite special. I think you could be used for your face as well as your hands. Yes, all right

Adrian, tell her I'll call back in ten minutes.' She got to her feet, and I stood up as well. 'I'm going to send you to my friend Hiroshi.'

※

'That is good. That is wonderful!'

All the lights were on, and I was lying underneath the arc-lamps in Hiroshi's large white studio. I wore an Ossie Clark chiffon dress with smocking at the top, long sleeves, and a print of red flowers and dragons on a white background, which made me feel as though I was floating on fleecy white clouds. Hiroshi was a small, gentle Japanese boy, with silky black hair which he wore in a pony-tail. The compliments sparkled like champagne, and made me feel just as light-headed.

A few days later, it was Karl Stoecker's turn. Karl was a friend of Nigel's, a good-looking American with long hair, about five feet eleven, and very well-built. He had agreed to take the photographs as a favour; but when I rang the bell at his studio flat in Marble Arch, he seemed surprised.

'Nicky – is that really you?'

'Sure – what do you think?' I had put some black soot on my cheeks, and I was wearing a black velvet cap, and a black velvet jacket and plus-fours which I had had made for me in Savile Row by my brother's tailor.

'I think you look fabulous – very sexy – and I love the Oliver Twist cap – but what's the rest of the image?'

I walked into the flat, and said hello to Clare, his girlfriend. 'It's Chatterton,' I said. They looked blank. 'You must know, Chatterton: the boy-poet and faker – he committed suicide in London about two hundred years ago at the age of eighteen. Brilliant, but too poor to eat.'

'All right!' said Karl. 'But let's not do the shots in the studio – let's go for some authenticity here!' We were soon on location in the back streets of Notting Hill Gate.

Where Hiroshi had been dreamy and romantic, Karl was down-to-earth and gritty. Being photographed by Karl was less like drinking champagne, and more like having sex, and being told how good I was in bed. As the session went on, I began longing for him to kiss me, and I flirted madly to camera.

Before long I had an unusual portfolio of pictures; but no-one was clamouring for me; and since I didn't relish the idea of going round trying to sell myself, my career as a model appeared to be over before it had really begun.

※

My brother Nigel had returned from Trinidad crazier than ever. "The Revolution is coming!" he told me over a large whisky. "Michael will be at the head of things – and he's asked me to be in his government. Daddy would have been proud, don't you think?" But at least his hostility to Nigel Waymouth had moderated. Indeed, he had been so impressed by some of Nigel's designs, that he had commissioned him to paint a large mural on the exterior of his Cornish castle, which led at the start of August to our having a brief but very happy holiday in a caravan in the castle grounds.

And then one evening in Chesil Court Nigel pulled out his wallet and handed me two tickets to the Bob Dylan concert on the Isle of Wight. "David Litvinoff gave me these earlier to-day, he told me.

I fingered the tickets thoughtfully. 'I may go on ahead of you for a few days. My friend Annie's parents have got a house down there.'

'All right – and while you're staying with Annie, I'll go back to Cornwall and see if I can get that mural finished.'

CHAPTER SEVENTEEN
The Isle of Wight Concert

I left for the Isle of Wight on Monday 25 August, and arrived at Annie's in time for lunch. She and her family were staying in a beautiful old Victorian house in Bembridge, with a large garden just by the edge of the sea. After lunch, Annie and I wandered down to the beach.

'What's up, Annie?' I asked, linking arms. 'You don't seem your usual sparkling self.'

'Oh, I don't know. I'm enjoying life at Hornsey. But all this…' She waved an arm in a large gesture which seemed both to encompass the whole of Bembridge, with its safe, secure lives and its polite middle-class values. 'I feel so hemmed-in, sometimes.' She turned towards me, and smiled. 'You're a breath of fresh air, Nicky. Shall we go riding?'

On Thursday, Annie left for London; and the following afternoon I met Nigel (in pouring rain) as he came off the ferry in Cowes. 'Hello, darling,' he said, giving me a welcome hug. 'Where are we staying? How was Annie? And have you managed to arrange any transport?'

'One thing at a time! I've got a car waiting for us. It was the only one left on the island.' Nigel looked aghast as the car door was opened by an elderly gentleman in a dark suit, wearing a top hat and white gloves. When we got in, there was a slight smell of formaldehyde.

'Nicky,' he whispered to me, 'This isn't…'

' I told you it was the only one left,' I whispered back. 'He's the local hearse-driver. The only problem is, that I can't persuade him to travel at more than five miles an hour!'

After leaving our things at the bed-and-breakfast I had found, we went on to the concert site which looked unutterably dreary. The storm had subsided to a steady drizzle; and when we stepped out of the car, it was muddy under-foot. There were dirty-looking hippies everywhere, and a host of ramshackle tents, with an occasional hamburger or fish-and-chip stall. To one side a wooden platform with an awning above it formed a kind of stage, on which people were scurrying about with sound equipment.

'God, it looks squalid,' said Nigel. 'Let's go over to the stage – David should be there by now.'

Just in front of the stage, I could see an area of muddy field which had been cordoned off with some posts and a length of rope. Inside this enclosure, groups of people stood and talked earnestly, or sat at one of half-a-dozen trestle tables. As we approached, someone barred our way. Nigel took no notice, but called: 'Hullo, Donald!' and waved towards one of the nearest trestle tables. 'It's all right,' he explained, 'we're with Donald Cammell, the film director.'

I thought he was bluffing, but much to my surprise someone with longish brown hair and a tense, slightly ravaged face had turned his head. He wore a red sweater, with a scarf round his neck, and looked unconventionally chic. When he recognized Nigel he smiled, stood up, and began walking towards us. As he drew closer, I saw that he was also wearing what must have been an uncomfortably tight pair of trousers, and that the trousers had teddy-bears all over them. They looked faintly ridiculous; and yet there was something powerful and attractive about the way in which he moved; and when he spoke, his voice was deliciously deep and guttural.

'So: you've brought Nicky with you?' Nigel nodded, and Donald turned to me with a smile, and laid a hand on my arm for a moment. As our eyes met, I felt a powerful sexual charge run right through me from stem to stern. My whole body seemed to be tingling. I was half expecting a compliment; but Donald went on: 'And you've both made it into the groupies' enclosure! Do you like it here?'

I was so thrown off-balance that I couldn't think what to say. Fortunately, Nigel rescued me by asking him about David Litvinoff, who evidently hadn't yet arrived. As for me: the tingling became a lustful ache; and as we walked over to join Donald's friends at their trestle-table, I deliberately took Nigel's arm. 'The last thing you need,' I said to myself, 'is another Jim Haynes in your life!' And yet while my mind was saying one thing, my body was saying another; and I felt absolutely certain that (despite the teddy-bears on his extraordinarily tight trousers) Donald Cammell and I would end up in bed together.

After sitting down, I tried hard to concentrate on the other people around the table, most of whom greeted Nigel as though they had known him for years. Donald made only one introduction. 'I don't think either of you know Roger Vadim?'

A small, very dishy Frenchman with a polo-necked sweater heard our names, and acknowledged us with a friendly wave of his hand. Then he looked as though he had forgotten something, and turned to the woman who sat by his side: his secretary, I presumed. She listened attentively. She was extraordinarily attractive, with a lovely face and large green eyes, and my heart went out to her because she had a perfect-looking bust that was just as unfashionably prominent as mine. After a moment or two she reached down to the ground beside her, and picked up a leather box which she placed carefully on the table. When she opened it, I could see that it was full of brandy, whisky, and crystal glasses; and she poured Vadim a large whisky.

Later that evening, when Nigel and I were snuggled up together in one of the twin-beds in our B&B room, talking about the people we had met, he asked me what I thought of Donald Cammell. I was glad that the light was off. I just said: 'I can't think why he wears those awful trousers. But God, Nigel, what a lucky man Vadim is, having such a pretty secretary who is so efficient.'

Nigel laughed uproariously.

I sat up, switched the light on, tickled him in the ribs, and demanded to know what was so funny?

'Ouch! Stop it! Some secretary!' he said through his laughter. 'That wasn't a secretary, you innocent abroad, that was Jane Fonda! The star of *Cat Ballou* and *Barbarella*!'

※

On Saturday evening, Martin Sharp arrived, wearing another one of his T-shirts covered with cartoon characters. With him was Ejo, his tall and beautiful but virtually silent Finnish girlfriend, with whom he would be sharing the other twin-bed in our room.

Sunday was the day of the concert; and soon after breakfast Nigel and I went to the airport to collect my brother and Hazel, who arrived looking cheerful, and walking arm-in-arm. We drove them straight to the concert site, where David Litvinoff ushered us into the VIP enclosure. The famous faces there included Mick Jagger and Keith Richards of the Rolling Stones. I didn't dare to talk to either of them, and I was glad of Hazel's company. After a while, she and I sat down on the row of seats closest to the stage, and I asked her about Nigel and Michael X.

'They're orf ter Trinidad again soon,' said Hazel cheerfully. 'Michael's bin dahn ter Cornwall – 'E's seen your Nigel's mural – said it was "Great, man!"'

Litvinoff, who had also sat down next to me, sighed at her remark. 'Ah, yes. "Great, man!" Most perspicacious. So good that the colonials are being properly educated, don't you think?' Before either of us could answer, he went on:

> So. You and Nigel. Bed-and-breakfast. Highly commendable: seeing how the other half lives. But I fear I shall have to eschew such delights. Keith Richards has just invited me to spend the night on his yacht – we're going to write a movie together.

At that moment the folk-singer Tom Paxton stepped onto the stage. There was a cheer from the audience, and everyone settled themselves down for the start of the concert.

After Tom Paxton came a big black man, Richie Havens, who had come almost straight from his triumph at Woodstock; as had the next rock group, The Band, who had once been Bob Dylan's backing group. At some stage, Litvinoff disappeared for a while, and the seats were so uncomfortable that I wished I had gone with him. When he returned, he said that he had:

> Gone among the poor. I found them in a large tent, sad creatures, taking acid and getting themselves arrested for wandering around with no clothes on! I tried to explain to the officer in charge that

they were taking advantage of the slight drizzle to make up for having not bathed for a month. "Medically sound," I told him, "but morally dubious. But should one put morals before health?" His answer, I regret to say, was curt.

As the day wore on, there was no sign of Bob Dylan. The rumour spread that he was behind the scenes, negotiating for more money. At last he appeared, and sang for about an hour; and then it was all over, and everybody was saying how great it had been, and smiling at each other, and we were being driven away in our hearse.

David Litvinoff sat in front with the driver, who still wouldn't go at more than five miles an hour. 'You know the island well, my good man?' The driver nodded. 'I imagine so.' Litvinoff sighed heavily. 'Ah, yes… Death the Great Leveller. Of course, I may yet prefer the grave to Keith Richards's yacht. Do you think you can find it, going at this tremendous speed?' We drove for hours without success, until I felt that we had seen every cove and inlet on the island three times over. David began a new game. 'I hardly like to say so,' he gasped between coughs, 'but a hearse begins to seem strangely appropriate. I've got this terrible chest condition. There's only one thing for it: a herbal cigarette.' He lit a joint, and took a long draw. The scent of marijuana filled the air. 'Disgusting things, but my doctor insists. Would you like to try one, driver?'

We never found the yacht; and at midnight, in desperation, I asked to be taken to Bembridge, where Annie's parents came to the rescue by agreeing to put up my brother and Hazel for the night. 'And what are you going to do, David?' asked Nigel Waymouth.

'Don't worry, man – I'll stay with you.'

'That'll be a little difficult. We've only got one room, and the other bed's being used by Martin and Ejo.' This didn't deter him: so we drove up to our very conventional bed and breakfast establishment at one o'clock in the morning with an uninvited guest. Fortunately, the proprietors were very good-tempered, and even gave us a camp bed for David to sleep on.

'Thank you so very much, most kind,' he said, staring at it rather dismally. Then as we walked up stairs he muttered to me: 'You don't think that I could possibly sleep on that thing all night?'

As soon as we reached our room (where Martin and Ejo were already sound asleep) David turned on his cassette recorder full-blast, and began playing the tapes he had recorded at the concert. At the same time, he delivered a running commentary which meant that no-one could hear any of it properly. Every other word was: 'Listen to this, man! It's great!' Before long Martin and Ejo were awake: which was just what David had intended. Turning down the volume on his cassette, he began talking to Ejo, leaning over her menacingly as he spoke.

'Ejo – what an enchanting name for a very, very naughty woman. Haven't you realised by now that Martin doesn't like you? That he doesn't like any woman? That the sight of a naked breast prostrates him for a week? Hasn't he confessed that pretending to love you is just a pose – a game? That he's really in love with me?'

'Take no notice of the Pommie bastard!' said Martin sleepily, rolling over and burying his head under the blankets. Ejo, as usual, said not a word and eventually David gave up and resigned himself to the camp bed.

※

The next morning, as we left for London on the Hydrofoil, David was complaining bitterly. 'It's not that I mind; but for a man in my position, doing a film with Keith Richards, a private plane would have been so much more suitable. A Hydrofoil – and then British Rail!' He shuddered. From his breast-pocket he drew a thick wad of money. 'It's not, as you can see, beyond my means.'

Later, in our railway carriage, he described the concert as: 'Ghastly! A symptom of a civilisation in decline. The hippies are the storm-troopers of cultural decay.' And later on: 'You people are always going on and on about money, as if that counts for anything.' As he spoke, he pulled some bundles of bank-notes out of his blazer pockets. 'Do you want to see someone with a truly hippy attitude towards money? Just look at this!' And he began flinging notes out of the carriage window.

'David,' I cried, sitting up in alarm, and watching as five- and ten-pound notes hovered for a moment just outside the carriage window, before being whirled away towards the telegraph wires. 'For God's sake! You can't do that!'

'Why not? It's only money!"'

For a moment it seemed like a magnificent gesture; and then one of the notes was somehow sucked back into the carriage. Nigel picked it up, looked at it closely, and smiled.

'Don't worry, Nicky – it's stage money!'

I looked at David, expecting him to join in the laughter; but all the warmth and animation had drained out of his face, and he looked suddenly old, isolated and alone, with all the cares of the world upon his shoulders.

※

After the excitements of the Isle of Wight, London seemed very dull, apart from preparations for our descent on the U.S.A. Clothes were bought, addresses collected, visas and travellers' cheques arranged; and by 23 October 1969, when we set out for London Airport, we had been joined by Miles, Caroline Coon of Release, and Hazel and Nigel.

My brother was moody in the taxi, and kept pulling at a hip-flask. 'Oim really worried.' Hazel whispered to me. "E don't look ready ter travel…' Miles and Caroline were deep in conversation with each other. From the way they were sitting it was difficult to tell whether or not they were holding hands; and Caroline, with her clear skin, her bright red lipstick, her long curly black hair and her wonderful figure, looked absolutely beautiful.

As we queued up to have our luggage checked at the Air India counter, my brother suddenly gripped me by the shoulders. 'It's no good, Nicola – I can't go. Got to see my son tomorrow. Promised Suzy. Try and follow with Hazel in a few days. Come on, Hazel.' And he staggered off with his suitcase back towards the taxi-rank. Hazel shrugged her shoulders despairingly, and followed. I burst into tears.

Don't worry,' said Nigel Waymouth, comforting me. 'He's so drunk they probably wouldn't have let him on board in any case.'

CHAPTER EIGHTEEN

The Chelsea Hotel, the Chateau Marmont, and Mexico

After touching down safely at Kennedy (the pilot fortunately having resisted my efforts to ply him with champagne), we took another taxi. I felt a thrill of pleasure as we crossed the East River into Manhattan, and the familiar sky-scrapers loomed up once again. I was also excited: because we had arranged to stay at 222 West 23rd Street, between Seventh and Eighth Avenues, in the heart of New York's colony of writers and artists, in the red-brick buildings of the Chelsea Hotel.

Going in through the main entrance, we found ourselves in a large area with a number of battered old sofas. For a moment or two it seemed disappointingly like any other slightly seedy hotel lobby. Single people waited and read newspapers and looked anxiously at their watches; married couples ignored each other; and lovers held hands and gazed into each other's eyes.

But then Caroline Coon pointed to one of the numerous pictures on the walls: 'Look, Nigel: that's a Jasper Johns, isn't it? And that's definitely a Warhol. And over there…' She and Nigel began walking excitedly from picture to picture. Miles explained that when one of the artists living in the Chelsea Hotel couldn't pay the rent, the management would sometimes accept a picture instead. So the hotel lobby had almost as many fine Warhols as the Museum of Modern Art.

The Chelsea Hotel, the Chateau Marmont, and Mexico

We walked over to the front desk to check in. 'I think you'll find that Sandy Daley's arranged everything for us,' Nigel told the desk-clerk. 'Could you tell her we've arrived?' The clerk didn't seem at all impressed by Sandy's name – she was an avant-garde film-maker whom we had met in London – but he dialled her room number.

A few moments later we had the keys to our rooms; and then the lift doors opened and Sandy appeared. She was a tall girl with long straight appropriately sandy hair, dressed in a black T-shirt and jeans, and beaming all over her pleasant, open, slightly freckled face. Her arms were wide open, and she gave Nigel and me a tremendous hug. 'Nicky! Nigel! It's great to see you again! When you've settled in, come down and meet me in the bar. It's over there.' She pointed to a doorway at the side of the lobby. 'I'll introduce you to some people.'

A Puerto-Rican porter helped us with our bags; and when we followed him out of the lift, we found ourselves in a long, wide corridor, full of children. Two of them were racing down it in Go-karts; and they swerved to one side as they passed us. The porter smiled. 'Plenty families here – young girls, two, maybe three kids.' We reached our room. It was unbelievably small and squalid. 'No room service,' said the porter, in answer to a question from Nigel. 'But you can always send me out for a sandwich.' A few minutes later we were down in the lobby again, where the clerk made a note that we wanted a larger room as soon as one became free. Then we went to join Sandy.

We found her sitting at the bar, which stretched all the way down one side of a long, dark room filled with small tables. Just beyond her, hunched over a drink, sat a squat figure with glasses and grey hair, wearing scruffy old corduroys and a still more scruffy pullover; and beyond him sat a smartly-dressed woman in her thirties, with long black hair swept back, and a slash of bright lipstick. 'Come and meet my friends,' said Sandy as we approached. 'This is Harry Smith – he's an artist –

"Some people might dispute that,' said Harry aggressively, swivelling round on his stool to face us. 'So what's new in England?"

'And this is Peggy Biderman. She works in the Museum of Modern Art.'

'Welcome to the El Quijote Bar!' said Peggy, raising her glass. 'It's about the only part of this tumble-down establishment which seems to function.'

'There's a good reason for that, you chump' said Harry more cheerfully. He drained his glass and slid it across the counter, where it was promptly refilled. 'It's nothing to do with the establishment. Separate management altogether.'

'Nigel does posters,' Sandy was explaining; 'and Nicky...' Her voice tailed off.

'Just come along for the ride, have you?' asked Harry.

Instead of answering him, I began talking to Peggy about her work at the Museum of Modern Art, where she spent most of her time restoring old films.

Later on, Harry said something grumpy and walked away. 'Harry's a resident,' Peggy told me. 'He's tetchy, I know; but he's a fine artist.' And then two more of Sandy's friends arrived. 'Robert! Patti! So here you are! Let me look at you! Nigel, Nicky, this is Robert Mapplethorpe and this is Patti Smith.'

They were so extraordinary and yet so alike, that at first I thought they must be twins. Both were thin and gaunt – Patti had tiny hips, and virtually no bust. Both wore black jerseys and black trousers – Robert's extremely tight, and made of leather. Both wore ear-rings. Both had long, black hair. Robert was handsome; while Patti had a stunningly beautiful face.

'Are you staying here at the hotel?' I asked her.

'No – but we've found a two-roomed apartment above Horn & Hardart just down the road. Oh my God! Last night we were living in Brooklyn. And now we're here!'

Having just flown all the way from London, this didn't seem like a very big change to me; but I soon realised that for Robert and Patti moving across the East River was the most significant move they had ever made in their lives. Patti told me that Robert was a sculptor. She had a job at Scribner's, the book-store on Fifth Avenue, to keep them in funds; and in her spare time, she was writing and drawing. 'And what do you write?' I asked nervously.

'Lots of poems. Lately, it's all been about The Rolling Stones. Wasn't it just so terrible when Brian Jones died? I must have cried for a week.'

'You'd better talk to Nigel, then – they were friends.'

'No! Really?' She clutched the sleeve of Nigel's tartan jacket, and pulled him away from his conversation with Robert and Peggy. 'You knew Brian Jones?'

Nigel admitted that this was so.

'Oh God, Oh God! Robert, did you hear that?' Half laughing and half crying, she made us sit down while she fished in her pocket for a poem she had been writing about Brian, and then she read it out to us. She seemed deeply moved by the experience, and afterwards she told us: 'It's so good that we've met. Robert and I like you, don't we Robert, and we're going to see a lot more of you.'

※

Soon we had moved into a slightly larger but equally squalid room in the Chelsea Hotel; and we had fallen into a kind of routine: getting up at ten or eleven in time for a late breakfast of coffee and cornflakes at the Schwarz next door; spending the middle part of the day getting to know New York; and then at five or six heading back for the hotel, and whiling away the rest of the evening drinking in the Quijote Bar, or listening to records and smoking hash in someone's room.

We saw Sandy almost every day; and one afternoon she insisted on taking us up to the top floor of the hotel to meet the composer who was its strangest resident. 'You won't believe it,' she told us as we went up in the lift, 'but George Kleinsinger has a private zoo up here.' As we approached his door, I could hear strains of classical music filtering out of his apartment.

'Mozart, I think,' said Nigel.

Sandy knocked on the door; and it was opened by a kindly-looking man in his mid-forties. 'Oh, good,' he said softly. 'Come on in.' We followed him into a small entrance hall. 'I hope you like opera,' he went on. '*The Magic Flute* is a great favourite of mine.' He began opening another door. 'I only have three rooms up here, but fortunately for me and my friends the sitting-room is extremely large.'

It was like finding oneself in a different world. George had not only an aquarium, its huge tanks containing limpid water through which swam a host of exotically-coloured fish; but he also had tropical plants right up to the 12-foot ceiling, and monkeys and parakeets and macaws – and snakes: snakes of all sizes and colours, writhing away in their enclosed spaces – or even outside them. For George particularly loved snakes; and when he had sat us down, one of the first things he did was to produce an extremely large and threatening specimen, and encourage it to slither all over me.

I've always hated snakes. I tried to be brave, but I felt like screaming.

'Oh, I'm so sorry,' George said very gently, detaching the snake with expert hands just as it was trying to nose its way down the back of my dress. 'I'm not sure that I've milked this one to-day; and he's extremely poisonous.'

☼

On the Tuesday after our arrival, Nigel and I visited Peggy Biderman at the Museum of Modern Art, where she asked Nigel to give copies of some of his posters to the Museum to add to their collection. Later that day, I arrived in the bar to find Nigel deep in conversation with Sandy Daley and a thin, gaunt but quite good-looking man with glasses and long brown hair. Nigel introduced him as: 'an old friend of mine – Nik Douglas. He's just arrived in New York with a film he shot in India with Robert Fraser, the art man; and Mick Jagger. Nik, you tell her all about it.'

Nik smiled shyly. 'It's called *Tantra: Indian Rites of Ecstasy*, and it's all about Tantric Art – have you heard of that?'

I gave a non-committal shrug.

'Tantrism is a kind of magic – white magic. In one way it's about worshipping the Goddess; in another it's about gaining spiritual power…'

'Maithuna, that's the word,' said Nigel, coming to Nik's rescue as he appeared to be floundering. 'A kind of ritual love-making – and better if you do it with someone normally forbidden to you, like a sister or an aunt. But you have to be in a state of grace.'

'And the Art?'

'Figures of Indian Gods, on the whole,' said Nik.

Sandy joined in. 'I think Andy Warhol might be very interested in the sexual imagery – if I can arrange things, we'll go round to the 'Factory' on

Thursday afternoon, and show him the film. Nigel, Nicky: you guys are welcome to join with us.'

So two days later (on Thursday 29 October), the four of us set out for Andy Warhol's headquarters, some warehouse space at 33 Union Square West, which he called 'The Factory.' It was only sixteen months since Warhol had been shot and almost killed by Valerie Solanas, a radical feminist who had written the manifesto for SCUM, otherwise known as 'The Society for Cutting Up Men', and who had somehow become convinced that Warhol was trying to steal her work.

'What sort of state is he in now?' I asked Sandy as we rode a large warehouse elevator up to the third floor. I didn't tell her that Warhol's Pop Art paintings had been a favourite of mine at school; and that one holidays, when he came over to London for an exhibition of his work at the Tate, I'd queued up to have him sign a copy of one of his books for me.

'You'll have to judge for yourself,' she said; and then the elevator doors opened, and we had arrived. The first thing I noticed was the intense heat; and then I saw that right in front of us was a desk; and at the desk (apparently all alone) sat Andy Warhol. He looked just as I had seen him before, in his black T-shirt and black jeans; and he wore the same welfare glasses with pink rims. Perhaps he was a little more fragile? But I could have been imagining that.

'Hi!' said Sandy enthusiastically.

'Hi, Sandy!' Warhol replied, without a trace of warmth in his voice.

While Sandy was introducing him to Nik Douglas, I looked around. We were in a large area, completely devoid of furniture apart from Warhol's desk and chair. But over in the far corner there was a six-foot four-inch blond hunk, wearing shorts and waxing a surf-board. He took no notice of us at all: it was as though he was a piece of living sculpture.

Then a door opened, and in came a man in a suit. This turned out to be Paul Morrissey, an avant-garde film-director who was also one of Warhol's principal assistants. He took charge at once, and ushered us into another room where we could watch the film. *Tantra* looked impressive to me; but when I glanced at Warhol to gauge his reaction, he seemed unmoved. At length the lights went up. Warhol remained absolutely silent. Finally, Paul Morrissey said: 'Yeah that's very interesting. We did a film on India too; we did a film on the Maharajahs and their Rolls-Royces. I don't know about all this Tantric stuff.'

I looked at Nik, whose mouth had fallen open a little. He looked as though he was trying to speak, but something had just gone seriously wrong with his vocal cords. And then Warhol was saying: 'Well, goodbye Sandy. It was so very sweet of you to bring your friends over.' Stepping into the elevator, I turned and noticed that Warhol had followed us out. He was staring at me quizzically. I felt a thrill of excitement. I hoped he was wondering whether he had seen me before. And then the doors slid shut.

※

Patti Smith was a fine singer, and the evenings would often find us listening to her accompanying herself on the guitar while she sang a melancholy song. I much preferred her singing to her poems: she was an amusing person, with a sharp Brooklyn sense of humour; but her poems about the Rolling Stones bored me to tears. She kept on writing new ones, and reading them out, and asking Nigel all about Brian Jones, clutching at his arm while her eyes filled with tears.

One morning she took us to see Robert Mapplethorpe's studio. Some of his sculptures disturbed me: the fierce little men in jock-straps; the women screwing each other. Others were simply obscure, with lots of small objects somehow grafted on to each other. Fortunately, Nigel had something to say about them. 'Ah, construction pieces,' he said knowledgeably. 'A little like Joseph Cornell's sculptures – fetishistic in a way.'

Robert's eyes lit up at this; and when Nigel asked what he was currently working on, he replied: 'Just at present, Nigel, I'm very attracted by what's going on in Greenwich Village – and up on 42nd Street – the people – the leather – they're expressing something I'd like to capture.' He laughed. 'It sounds kinda voyeuristic, is that what you're thinking?'

'Not at all,' said Nigel. 'Why don't I come with you? I might bring a camera with me. I'm quite interested in photography at present.'

'I don't even own a camera,' said Robert. 'But yeah… Come along, and give me some ideas.'

Nigel became equally fascinated by the marvellous vulgarity of the area around 42nd Street and Times Square; and this was how he came to accompany Robert Mapplethorpe on the first few steps of Robert's personal journey through the half-world of New York, an odyssey for which he would later become famous.

※

A few days later, Hazel arrived in New York. She lightened the mood, and I was really pleased to see her; but she was alone. Once again, my brother had failed to board the aeroplane. Hazel showed me the wonderful ticket he had given her. She could have used it to fly the rest of the way round the world, but Nigel hadn't thought of giving her any money: so after a few days she flew back to London, and Caroline Coon went with her.

After their departure, the Chelsea Hotel seemed increasingly sinister. I came to realise how many of the residents were on hard drugs. In the hotel corridors, I would pass people looking not just ill and exhausted, but desperate – and they frightened me. I felt still worse after a visit to Harry Smith's room. The evening before, at the bar, he had been drunk but witty, talking brilliantly about his interest in rock-and-roll and blues music, and asking me to go to his room the next morning to listen to some music, and perhaps to see his paintings. 'Number 731 – don't forget!' he called out over his shoulder as he left the bar.

'That's a rare privilege,' said Peggy Biderman. 'Take him up on it – but don't be surprised if he kicks you out after ten minutes!'

She wasn't far wrong. My first knock on the door was greeted with angry shouts of: 'Who the fuck is that?'

'Nicky Samuel – but I can come back another…' As I spoke, I heard bolts being drawn back; and there was Harry, only inches away from me, looking hung-over and smelling bad.

'What a privilege,' he said sarcastically, and pinched my cheek. 'The lovely Miss Samuel, the sweet English rose whom everybody wants to take to bed.'

'I was hoping to look at your pictures,' I said, as brightly as I could manage.

'Well, come on in, damn you, and see how an artist actually lives in this godforsaken hell-hole.'

I went in. It was a disgusting little room, filled with empty bottles and half-smoked cigarettes. Against the far wall, a pile of canvases showed their backs to me. I wandered over towards them; but as I laid a hand on the first, Harry's hand slapped down on mine. 'Where's your manners! Weren't you brought up to say please?' I was frightened now, and perhaps he sensed it; because he released me, and went and slumped down on his bed with his head in his hands. 'Go away, Miss Samuel. Go away back to some safe secure little English tea-party on the other side of the Atlantic. Don't you know what kind of a place this is? Don't you know about the drugs, the murders…'

From then on, I was perpetually scared. Whenever I went into a room, I felt that it contained some dark secret; that something horrific had happened; that the blood had only just been whitewashed off the walls. Finally, in mid-November, I became so tense and ill that I had to see a doctor; and soon afterwards Nigel and I went to the airport and flew to Los Angeles.

※

Our little motel (just off Sunset Boulevard) felt even more dangerous than the Chelsea Hotel; and the next morning, I was on the verge of telling Nigel that I wanted to fly back to England, when we bumped into Donald Cammell. Just as he had done at the Isle-of-Wight concert, Donald was wearing what looked like an uncomfortably tight pair of trousers. As I gazed at them, I couldn't help thinking of Mae West's famous joke: 'Is that a gun in your pocket? Or are you just happy to see me?'

'Are you still working on the film?' Nigel asked him.

And then Donald's first words were so deliciously deep and guttural that I felt an instant melting sensation between my thighs.

'*Performance.*' He smiled and looked down at the ground for a moment. 'Yup – the final cut's taking a helluva time.' He stared lazily at Nigel. 'And what are you doing out here, man?'

Nigel laughed a little uneasily. 'Great to see you, man. I'm doing a record cover for Denny Cordell.'

This registered. Donald looked impressed. 'Denny Cordell – the guy who's started a new record label?'

'That's the one.' Nigel looked happier. 'He and Leon Russell have set up Shelter Records, and they want me to do the record cover for Leon's first album.'

When he heard where we were staying, Donald shuddered. 'The two-murders-a-week-motel! Don't stay there. I'll tell you where to go: but first, come and spend time with me. I'm down on the beach with Christian Marquand.'

Donald drove us out to the point at Malibu. The sea was as blue as the sky; and the surf pounded up the beach towards a row of timber-frame houses as dramatically as though it was under contract to Cecil B. de Mille. Christian Marquand, a French heart-throb whom I had seen in *The Flight of the Phoenix*, was a small, dark man who wore a heavy gold necklace; and when we arrived he was discussing business with Tom Keays the script-writer (someone else whom Nigel had met in London), and Roman Polanski.

Polanski didn't say much to begin with. He looked lost and desolate. I wasn't surprised. It was only a few weeks since his wife, Sharon Tate, had been brutally murdered; and the police were still hunting for her killer. I'd seen *Repulsion* and *Cul-de-Sac* in London; and I'd seen the reviews. His critics had accused him of having a grim view of the world. I wondered what they would say now.

Then suddenly Polanski came over and sat down next to me. He was small, but intense. He started telling me about some strange scene on the highway going down to Malibu the night before. 'I lay down in the middle of the road,' he told me. 'But I was lying the wrong way, and no-one came to make love to me.' He spoke with such force that he scared me; and what he said didn't make any sense.

After a while, I thought of Hardy's *Tess of the d'Urbervilles*, and quoted those lines from the end of the book about the President of the Immortals having finished his sport with Tess. They had always meant something personal to me; and I noticed that a flicker of interest crossed that melancholy face.

From Malibu, Donald Cammell drove us to the Chateau Marmont at 8221 Sunset Boulevard. This extraordinary Gothic hotel (with its outside painted white), looked less like a real building than a movie set. This was appropriate: it had a kind of faded glamour associated with the Hollywood of the thirties and forties when film-stars like Greta Garbo had lived there.

Now there were more people from the music industry than from Hollywood – Ray Charles was in the huge hallway the first time we set foot inside – but it still had its quota of actors, actresses, producers and script-writers; and behind the desk, in one corner of the hallway, sat Mrs. Voysey, a living relic of its fabled past. I heard that she had come out to Hollywood to be a film-star back in the early 1930s, when she was young and beautiful, had taken a temporary job at the Chateau Marmont, and had stayed there ever since. She still wore heavy make-up and bright lipstick, but now she was a small, sparrow-like old lady with her hair drawn tightly back in a bun; and she gave us a fine suite of rooms, with a double-bedroom, a sitting-room and a bathroom.

When we managed to make contact with Denny Cordell, he told us that he was tied up on some other business just then; but his wife Mia would join us at the Chateau Marmont in about ten days' time. Neither of us could drive, which would have seriously restricted our freedom of action in the meantime, but fortunately Nigel came across an old chum of his known simply as H, a squat stocky-looking man with long blond hair who had once been road manager to Jimi Hendrix. H was at a loose end, and told us that if we hired a car, he would drive us wherever we wanted to go.

'What do you think, Nicky?' asked Nigel.

'I think it's a great idea,' I said. 'How about a trip to Las Vegas – and then perhaps the Grand Canyon?'

So the very next day we hired a car, and the three of us set off for Vegas. I felt a little out of it, sitting alone in the back of the car, because H totally ignored me, and spent the whole time talking to Nigel. When we arrived at Las Vegas, H even suggested that the three of us should share a bed-room together. 'I'm sorry, but I draw the line at that,' I said in the hotel lobby. 'But let's meet in half an hour, and we'll go out on the town together!'

So that evening we immersed ourselves in the slot machines and the bright lights and the raw nervous energy of this cross between a giant Blackpool and the old Wild West; the next day we drove out to the Hoover Dam; and the day after that found us looking down into the Grand Canyon. Seeing that great gash in the ground was mind-blowing. And then I began absent-mindedly stroking the muzzle of one of the mules on which we were about to ride down into the Canyon, and it got my hand in its grip.

It was a terrifying moment. I felt all the hatred of that mule concentrated in its attempt to bite off my fingers. When I finally got free (someone prised its jaws open) I felt hysterical. Nigel held my hand, examining it. 'That ring saved you,' he said. 'Look, how it's been squashed down.'

※

We celebrated Thanksgiving Day on 27 November 1969 and, the very next day, Denny and his wife Mia and their two little boys moved into a cottage by the swimming pool of the Chateau Marmont. Denny was tall and thin, with long hair; while Mia was young and blonde and pretty, and soon became a friend of mine.

Nigel was now spending a great deal of his time away from me: either discussing things with Denny, who promised him a great deal of work; or going off with H to music concerts with performers like Frank Zappa, 'The Byrds', and 'The Mothers'. Once I spent almost the whole day in our room alone, watching television and feeling very dismal.

The next two days, I went over to see Mia, and talked to her for hours each time; but it didn't make me feel any better. 'I just feel such an outsider,' I explained to her on the first day. 'Nigel seems to know everyone, and they're all something to do with the music business. Which means absolutely nothing to me!'

'Listen, honey,' said Mia, pulling a jersey over the head of one of her boys, and removing it for washing, 'just be glad he's doing so well. Denny really cottons to him, I can tell. And if you're getting real bored, come and help me hang out the washing!'

On the second day, Nigel was over in Malibu on some business or other; and I was so depressed that after leaving Mia to her children I rang him up. 'Nigel, is that you?'

'Hello, Nicky! It's all going very well here. How are you doing?'

'I'm fine', I lied, not wanting Nigel to know how I really felt. When will you be back?'

'Difficult to say. But don't worry about me. If it's late, I'll stop off for a hamburger on the way home.'

'OK darling!' And I hung up. The minutes went by, then the hours; and in the end I felt so desperate that I swallowed half a bottle of sleeping-pills.

※

The pills knocked me out for about ten hours; and when I came round again the first person I saw was Nigel, who was holding my hands and looking extremely worried. I made light of what had happened; but word must have spread round, because the next day my room was besieged by friends and acquaintances. It was like holding court; and the joke was, that everyone who came round asked if they could borrow some sleeping-pills! Nigel sent out for some Chinese food in the evening; and the next day he took me out to dinner, and whenever I burst into tears, he was wonderfully kind and understanding.

Once, Denny and Mia took us a curious shop which sold only western gear: boots, Stetsons, saddles, anything connected with the old west. At the back of the shop stood a large man dressed in a cowboy uniform covered with rhinestones. 'That's Nudie Cohn,' said Mia. 'He's the owner. He's a real scream.'

When she introduced us, Nudie took off his hat and held out his other hand to me. 'Ma'am, it sure is great to meet you. I ain't seen such a purty lady since Gipsy Rose Lee herself stopped by. Hee-haw!' He threw his hat into the air, with a roar of delight. 'C'mon, now, folks – do you fancy a little ride in mah automobile?'

A few minutes later, the five of us were roaring down the highway in one of the longest and most plushly upholstered cars I had ever seen. As we drove, Nudie began commenting on the bad habits of other drivers.

'Tarnation, that coyote needs taking down a peg or two,' he exclaimed, when someone had shaken their fist at him as he overtook on a particularly dangerous corner. 'You think I'm horse-shit you mother-fucker? I'll give you horse-shit!'

Suddenly he slowed right down, so that the other driver was almost under our back wheels. Then he pressed a button, and out came a load of genuine horse-shit, which splattered all over the poor man's bonnet and wind-screen, so that he swerved right off the road, and ended up in a ditch. 'Hee-haw!' cried Nudie triumphantly, and roared on in search of another victim.

By now, Nigel had decided that the Leon Russell cover should consist mainly of dozens of photographs; and instead of leaving me behind each day, he took me along to assist him at several of the photographic sessions. It took ages; and when the preliminary work was finished, it was Nigel's turn to look exhausted: so I suggested that we should fly down to Mexico for Christmas.

※

When we arrived in Mexico City, Nigel was looking not just exhausted, but a little unwell. "I'm really not feeling too good, Nicky,' he said when we had settled back in the taxi which was taking us from the airport to the centre of the city. I had asked for the best hotel, and the cab driver was taking us to the Majestic.

'Don't worry, Nigel, once we've checked in, we'll get a breath of fresh air, and look at all the Christmas decorations. Aren't they amazing? You'll feel better then.'

Nigel said nothing, but coughed a little forlornly into his handkerchief; and later he trailed round the streets with me for an hour or two. On Thursday he seemed a good deal worse, and after a very dull day we had dinner in our room. When I woke up on Friday morning, I could hear him making odd noises and then I saw that his face was a strange colour, and he was evidently having trouble with his breathing. I suddenly felt very scared and rang reception. 'It's Mr Waymouth in room 209. I think you'd better send a doctor at once. He looks as though he's dying.'

Within a minute or two, the hotel doctor had arrived. Bending over Nigel, he felt his neck, put one ear to his mouth to listen to his breathing, and then stood up again.

'Well? Aren't you going to examine him properly?' I was trembling with fear.

He smiled a little grimly. 'Eez not necessary. Eez pneumonia. Double, I think you say. He very ill. I know what to do. You pay, I inject. B12. Also plenty antibiotic.'

A few minutes later, Nigel had been rolled onto one side, and the doctor was pumping his bottom full of injections. Although I was still frightened, I almost wanted to laugh. The doctor seemed to be trying every injection in the book, perhaps on the grounds that if one didn't work, another one might. At length (with Nigel looking as though he had sat on a rather large pin-cushion), the doctor began packing away the tools of his trade. 'Keep 'im here four days. Plenty water, no food. Then, if eez okay, take to sea.'

The injections worked. Nigel was okay in three days not four; and on Monday morning, only three days before Christmas, I followed the doctor's advice and took him to the sea. This involved catching a plane to Puerto Vallarta, which lay in the Bay of Banderas on the Pacific Ocean, some three hundred and fifty miles to the north-west.

※

The best hotels were already booked solid, but we found a high-rise package-deal hotel which still had some rooms vacant, and once we had settled in, we went for a walk. Puerto Vallarta is a lovely town; and we had just turned a corner, and were admiring a row of beautiful old Mexican buildings, when I heard a strange padding on the side-walk, looked down and screamed. I had seen what looked like a cross between a large lizard and a very small dragon.

' It's all right,' said Nigel, holding me in his arms. 'You can open your eyes. It's quite safe!'

'What the hell is it?' I was shivering.

'An iguana… look, there's another one being taken for its afternoon walk.'

I never quite got used to seeing iguanas on leads, and gave them a very wide berth; but the weather was wonderful, the bay was beautiful and Nigel's health improved so dramatically that on Christmas Eve we were both able to take a boat a few miles down the coast to the place where in 1964 John Huston had filmed Tennessee Williams's *The Night of the Iguana*.

One afternoon quite early in our stay, I had gone riding on mule-back along the beach while Nigel rested in the hotel, and had found it quite unlike anything I had ever seen before. As soon as one was beyond the town, jungle came down to the very edge of the beach, and I found this close presence of the jungle so curiously seductive that on Boxing Day I persuaded Nigel to ride with me up one of the jungle trails which led away from the beach. Within seconds we were in a completely mysterious world. On every side, thick green foliage climbed up towards the sky; our own voices seemed muffled; but overhead flew screeching macaws, bright red with blue and yellow wings, or deep blue with yellow rings around the eyes.

We stayed on at Puerto Vallarta for another week, riding, sunbathing, and going to beach-parties night after night. But then came New Year's Day 1970; and after a farewell dinner with some of our new acquaintances, we flew back to Mexico City.

※

Now that Nigel was cured, we travelled up to the north of the city to visit the famous shrine of the Virgin of Guadalupe, where the Mary the mother of God was said to have appeared back in December 1531. To my surprise I found myself unable to discount the possibility that this had really happened: Mexico was a land where anything seemed possible.

Another day, we went still further back in time, making an expedition to Teotihuacan, some thirty-three miles northeast of Mexico City, where we gazed with wonder upon the remains of a pre-Columbian civilisation which had lain in ruins for over a thousand years. At the northern end of the deserted city, we visited the Pyramid of the Moon; at the southern, the Temple of Quetzalcoatl; to the east we saw where the great Pyramid of the

Sun rose red above the plain to a height of more than two hundred feet; and we walked in silence along the Avenue of the Dead.

After this experience, the remainder of our holiday was an anti-climax. We flew back to the USA, where we stayed briefly once more at the Chateau Marmont, and the Chelsea Hotel; and by Sunday 11 January 1970 we were back in London at my flat in Chesil Court. I telephoned Arnold Goodman. 'I'm coming to breakfast to-morrow,' I told him. 'It's time for me to know about my inheritance.'

NICKY SAMUEL

ANDY WARHOL

BOB COLACELLO

JIM HAYNES

JOHN LENNON
& YOKO ONO

JOHN PAUL GETTY JR

KENNY JAY LANE

MARIANNE FAITHFULL

MICK JAGGER

NICOLAS ROEG

OSSIE CLARK

PALOMA PICASSO

PATTI SMITH

SALVADOR DALI

CHAPTER NINETEEN
An Inheritance and a Wedding

It was a cold winter's morning. A slight but steady drizzle seeped its way through an early-morning fog. I remembered the heat of Mexico City, and shivered. I had returned to London to find a whole host of questions waiting to be answered. The future seemed as uncertain as the fog-shrouded outlines of the mansions in Portland Place.

The thought of my inheritance was curiously oppressive. I had been so used to my trustees at Coutts looking after my financial problems. I already had an allowance of two or three hundred pounds a month; and if ever I wanted any more, I only had to go to Mr. Ransom. Admittedly, I always felt nervous on those occasions, feeling that I had to convince him of my need. But he always gave me whatever I asked: probably he had no choice; though even if (from his point of view) the relationship was purely a business one, I enjoyed the feeling of being answerable to someone for my behaviour. Now, I supposed, I would lose Mr. Ransom's guiding hand, and be entirely and solely responsible for my inheritance.

Gloomily, I walked up to Arnold's front door, rang the bell, and went in for breakfast. It was not unlike our other breakfasts together: the same slightly dreary dining-room; the same eggs swimming in fat, which I hardly touched, but which Arnold wolfed down with enormous relish; the same joke about Nigel Waymouth: 'So you've been to America again? And how did your – um – your seaside resort enjoy himself?'; the same small-talk about my family: 'Jane, I believe, is now living in Devon with her Major Artist?' I nodded. 'And brother Nigel?'

'Not very well, I'm afraid. He came to see me at the crack of dawn this morning. He was very hyped-up.' I didn't tell Arnold that Nigel had wanted to tell me all about a black girl, Jasmine, by whom he appeared to be completely besotted. 'I'm seeing him again for lunch to-morrow with Mummy – she's up in London doing some shopping.'

'Ah…' He pushed his chair back, with a regretful sigh. Then his manner changed completely. The usual note of affection went out of his voice. He picked up a thick document which had been lying near him on the table, perched some glasses on his nose, and began telling me about my money in a chillingly business-like manner.

'Your Trustees estimate that the current value of your holdings is some £550,000. Your brother agrees with me that it was a mistake for him to receive his money in full. So I have drawn up this document, which will place a third of the money in trust until your twenty-fifth birthday; and a further third until your thirtieth birthday. The remainder is immediately available.'

He pulled a fountain-pen out of his breast pocket, pulled the cap off so that it was ready to use, and then pushed it and the document across the table towards me. 'All you need to do is to initial all the pages, and then sign at the foot of the last page. There's a second copy for you to keep.'

I picked up the pen, and looked at the document in horror. So, everything had been arranged. No asking what I wanted, no consultation of any kind, no advice from this ugly old bachelor other than to sign this piece of paper. I looked up. He was smiling encouragingly, apparently feeling that he had done me a tremendous favour.

I signed, and pushed the document back across the table.

'Well done,' he said, getting up and looking at his watch. The interview was obviously at an end. 'You're now a very rich young lady. And even if you do spend it all at once, which I'm sure you won't, there's lots more to come when you're older.' So that was all right, then. I would no longer be a problem to anyone. It was as if he had snapped a vital link between us, and for a moment I felt so angry that I wanted to kick him.

But then, standing outside his door, I felt a sudden excitement. It was still cold, and I pulled my Angora coat tightly about me; but the fog had cleared away, and a few shafts of winter sunlight illuminated the Square.

After living extremely well on £300 a month, I now had the better part of £200,000 at my immediate disposal.

'This is really strange,' I thought to myself. 'I shall never have to think twice about taking a taxi, or doing anything I like. I could go straight to Bond Street and buy all the jewellery my father promised me from Cartier and no-one would question me.' And then I shivered again, and thought of the Angora coat I was clutching; and I took a taxi straight to Bond Street. But instead of going to Cartier (I still felt instinctively that jewellery was something one should be given) I went to Maxwell Croft, the furrier.

For a while the assistants could hardly believe that an eighteen-year-old hippy was asking to see their stock; but I was determined. Not long ago I had seen Greta Garbo in the title rôle of *Catherine the Great*. I had admired her passionately, and had immediately longed for the fur coat which would transform me into that magically romantic figure. Now I could have it. A sight of my Coutts cheque-book banished any doubts; and soon I had ordered a coat (with my initials inside) to be made up from the rarest of Russian furs.

Exhilarated by such extravagance, I made my way back to Chesil Court, and told Nigel that we were rich. Slightly to my disappointment – and then greatly to my relief – he didn't seem either shocked or surprised. He simply took the news in his stride, gave me a little hug, and began talking about his latest set of photographs.

I felt very protective towards Nigel at that moment. It was clear to me that he had no designs upon my money. I had already begun to think that my most sensible move might well be to marry Nigel and give myself some security; and as he discussed some detail or other in a corner of one of the photographs, I came to a decision. All that I told him was that he needed a proper studio to work in, and I was going to buy him one.

Not surprisingly, Nigel was over the moon; and we had very soon found a lovely mews house at Farm Place in Notting Hill. There was plenty of space, with a garage below, and a huge upstairs room which would make a perfect studio; and once a surveyor had checked it out, I bought it on a twenty-five-year lease.

We were in Chesil Court one evening, when there was a knock on the door. 'Get that, Nicky, would you?' Nigel called out. I opened the door to a man whose face I vaguely recognised. He had long black hair and hippy clothes: tight trousers, beads, and a jacket. With him was a very pretty girl also dressed quite casually.

'Hello – Is Nigel in? Oh, there you are, you old sod!'

'Mickey! Great to see you! Come on in! Nicky, this is Mickey Finn the drummer – Marc Bolan's brought him into Tyrannosaurus Rex in place of Steve Took.'

Mickey smiled. 'And this is Sue – Sue Worth. But I gather,' he said to me, 'that Steve was a friend of yours?'

I thought grimly of those nights with Hazel and Steve Took noisily making love in the bedroom of my flat in Argyll Mansions. 'No, not really!'

'We were just going out to the Baghdad House,' said Nigel. 'Would you like to join us?'

After this we saw them almost every evening. Micky had known Nigel for years. Sue Worth, his girlfriend, was not only a successful model, but also came from a good background, and she and I became close friends.

I also continued to see a good deal of Hazel, despite the fact that she and my brother had split up. We were having lunch one day at the Casserole, and talking about Nigel, when she leaned over the table and squeezed my arm.

'Gawd 'elp us, darlin' – 'if it's bad for me, what's it like fer you? E's out of control. It's Michael wot's done it – taking 'is money, and pushing them black bitches dahn 'is trahsers.' And then she squeezed my arm again, and gave me a radiant smile. 'Yer know I'm seeing one of yer old flames – Nicky Ryman? 'E's a bit mystical, but I'm really fond of him, poor bugger! I 'ope you 'n me can still get on?'

I didn't mind at all about Nicky Ryman, but I was very anxious about my brother. I had called on Suzy quite recently to admire Howard, her baby and my little nephew; and she had suddenly blurted out her fears about Nigel:

'You saw him, Muffet. You know what a state he's in. Michael X is at the bottom of it. He's back in England, up to some mischief or other. There's another girl involved, of course. But there's something else, something I can't work out. I'm always afraid, now, that one day he'll be pushed too far.'

Having heard what Hazel had to say, I called on Michael Davys. He was sympathetic, but said there was nothing to be done at present. 'A breakdown needn't be a disaster,' he added. 'In some ways, the sooner the better. Once he admits he's got a problem, we might be able to do something.'

A few days later, Nigel Waymouth and I went down to Devon to see my Mother's new home; and that was where I first met Jasmine. She turned up with my brother late on Saturday evening. We took an instant dislike to each other; and although I could see that she was very attentive to Nigel (who treated her with absent-minded good-humour) I didn't see how she could begin to understand or cope with his problems.

'I hear that Michael X is back in England,' I said to my brother over a night-cap. We were all sitting slightly awkwardly in my Mother's new drawing-room. 'Are the two of you going to complete your work on the Black House?'

He smiled vaguely. 'Not on *the* Black House. There are going to be *dozens*! All over the country. Probably one down here, somewhere.'

Mummy looked anxious. 'But, Nigel darling, isn't that going to be fearfully expensive?'

'Thass all right,' said Jasmine. 'Michael knows what he's doing.'

'Of course he does,' said my brother, patting Jasmine on her knee. 'He's going to start fund-raising in March. It's all going to be registered as a charity. He's writing to everyone – the Bishop of London, Charles Clore, the ambassador of Kuwait. It's all going to be tremendous: you'll see!'

'Bloody Hell!' Nigel Waymouth said to me later on, in the privacy of our bedroom. 'Your poor brother's going completely loopy.' I hugged him tightly. In an increasingly dangerous world, he was clearly my only real security. I decided that I would buy a large house in London, and marry Nigel, and live there with him. Perhaps we might even have children – though I was frightened of that, because I was now taking Mandrax very regularly, and if I was going to have a baby I would have to come off any drugs for a long period. However, I would meet that problem if and when it arrived.

'Come to bed,' I implored. He needed no second invitation. I believe

I was making him very happy at that time; and early in March, while we were enjoying lunch at the Casserole, Nigel asked me to marry him.

I accepted at once. Nigel had one hand in mine; and with the other, he summoned a waitress, and asked for a bottle of champagne.

'Let's make it a quiet wedding,' he said. 'It's really no-one else's business.'

'I don't see how we can. As soon as our families know, they're bound to want a party.'

'Then let's get married straight away!'

After lunch, we went straight to the nearest registry office; but were thrown out, and told to come back when we were sober.

'Well then,' I said, 'Perhaps we'd better do things properly. Let's have all our family and friends, and get married on my nineteenth birthday!'

Both families appeared to be delighted; our friends congratulated us, and seemed genuinely pleased; and for a while it was all very exciting; but although I knew marriage would make me safe, I sometimes wondered whether I was being fair to Nigel Waymouth. I was capable of infatuation, that was obvious. But was I capable of unselfish love? The more that Nigel loved me, the more I wanted to keep him at a distance, knowing that anyone I loved deeply was liable to be snatched away from me just as Daddy had been.

When I was thinking gloomy thoughts like these, I would often visit the one place where I always felt happy and secure: Christopher Gibbs's shop in Eccleston Street. I enjoyed my cups of tea with Bouclant the Moor; and Christopher himself had begun to take a friendly interest in me. It was now that my proper artistic education began, with Christopher teaching me what was good and what was bad, what to look for and what to avoid. My Grandmother Ailsa Lane lived just over the road, so I often combined a visit to her with a visit to the antique shop, where I had now purchased a number of items, including a glass Tunisian lamp, an old Moroccan table and a Moroccan mirror. My credit increased still further when I sent Ailsa into Christopher's shop, which she loved, to buy me a wedding present of Moroccan curtains in the most wonderful gold embroidery.

There were other distractions: in mid-March, I finally passed my driving-test; so I bought a car, and drove Nigel Waymouth, Mickey Finn and Sue Worth down to Fulking for Easter. Michael Davys had loaned us my old home for a few days; and I so much enjoyed being back that I began to think I might look for a village property as a bolt-hole from London life – and perhaps I could even keep a pony again.

After Easter, wedding arrangements took over. We couldn't get married on my birthday, because by the time we contacted the Registry Office they were fully booked; but everything was fixed for the very next day.

※

On my wedding-day, Tuesday 23 June 1970, I woke up feeling guiltily that I was probably doing the wrong thing in marrying Nigel Waymouth; but I kissed him goodbye cheerfully enough before leaving Chesil Court and hurrying over to Chelsea Park Gardens, where I had arranged to get changed at Annie's house. She had met Nigel, and liked him; and her family were so happy for me and so excited that I became excited myself. 'Nigel's a good man,' said Mrs. Griffiths that morning, 'and I think you're both very lucky to have found each other.'

I went up to Annie's room, where she helped me into my wedding-dress. It had been made by Thea Porter of Soho from an old lace bedspread or table-cloth, and was covered in ribbons.

'Are you sure everything's all right?' she asked me.

'Yes, of course!' I lied.

Then we were driven over to the Registry Office, to which we had invited just family and a few close friends. My mother was there with Basil, both of them looking wonderfully smart and tidy. Nigel had chosen David Litvinoff to be his Best Man; and when we were called up by the Registrar, Litvinoff immediately began a long conversation with him.

'Just a moment, my dear fellow – while they all have time to settle down – there's a certain rough element here today – ' (and here he glared over his shoulder at the assembled company, and waved them into their seats) 'could you just give me a few facts and figures?'

'This is hardly the time,' began the Registrar, but Litvinoff took no notice.

'You see, I'm a homosexual. So this is of considerable interest to me.

Just how many homosexual weddings have you personally carried out in the past twelve months?'

The Registrar's was now completely baffled.

'I'm not quite sure, Mr, er –'

'Litvinoff.' He raised his eyebrows, and looked quizzically at the people round about. 'Perhaps you'd like my telephone number? But is this the right moment, as it were, to come out of the closet?'

'Mr. Litvinoff, I really must insist upon your silence.'

'Yes yes, I understand. Discretion the better part of valour, and all that kind of thing.'

'Discretion has nothing to do with it. Silence, please!'

The reception was in my brother Nigel's house at 30 Pavilion Road. The catering was as good as money could buy; and the house was packed with a curious mixture of friends old and new, ranging from Queens' Gate friends like Eleanor and Podoff, to people like Christopher Gibbs and Mark Palmer. Mark was in a very friendly mood, and I talked to him about what it had been like to be a page-boy at the Queen's Coronation. He smiled. 'That was a long, long time ago.'

'And now you've come down to dealing in horses! Could you sell me one, do you think?'

'As a matter of fact, I could. I've got one down at Stargroves, Mick Jagger's house just outside Newbury. It belongs to Mick but he can't ride it!'

At that moment David Litvinoff began calling for silence. It was time for the cake-cutting.

'All right,' I said to Mark. 'We'll talk about it when I get back from my honeymoon.'

After the wedding, Nigel and I went down to spend another few days in Michael Davys's cottage in Fulking. I remember the drive very well. It was late at night, and there was no moon. The chauffeur driving us to Fulking got lost and I remember thinking: 'My God, I just don't want to get there, because this is my wedding-night and we're going to have to screw each other!'

We'd been screwing each other quite happily right up to the evening before our wedding. But now that we were married and Nigel was holding my hand in the back of the car and puffing on a cigarette and whispering in my ear that he was looking forward to being in bed with me, I suddenly realised that I didn't want him anymore. When he opened a window and threw out the last of the cigarette and its glowing end whirled away into the night, I felt that any sexual attraction he had ever had for me had also disappeared into the dark.

It rained all the next day. We were stuck indoors with nothing to do but make love. I went through the motions for Nigel's sake, and even though my heart wasn't in it any more he was so sweet and loving that I thought that perhaps I was quite lucky after all. Then the following day it was sunny and beautiful, and I took some of the LSD that Litvinoff had given me as a wedding present and set out for a walk over the Sussex downs.

I had never taken LSD before, and I was hoping to have great lightning flashes of inspiration; but nothing very exciting happened. It was just a happy, dream-like experience. The pleasure I felt from walking along paths I had walked countless times as a child, the pleasure I felt from having a man beside me who seemed genuinely to love me, the pleasure I felt from the sunny June afternoon – all these pleasures were intensified. And when we came to a small hotel where they sold cream teas, instead of immediately feeling on edge and wanting to leave, my usual experience in restaurants, I ate masses of scones and cream and jam; and felt utterly happy and contented. That was the effect of my first trip on LSD. My second trip would be quite different – but that story belongs later on, and I'd rather not think about it until I have to.

After our honeymoon, Nigel and I went back to London as a so-called happily-married couple; and perhaps we *were* happy for a while. Nigel certainly seemed contented and he was also working very hard. He'd go off to his studio in Farm Place at ten in the morning and come back at six or seven in the evening, like any normal married man. Life at Chesil Court itself was very easy, since Rita came in once or twice a week to clean up. But it was also very dull. I tried to enliven it once by giving Rita some hash cake with her morning coffee. At first, seeing her stoned was an amazing experience, as she had no idea what was happening to her; but after a while she lay down on the kitchen floor and began telling me stories about her poverty-stricken childhood, and I ended up feeling more sad than amused.

We hadn't been back long when I was so bored that I persuaded Nigel that since we saw very little of each other it would be good to have another short holiday, and so we set off for Ireland, with me driving. The journey round Ireland was quite uneventful; but on our way to the ferry-port we spent a couple of nights in a remote part of Wales with David Litvinoff, who had rented a tiny cottage some miles north of Lampeter.

Over supper on our first evening, as we sat on dilapidated old wooden chairs at a dilapidated old wooden table squashed up against the fireplace eating some overdone lamb chops in a quite passable mint sauce, Nigel was saying how charming it all was, when Litvinoff interrupted him: "You might not think so, dear friend," he said,

> "were you aware of the somewhat sensitive political matter in which you have unwittingly become involved! Can you imagine to whom this rustic dwelling belongs?" We shook our heads. "I must speak the name quietly, for fear of offending young Lenin here"; and he leaned across the table and said in a dramatic stage-whisper: "Enoch Powell! And do you know the name of the only book I found in the entire cottage? Little Black Sambo!"

At that moment there was a growl from Lenin, an enormous Labrador to which David was absolutely devoted.

"You see how sensitive he is? It is fortunate the door is well and truly shut. Lenin becomes quite upset at the mention of *that name* and then rushes out and begins savaging Farmer Jones's sheep."

"But that's terrible!" said Nigel.

"Indeed so. The matter comes to court next week. The cruel magistrates will undoubtedly wish to terminate Lenin's life."

However, Lenin survived. We heard later that Litvinoff had worn down the legal system with arguments of such complexity, and references to decisions of such obscurity, that the magistrates had spared the dog's life on condition that he was removed to another county, so that they would never again have to endure a similar harangue from his master.

Once we were back in London again, life was as dull as ever. Only one thing gave me real pleasure: I had bought the horse which Mark Palmer had promised me on my wedding-day, a pretty little thoroughbred called Fella which Mark had bought at some gypsy sale in south London. He had actually sold him first of all to Mick Jagger; but Mick had been thrown by him a couple of times, and had lost interest.

So twice a week I would drive down to Stargroves. The name was good, but it was the most awfully ugly Victorian house you could ever imagine. I heard that Mick Jagger had bought it on Christopher Gibbs's advice, but so much work needed doing on it that builders were always around – at this time they were putting in a recording studio, as well as working on the main bedroom and bathroom.

Mick himself was hardly ever around, but his mother and father often seemed to be visiting. They were rather sweet, very ordinary down-to-earth Londoners, who had been completely bowled over by Mick's success. They were both very proud of him; and he adored them. Unlike many stars from working-class backgrounds, he never turned his back on them, and I can remember his mother saying: 'Mick's very good to us – he always asks us to his parties, and we always go when we can.'

One of the fixtures at Stargroves was Maldwyn Thomas, Mick Jagger's groom, a beautiful young man in his twenties and a friend of Mark Palmer's from his gypsy-caravanning days. Maldwyn lived in the gardener's cottage in the grounds. Officially he was now Mick Jagger's groom and looked after the stables; but I think that at that time he knew much more about breeding greyhounds than about horses.

It was a very hippy community; and when I arrived from London in the late morning I used to go indoors for a coffee and a cigarette to find that nearly everyone was smashed – except of course for Mick's parents, who must have been quite bemused by our behaviour, but took it all in good part – and instead of being given the cigarette I wanted, it would always be an enormous joint. I've never actually liked hash that much, so I would pretend to puff at the joint; and then I'd go off and ride Fella.

That was the part of the day that I loved. It was the first time that I'd ridden properly since I was twelve or thirteen, and it was like being a child again. I was taken back once again to the island covered with meadows and leafy woods on which Annie Griffiths and I had been going to run a riding-school. I remembered how when I was a child, my father had nursed such high hopes for my future. And what was I doing now? Sometimes the present, being married to Nigel and being a good housewife, seemed like another dream, and dreams don't last. The real future was rushing towards me, dark and uncertain.

Driving back from Stargroves one evening, my mind full of these thoughts, my lungs full of hash, I was coming into London over the Chiswick flyover when I fell asleep. It was probably only for a second, but as I jerked my eyes open again and saw how close I was to the edge of the road, and saw the long drop over the side, and knew where it would lead, I felt a moment of such longing and such terror that flyovers and even bridges have frightened me ever since.

I also realised more than ever that I wanted a place in the country of my own. I told Nigel about it, and persuaded him to come down with me to Sussex. "Wouldn't it be lovely to have somewhere of our own?" I said to him. "I could keep my pony there, and I wouldn't have to go down to Stargroves anymore." So we went house-hunting together; and amazingly, we had only been searching for a few days when we heard of a cottage below the Downs just outside Fulking. When we went to see it, it seemed like a dream come true: a tiny little black and white cottage, so hidden-away that it wasn't even visible from the road. Admittedly, the local cricket-pitch was opposite, and they were playing that afternoon.

"That's rather a drawback, isn't it?" I said to old Mrs. Porter, after we had walked down the narrow little path to the front door, and she had come to let us in.

"Oh no, dear. Goodness, don't I remember you when you were a little girl? Always about the place with your brother? Oh, no, dear. They only play a few weekends in the summer – and listen to that sound – myself, I find it rather comforting."

I had to admit that the muffled sound of ball on bat and the occasional ripple of applause was rather agreeable. And Mrs Porter's memories made me feel that I had really come home. "You look happy!" said Nigel in a slightly surprised tone of voice.

"Darling, I really love this cottage."

"The only problem is that there's no room for anyone to stay." I probably looked very crestfallen at that, because he quickly added: "Still, I suppose we could always add a small extension downstairs – perhaps another sitting-room with a bedroom leading off? And what will you call it?"

"The Cabbage Patch!" I joked; and in September, when all the legal work was completed, the Cabbage Patch it became. Nigel and I started going down there for weekends, and not far away in Clappers Lane I found a livery stables where Fella could be looked after. It was run by a young couple, and the husband was not only upper-class but unbelievably good-looking. I immediately took a fancy to him. Although he made no move in my direction, as the weeks and months went by his restraint only heightened the erotic pleasure I felt in his company.

In the meantime, Nigel and I fitted in a brief pre-Christmas trip to Paris; and while we were there, Nigel telephoned his friend the fashion model Amanda Lear at the Hotel Maurice. She was staying there with Salvador Dali, whose Muse she had been for many years; and she said: "Do come round, Dali would love to meet you both. Come round for tea." And when we turned up, this startling figure with his waxed moustache and pop-eyes opened the door to us himself, wearing one of his famous velvet jackets, and carrying a marvellous jewelled stick, so that he looked more like a wizard than a normal human being.

Dali was very polite and welcoming, kissing my hand and saying in somewhat broken English: "'Come in, come in, come in. Sit down. Amanda's told me. Do sit down." We found ourselves in a roomful of people to whom he was evidently holding court: Amanda was among the audience, also someone whom Dali called 'Captain' who in one hand held a camera, and in the other a lead, on the end of which was a cheetah. There was also another couple; and a beautiful tall blonde wearing the shortest of mini-skirts.

We had hardly sat down when Dali turned to this girl, and asked her to hang some mistletoe on the chandelier in the middle of the room. To do this she had to stand on a chair and stretch upwards, and so of course her mini rode up, and Dali was almost beside himself with voyeuristic excitement, fluttering round her and making the Captain take photographs. In the background there was a huge lugubrious portrait of a child with the head of a man bending a fencing sword in his hands; and when Dali had helped the girl down from her chair and calmed down a little, he flourished his jewelled stick in the air like a wand, and said that it was a portrait of Aleister Crowley as a child.

Next to it was propped a giant fork (Nigel told me afterwards it was a soft sculpture by Claes Oldenburg); and then suddenly a gong rang, and tea was wheeled in on a trolley. It was a very formal rather British tea (perhaps in our honour); and I was just beginning to think that things had started becoming a little more normal when Dali insisted that if anyone wanted sugar, it was essential for them to put the sugar-lumps in without removing their wrappers. "Otherwise", he said madly, "the germs will get to you".

I found it rather like being in a play, and not being sure of one's lines. Because everything around Dali seemed to be orchestrated, organised and manipulated. Nothing was quite natural: it was as though he had created his own world with its own rules, and everybody had to fit in. Nigel was very impressed, and later told me that amidst all the madness he felt he had been touched by a powerfully creative force, that there was a genius in Dali's art, somehow mixed up in the conjuring trick of being himself. But Dali scared the living daylights out of me, just as his pictures still do: they all have a nightmarish quality.

※

Back in London that autumn we had continued spending our evenings in a hippy kind of manner, going to places like the Baghdad House and hanging out chiefly with Nigel's closest friends. Several of these friends of Nigel's had friends themselves, often not very interesting people, who would expect to be able to come back home with us and spend the night in Chesil Court. This was far too small for visitors, and I persuaded Nigel that we should start looking for a proper house in London. I also began spending more time with people who seemed to appreciate me for myself alone, like Christopher Gibbs and my new friend Ossie Clark the fashion designer, about whom more later.

The house-hunting was enjoyable. It was exciting going into the estate agents and saying rather grandly: "Yes, I'm looking for a house; my price margin is £50,000 to £100,000", which in those days made them pretty keen on my company. After looking with Nigel at several houses, including the one in Tite Street where Oscar Wilde had lived, it was alone that one November morning I went with the Hamptons' estate agent to see an extraordinary house in Mallord Street.

From the front it looked very much like any other small London mews house. When the agent let me in through the front door, I found myself in a very small, very beautiful Dutch hallway, with Dutch windows rather in the Lutyens style. On my left there was a sitting-room, also lovely but a little neglected, with another little room leading off that; and then there was a passageway which went down to a kitchen and a dining-room; and beneath that there was a self-contained basement flat with sitting-room, bedroom, kitchen and bathroom, and this was in better condition than any other part of the house.

But the great feature of the place was that at the back, where originally the garden would have been, there was an enormous studio with a lovely wooden floor which had been built by Augustus John, using a Dutch architect. The property as a whole looked in need of a good deal of tender loving care; but it was unique and beautiful and I knew immediately that I wanted it. I telephoned Nigel at once, told the estate agent I needed a second look immediately, and within two hours I was back at the property, and Nigel was agreeing with me that it was fantastic.

"The studio will be perfect for you", I told him; "and the downstairs basement's in such good condition that Rita and Jorge could move in straight away!" After that, things happened very fast; Rita and Jorge were safely installed by the New Year of 1971; and then I went to Christopher Gibbs and said to him: 'Look, I've just bought this house, will you help me decorate it?'

Christopher seemed genuinely pleased, perhaps because he realised immediately that unlike some of his other projects this one might actually come to fruition. I clearly wasn't doing this as a folly, or as a side-line to my real life. I truly wanted to live at Mallord Street and do it up properly and fill it with beautiful things. When Christopher came to see the house, he was particularly impressed by the studio. "I think we should connect it to the main house", he said to me. "We could knock a doorway through from that little room beyond the sitting room, and that could open onto a magnificent balcony, from which a spiral staircase would lead down into the studio." Then he looked at me inquiringly. "If it has to be a studio?" I nodded, not at all sure what he was driving at. "A pity – it would make the finest drawing-room in London."

He had soon found me a builder and decorator, Tony Wills, a lovely East-ender who had made good in the building trade. "If you've got Tony working for you", Christopher told me, "you won't need an architect or a surveyor." So Tony would turn up alone for site meetings, looking very spruce in his dapper little grey suit with a nice clean shirt on. In fact, he looked so smart that to begin with everyone in the street thought he was my father!

And then for a while it became very difficult to think about Mallord Street, because there was terrible news about my brother Nigel.

CHAPTER TWENTY
The Trouble with Nigel

I remember that it was in February 1971, only days after decimalisation had torn the historical heart out of our currency, and forever removed my beloved three-penny bits and sixpences and shillings and florins and half-crowns, not to mention Queen Victoria pennies dating as far back as the 1860s. It was on a Friday night, and my brother was up at the Black House, where Michael X was pushing him for more money.

It was a difficult time for Nigel: he'd been writing out too many cheques and his Trustees had been down on him quite heavily. So for once he'd said: "No, you're not getting any!" By this time, they had spiked his drink with acid; but before it took effect he had walked out and hailed a taxi. Unfortunately, Jasmine, who really liked Nigel, was not with him on this occasion; and when he wouldn't hand over any money, two other black girls followed him into the back of the cab, and then everything got seriously out of hand.

As the acid began to take effect, Nigel began tripping madly and lost control. His companions responded by slashing at his legs with a knife and cut him quite deeply. When the cab stopped at some traffic lights the two black girls jumped out, covered in blood. The taxi-driver drove Nigel straight to the Charing Cross Hospital, dumped him in the emergency ward, and cleared out. By this time Nigel was completely off his head, produced the thousand pounds in cash that he usually carried on him and started throwing it around like confetti. Within a few minutes he was being sedated and then sectioned by two doctors, and sent to Horton Down, a vast Victorian mental institution in Epsom.

I only learned about this the next day, by which time it was already too late for anyone to do anything. The papers had been signed, and that was it: he would be incarcerated at Horton Down for a minimum of 28 days. I drove down at once to see him; and it was like a journey into hell.

I found my brother in a locked ward with sixty other people, most of them elderly long-term patients. It was all filthy beyond belief. The green linoleum floor in the day-room looked as though it had never been cleaned; on it stood a few metal chairs, and here and there I could see ash-trays overflowing with fag-ends. One of the three Pakistani male nurses who patrolled up and down told me that Nigel was still in bed. They hadn't put him in the main dormitory, a long thin room with two rows of little narrow beds separated by bare tables. Instead, he had been placed in an area reserved for the most dangerous inmates.

It was obvious that Nigel's leg was bad, but when I asked one of the nurses to clean it up, he shrugged his shoulders and told me that he wasn't a medical nurse. "Then give me a first-aid kit!" I snapped. But when he brought it to me, it contained nothing remotely useful: just a stale egg sandwich.

Nigel himself was too doped-up to say anything intelligible; but I told him that I would get him out as soon as possible, and then I stormed into the office of the doctor in charge and told him "You must let my brother out!"

"No", he said quietly and firmly, and then took a puff at his pipe. "I fully intend to keep him here for twenty-eight days. I need him here."

"I don't understand. Why?"

"Your brother, if he is your brother? Oh, very well." Another puff. "Do you know, your brother claims that his godmother is Jennie Lee, that his solicitor is Lord Goodman?" Another puff. It was quite aromatic, and my fury cooled a little. "Well, young lady, if he's telling me the truth", and here he pointed at me with his pipe, "then I want these people to visit this hospital to see the circumstances in which I'm compelled to work. And then maybe we can get some money for this place!"

Before I could answer, he had walked up to a tinted window from which he could look out over the recreation room without being seen himself. "Just look at that! It's a national disgrace. A good many of them are just social misfits: they've got drunk once too often, they can't hold down jobs, social security and the prisons have given up on them, and they end up in here." He turned and glared at me. "It's a kind of human dustbin. Do you know, there are old ladies in the women's wards who were put away in here when they were thirteen or fourteen for having babies and disgracing their families! All I can do is to give them enough drugs to keep them peaceful enough for my three Pakistanis to stop them rioting. And we're using a lot of Electric Shock Therapy – that seems to help."

"You need permission for that, don't you?"

"It's true, officially we need consent."

"Then just make sure that Nigel Samuel doesn't have any of it! And I'm sending in my own doctor to look after his leg! His name's Dr. Rossdale. You won't object?"

"Oh – very well. You'll be back again, I hope?"

But I was already striding towards the exit, with tears streaming down my cheeks.

From then on, Nigel Waymouth and I went down there every other day. By the time of my next visit, Dr. Rossdale had already visited and cleaned up Nigel's leg. He reported to me over the telephone that it had already been going septic, and given another couple of days gangrene could have set in.

I hated it more each time I visited. The atmosphere was often so highly-charged that I felt that one wrong word might cause a riot; and I had to put up with some of the inmates running their hands all over me. I couldn't even go to the loo while I was there, because it was absolutely disgusting and seething with cockroaches. Also, I saw for myself the horrible truth of what the asylum doctor had told me. Virtually all the patients were sent for electric shock treatment on Mondays, Wednesdays and Fridays, regardless of what was wrong with them. This meant that they were sleeping it off for half the week; and, with the help of drugs, the staff could just about deal with them for the other half, especially as they were kept locked up for twenty-four hours a day, and were never even allowed into anything like a prison yard for a breath of exercise and fresh air.

Sometimes we were joined by Hazel, sometimes by Suzy – Nigel's private life was such a mess. And once Jasmine turned up uninvited, and I was so angry with her that I took her to one side and said that if ever I saw her again, I'd kill her in cold blood.

After three weeks, we got Nigel out. Michael Davys arranged for him to be given a bed by a private hospital, St Andrews in Northampton; and I arrived in a limousine with two male nurses (required by law since Nigel was still under the order) to pick him up. Nigel had been amazingly philosophical throughout; and when the doctor said that he was sorry to be losing him, Nigel replied: "That's most kind of you, doctor, most kind. But I really do believe that if I'd stayed here one day longer, I might have gone mad!"

I was happy to leave Nigel in St. Andrews, where he had his own private room and everyone seemed to be extremely solicitous. But I had found the whole experience devastating. Up to that time, whenever people had told me that there was something seriously wrong with Nigel, I'd pretended to myself that apart from being a little under pressure he was perfectly all right. Now I had to accept the fact that although he wasn't actually dead, in an important way I had lost him.

When I went to cry on Arnold Goodman's shoulder, he very wisely suggested that my 'seaside resort' and I should go away for a holiday in Rome to get over things. "Your brother will be all right at St. Andrews – it'll be like a rest cure!" he enthused. So we did; and although I was sexually disenchanted with my husband, whom I now found too gentle with me, we had a reasonably happy time.

※

I mentioned Ossie Clark as a new friend. I had met him through Christopher Gibbs, and he had started using me occasionally for photographs for magazines. When we returned from Rome, and I was complaining that I needed a new dress, Nigel said to me: "Why not go to Ossie Clark and ask him to make a dress just for you? Nothing to do with one of his collections.' So I did, rather nervously; and much to my surprise Ossie was frightfully excited.

"Yes, sure darling", he said, "I'll do anything you want."

So I said: "I want something stylish and fashionable". And he began making me a beautiful dress covered with moons and stars. While this creation was under way, he rang me up and asked me to pose with his models Gaylor and Carianne for a fashion spread in a magazine. I'm not sure that the photographs ever appeared in print; but from that time onwards, instead of buying from Ossie's shop, I would go to his workroom and buy from there.

The result was that I met his wife Celia Birtwell, who designed many of the fabrics he used; and also, his business partner Alice Pollock with whom I became quite good friends: partly, perhaps, because she was having a bad time with her boyfriend; and I was feeling increasingly unsure about Nigel Waymouth.

Now that Nigel Samuel was at Northampton it was usually Michael Davys who came with me to see him. We found that he had his situation well in hand. He was having an affair with one of the other inmates; and there was so little discipline that provided he was in his room in time for a roll-call, he could spend most of the day with her in the pub. It seemed to me that St. Andrews was more like a hotel than a hospital, and so long as the management were being paid their £100 per day, they didn't mind whether or not he saw a psychiatrist regularly or followed any sensible course of treatment. The result was that his stay at Northampton did him no good at all.

In the meantime, Mallord Street had completely gone to my head. It was wonderful. I'd go there every day to boss Tony Wills and his builders around; and then Christopher Gibbs would turn up, and since I never once dared to question his judgment, I let him boss me around. When he decreed that something had to be a particular colour I'd just say meekly: 'Yes, Christopher, sure, that's the colour it'll be, yes you're so right.'

More important, perhaps, I couldn't get out of my head what he had said about the studio possibly being the finest drawing-room in London; and I began to dislike the idea of Nigel using it for his art. "I hope you won't find it too much for you", I said to him one day.

He looked at me oddly. "What do you mean?"

"It's just that it's such a wonderful studio – perhaps it's too perfect?" The fact was that I had begun to want the whole house for myself. I already knew that I didn't have to go on being Nigel's second string. The pretence was still there, the game was still being played out. But it seemed to me to me more and more probable that I would move into Mallord Street alone.

And then one sunny spring afternoon Donald Cammell reappeared. I was walking along the King's Road enjoying the warmth when suddenly I heard this familiar deep guttural voice at my shoulder, and I turned and there was Donald with his longish brown hair smiling at me warmly out of his slightly raddled face. He was only saying something like "Hi Nicky – long time no see!" But as usual he stank of sex, and in a moment my legs were tingling, my tits were tingling, my ears were tingling, and he kept on smiling at me, and I felt completely naked under his gaze, and by the time he had got round to saying: "Come back to my flat for tea", I think we both knew that there was more than tea on our minds.

I walked back with him to where he was living in Royal Church Street; and we sat down for a moment, but he was playing with himself as he spoke to me, something he always seemed to be doing, and I couldn't stand it any longer and went over and put my hand over his prick myself. It hardened immediately, and I pulled down his zip and his prick sprang to attention and I held it with my hand and began pulling at it, watching the end grow larger and larger, sucking at it, licking at the pre-come, wanting to bring him to orgasm at once; but a few moments later he picked me up and carried me to his bed and lay me down, and I found myself having the most amazing sexual experience of my life.

What made it so special was that while most men ask for what they want, and only then give you what you want – and you know the whole time that they're going to hate it – he gave first. I thought he'd fuck me straight away. But instead, he pushed up my skirt and pulled down my pants and began sucking my cunt, and I could feel that he was truly enjoying it. And when I was caught up in the agony – or the ecstasy – of my orgasm, watching my pleasure seemed to give him a tremendous high. After that I would have done anything for him. And when he came inside me and fucked me, he was strong and powerful and I knew I'd been properly fucked.

Afterwards he told me that I could come to see him whenever I wanted; but to remember that he had a girl-friend called Myriam Gibril, and he showed me a photograph of an incredibly striking dark-skinned woman with long curly hair and high cheekbones. "She's Ethiopian", said Donald. "Do you mind about her? She won't mind about you." What could I say? I was still tingling with pleasure, and I couldn't help thinking that it might make things easier with Nigel.

Because for all my faults I'm reasonably honest, so I went straight back to Nigel and said to him: "Nigel, I've got to tell you something. I've met your friend Donald Cammell again; and I'm even more attracted to him than I was out in California. I shouldn't think anything important will happen, because he's already got a girlfriend whom he adores. But I've invited him round tomorrow evening, and he says he'll call in about seven."

Nigel looked very shaken. He knew me too well not to realise that something important had already happened. As for me, having gone to bed with Donald once, I knew that I would want to go to bed with him again and again, and that my marriage was in ruins.

CHAPTER TWENTY-ONE
Donald and Myriam

When Donald Cammell looked at me, I could only think of one thing: bed, sex, and more sex. I have never known any other man with such a gift, and I wasn't alone in being affected by him. I just made the mistake of thinking that it was anything to do with love. That evening he came round to Chesil Court. I don't recall anything very remarkable happening; but Nigel took some photographs; and when he showed me the prints the following afternoon, he said to me very miserably: "There you are. Nicky – some pictures of the man you love." He was right of course; but I didn't know what to say. I certainly didn't feel embarrassed. In fact I felt intensely excited whenever I thought of Donald. And hearing the misery in Nigel's voice I knew that there was only one thing to be done.

I left the room for a moment and came back with a package in my hand. "Nigel, I know it's not your birthday until tomorrow, but I think you'd better take this now, because I'm afraid that we're going to break up."

Inside the package there was a very fine photograph which I knew would please him, but he didn't open it; and he was so gentle and dignified, that when a few minutes later the front door closed behind him, I was the one who felt like crying. 'Damn it', I thought. 'Why couldn't you have been just a little angry?'

He couldn't go to Farm Place, because we'd sold it to help pay for Mallord Street. But before long I began trying to find him somewhere new in which to live. I soon heard that Catherine Tennant had moved out of her Glebe Place apartment. This was essentially a big studio with two bedrooms, a kitchen and a bathroom attached, and I knew that it would be perfect for Nigel. The only problem was that Catherine had become very fond of Robert Mapplethorpe; and by the time I contacted her, she had already had him installed in Glebe Place. However, knowing how much I owed Nigel, I began negotiating with her.

In the meantime, I was going on endless visits with Christopher Gibbs to antique dealers. We used to go down the Fulham Road to Arthur Brown, then up the Pimlico Road where Geoffrey Bennison would urge me to blow the cobwebs off my cheque-book, and we stopped at any other places which took our fancy. I'd buy a few things myself, at which Christopher would shriek and scream and say they were awful; but I left most of the purchases to him because I knew he had a wonderful eye.

He would see furniture that looked all bashed up and totally rotten and he'd say: 'That's perfect – that's just what you want!' We'd buy these enormous sofas and chairs, and I'd say: 'God, look at the state of them!' And he'd say: 'That's okay: you can cover them all in blue denim.' This was a brilliantly simple idea. No-one, not even David Mlinaric or John Stefanidis had thought of anything so simple as upholstering all the furniture in a house in blue denim – but later it became almost a cult.

Mallord Street still wasn't completely ready; but by now the balcony had been installed, complete with an enormously long Regency sofa; and from the balcony I could walk down a new spiral staircase into the studio which Christopher was turning into the most wonderful sitting-room in London. We polished that lovely wooden floor; and then most of it was covered by an enormous carpet decorated with tigers, lions and monkeys. On that carpet, we placed a number of other carpets, and then came the furniture.

At the far end of the room from the balcony was a massive desk. On one wall there was an intricate Grinling Gibbons carving into which an old mirror had been set. In the four corners of the room there were marvellous Chinese tables; and then came oak tables and bookcases, those sofas covered in blue denim, another antique desk with twenty secret drawers, a beautiful set of chairs, and an elegant chaise longue on which I planned to recline when receiving my guests.

Beneath the balcony, there had been another small room. The story was that it had been the bedroom where Augustus John had seduced his models; but we pulled down the wall between it and the studio, installed a large fireplace on the end wall, and then covered the floor with cushions. There were also candles everywhere; and by the time it was finished it had been transformed into a small sitting-room where I could feel comfortable when there were only two or three of us present.

By mid-July 1971 I had moved in; and with Rita and Jorge downstairs to cook my meals and look after everything, I was extremely free and independent. But instead of making any sensible use of my freedom, I was so besotted by Donald Cammell that I was seeing as much as possible of this man whose eyes just looked at me and said: 'Jump into bed, Nicky – no roses and chocolate about it – just pure desire!'.

One weekend very early in our affair, Donald came down to the Cabbage Patch with me. He insisted that Myriam should come too. Deep down, I loathed her; but I was so passionate about Donald that I pretended not to mind. Inevitably, the three of us went to bed together.

Later on that day, I felt much happier when Donald came for a walk with me on his own. The hay hadn't yet been cut, and we ended up in a hayfield. What followed was unforgettable. Donald began by sucking my cunt for at least an hour and he would not let me come. Every time I nearly did, he would stop. It was heaven and hell at the same time. For some reason he desperately wanted me to pee. I never understood this, and no-one has ever wanted it again; but it was a great feeling, having this wonderful lover sucking me off and asking me to pee at the same time. We went on and on. We must have been lying there under the blue sky and the occasional drifting clouds for three hours or more. During all that time, he never once asked me to do anything to him. He continued to give himself to me until the agony was so great that finally he put his large and wonderful prick inside me & came. Afterwards I was on air; and sex has never again been so good as it was that afternoon.

Sex is certainly no romantic dream, and I don't believe that most women usually enjoy it. But it's all right if they can find someone like Donald, someone with his heathen power. Then they know they've genuinely been used, but while they've been used, they've also been loved; they've been genuinely wanted, and the man has been desperate, and he's known how to bring them to such a height that all they want is more, and they fall asleep still wanting more.

Back in London, I started visiting Donald and Myriam in their flat in Old Church Street. To start with it was usually the three of us sleeping together; but then one afternoon I found Donald alone. He seemed a little on edge, but he made me a cup of coffee and then pulled me down to sit on his lap, and casually put his hand inside my dress and began caressing my breasts while he talked. It wasn't long before my nipples were like bullets under his expert attention; but when I began trying to stroke his cock, he pushed my hand away.

"What's the matter, darling?"

"Let's wait for Myriam – she may be bringing a friend home." The air was suddenly alive with sexual tension.

"Who do you mean?"

"I don't know yet – a new friend, probably a very young one."

Before long, we heard voices – I recognised one of them as Myriam's – and then a key was turning in the lock and the door opened and in came Myriam with a pretty girl of only about sixteen; but although she was in uniform and carrying a satchel, her school frock was at least two sizes too small for her, and you could see that beneath the tight blue cotton she had already developed a wonderful figure. She looked at us all quite knowingly, took some chewing-gum out of her mouth, and said to Donald: "You the one with the grass, then?"

"This is Rose", said Myriam protectively, putting an arm round Rose's shoulders, and letting one of her hands fall as if accidentally onto one of Rose's extremely prominent breasts, which she then stroked gently.

Rose didn't seem to notice. She was already transfixed by Donald's gaze. "Don't he talk?" she appealed to Myriam, while still looking at him.

"Come and let me show you my clothes", said Myriam

They had to squeeze past where Donald was sitting. Myriam went first, and then Donald shot a foot across to block Rose's way. Before she could protest, he took her hand and began examining it, finger by finger. 'Ere, you're a saucy one', she giggled at him.

He looked her in the eyes again. "I'll come through and see you in a minute. Nicky will make us some tea."

Then Myriam and Rose went into the bedroom, and the door closed behind them. We could hear girlish giggles and shrieks; and then after a while silence; and after another while, moaning. Donald turned towards me and as usual I began to tingle inside. "Myriam's very good to me", he said, getting up from his chair to follow her. He half-opened the bedroom door, and then turned to speak to me again. Beyond him I could see Myriam and Rose on the bed. They were both naked. Myriam's head was between Rose's legs, while Rose's head was thrown back in ecstasy, and she was kneading her own breasts. "Go and make that tea", said Donald; "and then come and join us, if you like?"

I nodded, making the tea with such trembling hands it was a miracle I didn't burn myself.

When I joined them, with four mugs of tea on a tray, Myriam and Rose were sitting up on the bed, still naked, with Myriam's arm once again protectively round Rose's shoulders; while Donald sat on the chair next to them dressed only in his underpants, at which Rose was staring with considerable interest. 'You must 'ave got a big 'un in there, mate!'

He didn't answer her, but just smiled and said "Thanks for the tea, Nicky."

"Heavens", I joked, moving in front of Donald to hand the other two their mugs of tea, "I feel awfully overdressed in here!" And then I could feel Donald pulling down my pants from behind, and raising my skirt to show Rose my naked pussy. Somehow at the same time he had dropped his pants, and I could feel his prick moving deliciously up against my bottom. "Don't you think she's lovely?" he asked Rose. "She's done some modelling you know." Much to my disappointment, he let me go. "You could probably be a model too, Rose, you've got a very beautiful body. May I come a little closer?"

Rose blushed and put down her tea. Donald knelt down by the bed and began kissing the tops of her legs.

"Ere, are you goin' to do what she did?"

She lay back and Myriam, a look of intense pleasure on her face, began caressing Rose's breasts; while Donald moved gradually closer and closer to Rose's cunt and then began sucking it. By this time, I had taken off my clothes too, but although I was trying to smile, I was feeling in terrible pain as I watched Donald begin doing to Rose what he had done to me. He must have sensed what I was feeling because he stopped his sucking and sat up, and said to me: "Nicky: you have a turn. She's so gorgeous."

I've never liked sucking women's cunts, but I did so for Donald's sake, lying down on the bed and pretending that I was enjoying it. But then Donald was behind me and he pushed my knees under me so that my bottom was up in the air and then, joy of joys, while I was going on sucking at Rose, he slid his prick into me and began fucking me from behind so fiercely I thought stupidly that I was in danger of disappearing up Rose's cunt.

"And then you could be reborn!" Was it Donald saying that, reading what was going on in my head, or was it my imagination? I've never been quite certain; but a few minutes later I lay wrapped in a rug on the floor, smoking some hash and watching Donald doing his slow wonderful work with Rose, and I thought to myself: "She may only be sixteen, but this isn't an offence. Losing her virginity to him – he's like a heathen god, and there's something sacred about it."

The next morning, I said something about this to Donald. I spoke rather nervously, because it all sounded so silly over a mid-morning coffee; but he looked at me very approvingly and said: "Nicky, I always knew you would understand. There *is* a kind of magic. But you have to want to know about it." I explained that I had been fascinated by the occult for years, and he began telling me about a film he had been making in Egypt earlier in the year. "It's called *Lucifer Rising*. It involves all kinds of interesting people like Marianne Faithfull, and Kenneth thinks it can be a real block-buster."

"Kenneth?"

"Kenneth Anger. He's not only a film-maker, but also someone who knows a great deal about magic, both white and black." He looked at me speculatively, and I began to tingle again. "Good sex, the right kind of sex, is a very important part of white magic – but listen, come and eat with us tonight. And afterwards we'll go and call on Kenneth. He's not personally very interested in women – but I'm sure he'll be happy to meet you."

So that evening found Donald and Myriam and me going over to 23 Mount Street. "It's a strange flat", said Myriam, "but very elegant. "It belongs to his friend Robert Fraser, who ran a famous art gallery in the sixties."

"So where's Robert Fraser now?"

"In prison", said Donald bluntly. "Out in India – the result of some drug offence or other."

Myriam was right about the Mount Street flat, which was curiously elegant. It was still reached by an old-fashioned lift; and the whole place was painted black. When we knocked on the door, we were admitted easily enough; and there in the drawing-room, surrounded by half-a-dozen acolytes, was Kenneth Anger in long flowing robes and flaming red hair sitting on his throne casting spells. This was evidently the real thing and it made me shiver. And then, just when I was hoping I wouldn't be noticed, he stepped down from the throne, and came over to me and put his hands on my forehead and gazed into my eyes in a sinister kind of way. I felt scared out of my wits; and when my eyes wandered away from his face, I couldn't help noticing that beneath the robes he was wearing a green tweed suit with an unusual design.

"Most perceptive, daughter of Eve, most perceptive. Touch it if you like!" It was certainly good quality, though well-worn. "This jacket once graced the shoulders of my master, the great Aleister Crowley!" This was even more sinister, and I was so scared and (by this time) so stoned that I don't remember much of what followed.

Curiously enough, as I got to know Kenneth Anger better, I found that beneath all the sinister incantations and the lavish robes there was a very gentle and delightful man. It was only if he really disliked someone that he'd talk of using any black magic – and I very much doubt whether any of his spells really worked. He was just so besotted by Crowley that magic had taken over his life. For my part, I came to trust him; and Kenneth would be one of the very few people I invited down to the Cabbage Patch over the next few years.

I was learning as much as I could about Donald Cammell; and my first surprise was that this independent jet-setter had a mother living practically round the corner from him in a large house in Edith Grove. I began visiting her, and she told me that Donald's father had died in the war. She herself appeared to be highly sensitive; and perhaps Donald had inherited something of her temperament, because my second surprise was that he was a considerable artist.

"He was tutored by Annigoni," said his mother. "The portrait painter, you know? Come, let me show you some of Donald's paintings!" And she took me into a room piled high with his canvases.

"Oh, they're beautiful! The colours are so rich!"

"They're for sale, you know? Would you like to buy one? I'm terribly broke just at present."

She was a lovely old lady; and so kind to me that on my second visit I broke down in floods of tears. Out it all came: "I love your son. And I want a family. But it all seems so hopeless!"

She listened patiently, handed me a clean linen handkerchief and said: "Nicky, my dear, I'm his mother and I love him, so it hurts me to say this, you know? But don't be in love with my son, you're too good for him, you need a life of your own." I burst into floods of tears again, but she went on: "Don't play his game, don't love him, he's not going to give you anything."

Naturally I didn't want to believe her. I fantasised about Donald all the time; and having seen some of his pictures, I imagined him painting a vast richly-coloured canvas showing King Arthur screwing Queen Guinevere. Arthur would be on top and facing towards us, pagan and magnificent, with Guinevere beneath him as seductive as hell; and Arthur would have Donald's face, and Guinevere mine.

The reality was very different. Apart from when he was giving us sexual pleasure, he wanted any woman of his to be an under-dog. Myriam whom I had started thinking of as 'the Ethiopian slag', actually seemed to enjoy his life-style, and of course, because I loved Donald so much, it became my life-style too.

Sometimes there seemed to be an endless stream of sixteen-year-olds coming into his flat and losing their virginity to him, and sometimes I would be the one to take the girl into the bedroom and encourage her, while it was Myriam's turn to make the tea in the kitchen. For most of the girls, it was a wonderful introduction to sex; but for some of them, who were lonely and lost, I felt sorry. Donald, like some heathen God, loved us all indiscriminately: that was his nature.

CHAPTER TWENTY-TWO

An Interlude in Venice; and Meeting Bill Willis and Victoria Brooke

Not long after my first visit to Kenneth Anger, Donald came round and invited me to join him and Myriam on a holiday in Majorca. The holiday itself, with a wealthy writer-friend of theirs, was quite unremarkable except that by the end of it I felt that I had seen enough olive trees to last me a lifetime; but before it had properly begun, I was arrested on suspicion of drug-smuggling. The problem was that my handbag was too full of bottles of pills: Valium, barbiturates and Mandrax; and some of them were in the name of Samuel. The immediate result was that I was carted off to Hounslow Police Station where I had to hang around for four hours before they realised that I wasn't a dangerous international criminal.

Then about a week after my return, I was with some of my friends in Mallord Street, sitting on cushions listening to music and smoking joints when Rita announced that there was a detective from Scotland Yard at the front door. The whole house stank of marijuana; and when I opened the door to him, he began sniffing the air, and then he asked: "What's that smell?"

Fortunately, I was wearing my favourite perfume and not much else, and I had quite large tits in those days, so I simply thrust them under his nose and said 'Fracas' in as silky a voice as possible.

"Mmm. That smells good. I've just come to bring your pills back", he said.

"You'd better come in, then."

He handed me my pills, and told me: "I'm with Scotland Yard's drug squad – if you ever need any drugs, I'll get them for you. In fact, I've got a case here full of cocaine and LSD. Do you want any?"

It was an odd day altogether. The friends I was sitting with were Michael Rainey and Mark Palmer and Catharine Tennant, and I was having problems with Catherine. This was because I'd moved all Nigel Waymouth's things into her house in Glebe Place, but Nigel had suddenly taken it into his head to go off to India.

"How do you feel about that?" Catherine asked me. "You see, I don't want the building staying empty. Perhaps I should ask Robert Mapplethorpe to move back in?"

That was the last thing I wanted, but it was important not to annoy Catherine, so I just said: "I shouldn't think he'll be out there for long – perhaps I might even go and join him for a while."

"You're not thinking of getting back together with Nigel, are you?" asked Mark, shooting a glance at Catherine while he spoke.

"No – but I feel worried about him; after all, I am still married to him! And Nicky Ryman knows a Prince I could stay with."

No-one seemed very interested by this; and I noticed that Catherine looked away from Mark, and kissed Michael on the cheek. It was all so confusing that sometimes it made my head spin. Of the two men sitting in my room that evening, Catherine seemed to favour Michael, who was already married to Jane; while Mark would be the one whom she later married. In the meantime, Jane Rainey (who was away in Oswestry busily having Michael's babies), appeared to be terribly fond of Mark.

It wasn't much use turning to my brother Nigel Samuel for help. He had been released from St. Andrews, and was back in Pavilion Road; but the world into which he had moved with Suzy had completely fallen apart during his incarceration, and he was now living with some complete nutter he'd picked up from Horton Down, and (still worse) he was talking quite seriously of having Jasmine back again.

My chief problem remained my increasingly nightmarish obsession with Donald. My whole life hinged on whether he'd ring, and whether I could screw him; and I'd still go and see him and Myriam. The whole thing was making me feel desperately lonely and slightly mad. I remember being in Jermyn Street late one evening and trying to smash shop windows because I hadn't heard from him; and another night I took some acid, and in the middle of the trip I rang up Donald, telling him that I wanted to kill myself. He came round and found me in my bedroom lying on a wonderful iron Italian bed from Bennisons which still had wooden slats and no mattress, and I was crying out: 'Screw me, screw me, screw me! I love you, I'm totally in love with you!' Another night, I became so distressed that I seriously thought of killing Donald, and even fetched a knife from the kitchen.

Alice Pollock was a life-saver. She came to see me one day, found me in floods of tears, and said to me:

Look, why not come to Venice with us? I'm doing a show there with Karl Lagerfeld and some other designers – it's all being paid for by a wool factory, so I've done woollen coats and trousers and jerseys – all very patterned. And they've arranged a launch in Venice. How about it?"

Anything would be better than my present misery, so early in September, three or four days before the show was due to start, I travelled to Venice with Alice and another Nicky, a fashion journalist who worked for the Observer.

The three of us lived it up at the Hotel Danieli, where Karl Largerfeld was also staying, while the eight or nine models (including Carina Fitzalan Howard, who later married David Frost) stayed somewhere cheap and cheerful. I liked Largerfeld, who always looked immaculate, with his fine clothes, his pony-tail, his gold walking-stick and his very sleeked-back hair. In those days he was very open and approachable; and he was designing amazing ball-dresses which looked magnificent, though they were almost impossible to wear, with frills and flounces everywhere.

I had never been to Venice before; so in the mornings we toured round the city, admiring all the usual sights; then there would be rehearsals for the show; and in the evenings we enjoyed long dinners in Venetian restaurants, always in private rooms which had been completely taken over by our party. This included Karl's models, one of whom was the most beautiful black French lady I've ever seen in my life. When we had finished eating, she would suddenly get up on the table and do the most amazing strip-teases, wandering up and down between the glasses. They weren't crude but beautiful, and after the first evening I summoned up the courage to climb up onto the table myself and join in.

Everyone seemed surprised but pleased, and I found it incredibly thrilling to be stripping off my clothes in front of such a supportive audience. Of course, we had given up wearing bras, and we had tights instead of stockings and suspender-belts, so it didn't take long. First I took off my skirt or trousers, and threw them to one side; then my tights; and then I began teasing the audience with my top, until at length I pulled it over my head (and I must say that the sight of my large firm tits always excited plenty of favourable comment) and finally off came my pants. I found it so exciting myself that my nipples were usually fully erect by this time; but it wasn't so much about turning anyone on sexually, as about the freedom of women and the freedom of love.

On the day of the show itself, Alice was short of one model who had gone sick; and it was probably because she remembered my gyrations on the table-top that practically at the last moment she asked me to stand in. After baring my tits to Alice and Karl and Karina and the rest, parading up and down fully-clothed seemed like a doddle, and I managed quite easily both to please Alice and to entertain the audience.

After all that camaraderie, my return to Mallord Street was a dismal one. I suppose that this was the first time I fully realised what I'd done in leaving Nigel; and I suddenly felt very lonely. This was the time when I started going more and more frequently to the Casserole, Keith Lichtenstein's restaurant on the King's Road, whose back door (which I used as my entrance) was just around the corner from Mallord Street. It was clean but tatty, and I didn't much care for the food. It was also very small, with wooden tables with chairs on one side and fitted seats on the other and a bar at one end; but it was the place to which everyone went and it was always packed.

I had had one narrow escape connected with the Casserole a few months before this. A man had begun talking to me over lunch, and told me that he would like to photograph me for *Stern* magazine. Even in those liberated days Stern was thought to be slightly risqué; but everything was rather tastefully done, so, feeling flattered, I went along for an interview and agreed to take part. It was only after a few photographs had been taken involving me and a couple of other girls that I realised it was going to be a highly pornographic feature. I abandoned the photo-shoot, and very fortunately for me nothing ever appeared in print.

Now I started spending a great deal of time there from about eight or nine each evening. I had soon made friends with Nicky Browne, widow of the heir to the Guinness fortune, her friend the actor Oliver Tobias and a girl called Hilary; and every night the three of us would go on from the Casserole to Tramps, which had just opened as the leading London night club.

In the meantime, my escapades in Venice had improved my standing still further with Ossie Clark, who began introducing me to people like David Hockney. There was a connection between them because Ossie's wife Celia Birtwell was one of Hockney's closest friends – in fact my impression was that he looked up to her as a kind of a mother-figure.

And then one evening I saw Nicky Ryman again.

"I've had some more news about Nigel Waymouth", he told me. "He's in Delhi, now. Apparently, he's been taken up by the Bihar brothers."

"And who the hell are they?"

"Devotees of Tantric art – and some people say they're also complete con-men. They have some kind of a shop in one of the hotels."

"God – I know what'll happen. They'll totally take over, and Nigel will become a complete hippy and end up in some bloody ashram or something crazy like that. I really think I'll go out there and see him. And I'll combine it with visiting that Prince you told me about? The one you were with at Harrow?"

"Prince Jagat Singh of Jaipur – I'll send him a telegram straight away and tell him to expect you – when shall I say?"

※

It was just before leaving for India that I had two of the most important meetings of my life. I was packing some clothes for my journey, agonising about what to take, and deciding as usual to take everything, when the door-bell rang. It was Christopher Gibbs. He was smiling wickedly, and there was someone with him: someone who exuded a sense of danger and fun, someone with the handsome, perfectly chiselled face of a 1940s or 1950s film-star, someone dressed remarkably well for a man, though with it he wore an orange shirt which didn't quite match his wonderful St. Laurent suit; and he seemed to be wearing a good deal of Roman jewellery.

Then I realised that Christopher was speaking to me. "Nicky", he was saying, "I am going to let you meet the Queen of all the Queens of cocaine, Bill Willis!"

He and I were like two live wires going off together. Cocaine was our introduction, and we almost fell in love, with a slight reservation on Bill's side, but none on mine. We had been talking in my den under the gallery for about half-an-hour when Bill said to me: "You must meet a wonderful friend of mine, Victoria Brooke. She's an amazing lady: she was married to Lionel Brooke, heir to the last white Rajah of Sarawak. I've just left her in Paul Getty's house over in Cheyne Walk. May I use your phone and get her to come over?"

I agreed; perhaps a little reluctantly, as I was enjoying being alone with Bill, since by this time Christopher had disappeared in his usual mysterious way. After a while, the door-bell rang again. "It's all right, Rita!" I called as I went a little wearily to answer it. I opened the door, and then…

Victoria hit me like a thunderbolt.

It wasn't so much her beauty that struck me, though she was undoubtedly very beautiful, with a good figure and very large appealing eyes. She had something else, something extraordinary and unforgettable: an aura which suggested that she was game for anything, that she was prepared to take anything that life threw at her. In her hands she was holding a wonderful tiger-lily.

"Are you Nicky?"

"Yes"

"This is for you." She handed me the tiger-lily, and I took it as though it were a votive offering. "Are you going to let me in, then?"

I pulled myself together, and welcomed her to Mallord Street; and soon I felt that something had clicked between the three of us. Victoria, I treated as though we were lovers. I took her to my bedroom and gave her a dress in return for the tiger-lily. I had fallen madly in love with them both; but it was already 5 November 1971, and within two days I would be on my way to India.

CHAPTER TWENTY-THREE
A Blind Date in Rajasthan

Arriving at Delhi airport, I found myself once again in an utterly strange world, this one full of heat and colour and noise and dust and crowds of people everywhere. To begin with, I found myself having to fill in dozens of forms, saying how many pieces of luggage I had, where I lived England, why I had come to India, what my passport number was – and every time I completed one form, they gave me another. There was one form to retrieve my luggage, another one to say that I had my luggage and it had gone through customs, another one to say that it could now be taken to a taxi – at one point I half expected a form asking me how many seconds I had been alive since arriving in India.

And then suddenly I found myself outside the airport, with fifty people running up asking me whether I wanted a taxi. I chose someone more or less at random, and he disappeared with my baggage, and was gone so long that I began thinking I would never see my hotel, and that I would be on the next plane back to England, having lost everything. Then miraculously he reappeared, in a taxi which seemed to be done up with string, and had all my suitcases practically falling out of the back; but we arrived safely at the Ashoka.

Although it was reputed to be one of the best hotels in Delhi, I found the Ashoka very dreary and drab. But it was good to see Nigel, who was living there; and that evening we had supper together, and I caught up with his news. Much to my relief, he was in great shape, despite spending most of his time with the younger of the Bihar brothers.

"It's been a wonderful trip for me", he began. "I must have told you I was born in India?" I nodded, though quite honestly I'd completely forgotten. "I spent the first three years of my life in Bombay during the war. I was curious to see it again; and so I jumped at the chance of teaming up with an old friend of mine who does a lot of business in India. I'd already decided to finance my trip by buying some Indian carpets and pictures and antiques; and he gave me an introduction to the Bihars, because they specialise in selling things like that."

"Well, be careful!" I warned him. "I've heard they're the most frightful con-artists. In any case, tomorrow I'm off to Jaipur to stay with someone called Jagat for a week or two, but I'll let you know as soon as I'm back."

The next morning it was a forty-minute flight to Jaipur, some 150 miles away to the south-west. Much to my pleasure there was a driver to meet me, and he drove me straight to the Rambagh Palace. This was one of the original homes of the Maharajahs of Jaipur (Jagat was the current Maharajah's half-brother), but when the family were in financial difficulties, they had decided to turn it into an hotel. Because I was Jagat's guest, as soon as I entered the hotel the little Indian boys and all the rest of the staff began bowing and scraping to me. Some of them were literally on their knees, practically praying at my feet, and I began to realise the extreme oddity of my situation.

I was taken to a part of the hotel which was particularly lovely because it had been left untouched. I found myself alone in the most enormous bedroom, about the size of a tennis court, with one single bed; and a bathroom leading off. I wasn't certain what I should do, and so I did nothing. Time dragged. I unpacked my eleven cases, and then time dragged again. Finally at about five o'clock that evening, Jagat rang me and said "Let's meet". So we did; and he turned out to be a stunningly good-looking Indian boy, only a year or two older than me. I think that at first we were both equally embarrassed; and then he suddenly said: "Mrs. Waymouth, we're leaving in an hour. We're going across to visit some of my forts: would you like to come with me?"

Naturally, I agreed.

"Excellent! We will be travelling into Rajasthan – an area in some ways like the Australian outback, so please to bring enough clothes for at least a week." He gave me a little bow and turned on his heel and then paused for a moment and looked back at me with his hands clasped as though in prayer and said: "Nicky Ryman is a very good friend of mine. He asked me to show you India; and you will indeed see parts of India that few westerners have ever seen."

I re-packed my eleven cases as hastily as I could; and before long Jagat was at the wheel of a Mini Moke, the Indian equivalent of a land-rover, and I was at his side being driven westward out of Jaipur. I thought him the most appalling driver: not that he could be blamed for this, as most of the time there weren't any roads for us to drive on, just thousands of acres of dry scrub-land. And it wasn't just the two of us: we were part of a considerable convoy which included dozens of people ranging from a senior official who ran the family estates down to the humblest of servants.

It was such a bumpy ride that I was glad when occasionally the convoy ground to a halt and everyone leaped out of their cars with rifles and began potting away at rabbits, presumably so that we would have something to eat for supper. After a very short time I had no idea at all where we were; but occasionally we would suddenly come across a little Indian village consisting of just a handful of small white-washed mud huts and a few people who, recognising Jagat as their prince, would bow and scrape to him before we drove on. And finally we arrived in a much larger village, above which was the most marvellous fort I've ever seen in my life.

But since we were on a kind of royal progress, Jagat's first task was to be greeted by his villagers. They had been warned we were coming, and it was an important visit, because it was some years since Jagat or any of his family had visited them, and there were many official duties for him to perform, some of them to do with confirming land-ownership. So as we approached the village and the fort, we were surrounded by crowds of cheering people; and among them was a large number of rather thin, feeble-looking camels who had been brought in from the desert and the surrounding lands to welcome their prince, to whom apparently they belonged.

The fortress itself was made of red Rajasthan stone. It hadn't been lived in since the days of Jagat's grandfather, a Maharajah of Jaipur who had died back in 1922, and nothing much appeared to have changed since those days. For one thing, time hardly mattered, and nobody seemed to mind when even the best-laid plans almost never came to fruition. Jagat himself, despite his English education, had very little regard for time. We had arrived very late in the day, and it was not until two in the morning that we ate supper, squatting on the floor of a large empty downstairs room. It had been decided that since I had only just arrived in India, I mustn't be given any curries: nor must I eat any of the rabbits or other creatures they had just shot. Instead, I was put on an extraordinary diet of nan, bananas and rice; and this turned out to be extremely sensible because the result was that, unlike most visitors to India, I never had a moment's sickness.

But where was I to sleep? Very few of the hundreds of rooms in the fortress had been opened up for our arrival. Clearly, I couldn't sleep in the same room as the men; but Jagat didn't want me sharing a room with the female servants. So in the end it was decided that I should sleep in the Maharajah's old bedroom, where a bed had been made up for Jagat, but which he decided was the only suitable place for his English guest.

Although it was in a poor state of repair, the Maharajah's bedroom was one of the most beautiful rooms I have ever seen. My first thought was that Christopher Gibbs would have given five years of his life to have been there. The room was circular, with a twenty-foot-high ceiling; it had the most magnificent chandelier made of every kind of coloured stone you could possibly imagine, and there were lovely old Indian things all around.

As for my bed: it had an Indian mattress filled with down. It was one of the most luxurious beds I have ever slept upon; and when I woke in the morning, I could hear the sound of singing drifting in from outside.

I had hardly opened my eyes when an Indian girl with gentle eyes and a beautiful sari asked me: "Would you be liking a bath, madam?"

"Yes, I'd love one, thank you!"

And then more girls came in carrying the bath and ewers of hot and cold water; and soon I was sitting in the bath being washed and feeling more cared-for than I have ever felt in my life before or since. It was a truly wonderful experience, and I still dream of it to this day. Then I was dried and given cups of sweet tea; and all the while the sound of singing continued to rise up from outside.

Curious to know what was happening, I threw on some trousers and a chiffon blouse and went out onto the balcony. My room was right at the top of the fort and since it was circular it faced all sides of the village: and there down below me I could see that the streets were full of dancing girls and people singing. When they looked up and saw me, a kind of hush fell. I waved to them; but they seemed to be confused; and then I was being called back inside the bedroom, and found Jagat there, polite but for once rather steely.

"Please, this is not done. You must wear something more!" I looked down at myself and realised that my chiffon blouse was so transparent that my tits were showing. "Also, this is where the Maharajahs have always appeared to their people. It is not for you." He then went out onto the balcony himself to loud cheers and renewed singing; and I realised that the villagers had been waiting to see their prince, and must have been surprised and shocked when out onto the balcony in his place wandered a vaguely hippy westerner wearing a see-through top. Still more outrageous, the Maharajah's bedroom was in the male part of the house, and I had been the first woman in history to sleep there. Not even the Maharajah's wives had been allowed to use that room, let alone his courtesans, whom he had visited by way of a secret passageway which led from his bedroom down into the village.

By breakfast-time, I had exchanged my chiffon blouse for an orange silk shirt; and the Indian servants had produced some bread about which they were frightfully excited. Jagat passed some to me, and explained: "You see, Nicky, in the old days when we were attacked by our enemies, we used to bury everything. And my servants have just found this bread, buried beneath the ladies' quarters. It must have been there for a hundred years or more; and it's like stone on the outside – but on the inside, just like this piece I am giving you, it's totally fresh! Today," he went on, "we are going to go and have lunch by this rather wonderful waterfall and lake".

Which we did. I remember chiefly the cheering crowds on our way out of the village; and then we reached the edge of the vast Sambhar Lake in a wild and beautiful place where I saw a colony of thousands of pink flamingos in flight over the salt water. We were waited on by at least forty servants, but I could only look a little enviously at the picnic lunch, since because of the strict diet they had arranged for me, I wasn't allowed to touch any of it.

After another night spent back at the fort in the circular bedroom, we resumed our journey. As usual, there were frequent stops for rabbit-shooting; and it occurred to me that the men with guns – about twenty-five of them – were actually an armed bodyguard. Not that the Jaipurs were unpopular – far from it – it was more a sign of their power. Exactly where I fitted in was difficult to say. If I was writing a short story, I would call this adventure 'A blind date in Rajasthan'. But although Jagat was a handsome prince, I clearly wasn't going to become his princess. He looked at me strangely sometimes, but he was an Indian amongst his people, and if I was anything to him, I was a difficulty and an encumbrance. Besides, I found that I kept longing for Nigel to be with me: this whole exotic experience would have been so much more fun if I could have shared it with him.

The next fort was actually rather dismal. We reached it after travelling through an alien landscape using a map which seemed to have been drawn so long ago that the roads had changed and the villages had moved. The journey, said to be one of two hours, had stretched out to seven or eight. The only advantage was that I was too tired to be scared by the time its sinister roofs loomed up above us in the early hours of the morning. It had been uninhabited for so long that in that desolation I could feel the spirits of the past observing us full of anger at the way in which they had been abandoned; and I was miserable for them and miserable also for myself.

After a few more days of travelling through a much hotter and much damper landscape, in which we needed mosquito-nets at night, we arrived at Jagat's home. This contained hundreds of servants, and had been considerably westernised, but it felt more like being in a film-set than in an actual home. Because although my bedroom looked western rather than Indian, with an air-conditioning unit and a normal bathroom leading off it, the air-conditioning didn't work, and there wasn't any water in the taps.

From there we moved on again into an area of thick jungle, and for one night we stayed at an hotel that was normally full of American tourists. They would come here on photo-safaris, the shooting of tigers and panthers having already been banned throughout India. However no national rules seemed to apply to a local prince like Jagat; and during the next few days, as we visited more of his villages, our convoy became a shooting party.

I found it deeply thrilling. Some of the creatures Jagat and his men shot were rather like deer, with enormous antlers; and then one morning as we were driving slowly along, I saw a huge panther crossing the road ahead of us followed by its young. "Jagat!" I gasped, clutching at his arm, as it saw us and came loping towards us at speed. In the next few seconds our driver had halted and Jagat was reaching for his gun, and then the panther leaped towards us, and he fired!

The bang was deafening and I could smell the cordite and the panther was stopped in mid-air and fell to the ground. I felt sad for its little ones but I thought it prudent to say nothing, since Jagat and his men were all frightfully thrilled.

When we arrived at the next village, they showed off the dead panther and the children danced round it. Then we went into a tiny little mud hut, where there were already fifteen or twenty people milling about waiting for us to arrive. Then we all sat down, and we were offered tea. We accepted; and during the long wait that followed, the village elders (who were just as excited as the children by the dead panther) explained that several villages in the area had been losing their chickens and having their crops trampled by a wild boar, and they asked if Prince Jagat could shoot it just as he had shot the panther.

At last tea arrived, and I accepted a mug and took a sip of the milky liquid. I smiled. "Delicious!" I said. But actually, it tasted like sweetened mud, and during the next half-hour I poured away as much as possible when I hoped no-one was looking. By the end of that day, we had visited five more villages, I had drunk part of five more cups of equally disgusting tea, and Jagat had agreed to shoot the wild boar, which we had been told could be found each night at a particular spot.

Having made his agreement, Jagat turned to me and asked: "Miss Nicky: would you be caring to accompany us in search of the wild boar?"

"Yes, sure, I'd love to!" I said, rather fancying the excitement of being part of a night-time shooting party. At this, they had all begun clapping and cheering, and before long I understood why.

I had wrongly assumed that finding and shooting a wild boar, or even several of them, would take no more than about half an hour. In practice it meant another trip in our mini-mokes into the heart of the jungle, where the so-called 'particular spot' turned out to be a sort of paddock. But instead of being allowed to join Jagat and the others in the hunt, I was told to wait for him in the Mini Moke. So I was left alone, and although it had been hot and humid during the day, I was soon freezing cold.

However, I had often watched Jagat's servants collecting twigs to light fires – there seems to be dry wood everywhere in India – so I set about gathering some sticks. By this time there was a good deal of roaring going on, but I was so cold that I took no notice. And then, just when I had successfully lit a fire, and the flames were crackling up and warming me, Jagat's headman rushed out of the darkness in a panic, and began kicking my fire to pieces.

"Did you not hear the roaring, Miss Nicky? That was no wild boar. That was a tiger! A tiger! And tigers are attracted by a good fire!"

About a week after I had given both the headman and myself this severe fright, we came to a place where there was a railway line and a small station, and Jagat asked me whether I would like to go back to Jaipur. I decided that I had had enough of this strange combination of luxury and poverty, of cheering crowds and ruined forts; of panthers and tigers and muddy sweet tea; and I said that I would.

"My man Singh here will accompany you," he said, indicating one of his men-servants. "You will leave in one hour. As for me: I am off to Delhi." Then he looked at me anxiously, and briefly laid his hand on my arm, and said to me: "Nicky, I should not stay in India too much longer. You know we will soon be fighting with Pakistan? Already my half-brother the Maharajah is in the front line." And then he stepped back and bowed to me, and I bowed to him, and he drove away and sadly I never saw him again.

Before long, Singh and I were on the train, in a little compartment with a bench on each side of it. We had it entirely to ourselves: Prince Jagat's manservant was there to keep everyone out, and also to keep me safe. Having been living for a couple of weeks on nothing but nan, bananas and rice, I felt almost unbelievably hungry; but when we stopped at the next station and thousands of people surged forward and came up to the windows laden with all kinds of exotic food, Singh simply waved them away.

And then we were back in Jaipur, where before bidding me farewell Singh returned me to the Rambagh Palace. With his departure, my blind date in Rajasthan was over, but I found that my stock had rocketed up among the Indian servants, and there was more bowing and scraping than ever. I felt absolutely exhausted after my travels, but enormously relieved to be back in a place where I could lead a normal life and do silly ordinary things like washing my hair. Finding that I was such an honoured guest, I decided to enjoy myself; and almost the first thing I did was to ring up Nigel and ask him to join me, telling him: "Jagat's moved on, but he's left me with a wonderful room and you could share it with me."

When Nigel arrived at the Rambagh Palace wearing Indian clothes and saying that he was my husband, the staff were totally confused; but they showed him up to my room, and we began a kind of honey-moon in reverse. After all, Nigel was good company, we were still technically married, and now we were sharing not only the same room but also the same bed: so it was perfectly natural to begin having sex again, sex that was very warm and friendly and comforting.

I said that the staff were confused; but Nigel had soon won them over. He had brought with him all kinds of unusual artefacts such as cobra-vertebrae necklaces, things that are considered very holy relics in India; and a number of Tantric pieces such as small temple lamps. Using these he built an altar in our bedroom, which made the room-boys think that he was a religious guru. They began praying at it; and the bowing and scraping to us descended to floor-level.

Nigel had never visited Jaipur, and I had never seen it properly; and together we discovered that it is one of the most beautiful red-stone cities in the world. My memories are fragmentary, but intense. I remember the strong, exotic smells. I remember riding on an elephant out to one of the Jaipur forts, at the top of which we met a holy man who blessed us and told as that we were going to live for ever. And I remember visiting temples where we were garlanded with flowers.

Nigel was still hunting for antiques; and in Jaipur (slightly to his chagrin) he discovered a yard where 'ancient' sculptures were being turned out by the dozen, many of them by small boys sitting with chisels cross-legged over blocks of marble from which they rapidly created statues of multi-limbed Indian gods and goddesses. Nigel was impressed. "These are just as good as some of the things in the Bihars' emporium", he said. "In fact, this is probably where they come from! Well: two can play at that game. I'm going to ask them to make up a few Tantric Lingams." They were made in a morning, and aged by pouring sandalwood oil over them and setting fire to the oil. "There we are!" said Nigel triumphantly. "They look just as ancient and full of mystical power as the real thing!"

I had been hoping that we might have time to visit Agra and the Taj Mahal, but who should arrive in Jaipur but two of Nigel's friends: Kevin Delahunty and his girl-friend (and later wife) Arabella Sykes, the good-looking daughter of a Baronet. When we took them out to a restaurant that evening, they told us that they were on their way to Benares, on the banks of the Ganges almost five hundred miles away to the east.

"Why don't you come with us?" asked Kevin.

He made it sound so exciting that the next day (despite both Nigel and Kevin having gone down with food-poisoning) we all flew to Benares.

Here, on Kevin's insistence – I guess he was looking for an 'authentic' experience of Indian squalor – we found rooms in the most downmarket rathole imaginable before being caught up in a cacophony of bicycle bells, and a crowd of people going down through the twilight to the River Ganges.

We were now in the middle of a frightening scene straight out of the Middle Ages. At the edge of the river several dead bodies were being cremated; they had been covered with oil and sandalwood, and from the smoke and flames there came a terrible choking smell which stuck in my throat. Near the burning flesh sat limbless Sadhus, worshippers of the Lord Shiva, dwarfs with no arms or legs, meditating as they seek liberation from the cycle of death and rebirth.

A guide who had somehow attached himself to us, took us out on a boat into the centre of the Ganges. On one side the land was completely flat and desolate; and on the other side it was beautiful, like Venice, the land covered with palaces built by Rajahs for their holy rites and observances. Having landed us further up the river, our guide disappeared while we were watching another cremation. We made our way back to the hotel in the gathering darkness through a maze of streets, and somewhere near the Golden Temple I became separated from the others for a few minutes and felt absolutely terrified.

Both Kevin and Nigel were feeling much worse, and began throwing up, and it was now my turn to insist that we moved into a better hotel. Nigel, who became extremely ill, likes to tell the story of how his life was saved by Chowkidar number 21. "Chowkidar," he explains,

> "means a servant, a bearer, and he used to come to my room and say 'Chowkidar number 21. You go on, I get it for you.' And he put me on a diet of broth with special herbs in it; and a couple of days later I was well again and we flew back to Delhi!"

It was a relief to be back in Delhi but, just as Prince Jagat had warned me, the city was living under the threat of war with Pakistan. Air-raid sirens wailed from time to time and there were black-out practices every night – though they weren't very effective, since Delhi in a black-out seemed a great deal brighter than Blackpool with its illuminations switched on.

Over the next few days, we carried on as normally as possible, and spent many hours in the company of the Bihar brothers, with whom we were now playing an elaborate game, since they had heard that I was wealthy and might buy some of their things at an outrageously high price; while I wanted them to buy our fakes from Jaipur. But the streets were no longer as friendly as they should have been, and one lunchtime we were out at a restaurant, and then somewhere an argument started and fighting began and this was serious fighting with knives out and screaming and blood in the streets.

So, I said to Nigel: "I want to get out of India: it's the wrong time to be here. You must tie up your business with the Bihar brothers, because I'm booking us on a plane out of India tonight."

"But it isn't as easy as that…"

"Yes, it is!" And I booked the tickets at once, and then rang up Ritvik Bihar and said: "Look, we're leaving in two hours. This business has got to be settled." And I remember we sat on the floor in front of dozens of their Tantric pictures and I pointed at the one I liked best and said "Well, I'll buy that one." They agreed, though I felt that in the end they were rather angry that they'd sold it to me, because it was one of their better things, and I later made a fortune out of it in London. "Now how about our Tantric pieces from Jaipur?"

I could see out of the corner of my eye that Nigel was looking horribly embarrassed, but I was shameless. "They're thousands of years old", I lied, "and we were incredibly lucky to get them."

Eventually they agreed to a very good price; and then they asked me what else I wanted to buy from them. But at that point I said: "I'm sorry, but we're going." And after a very difficult and exhausting time with customs and excise we finally left Delhi at about one in the morning. The next day we discovered that my instincts had been right. Only a few hours after our departure, war had broken out between India and Pakistan, and ours had been the last international flight to leave Delhi.

※

We must have arrived in Beirut at about eight in the morning. It was the first of two stops on our enormously long and boring flight back to London. I looked out of the window as we landed, and saw that it was a lovely sunny day. "Nigel", I said, "Do you think we could ask them if we could stay here? It seems awfully silly to touch down somewhere and not see where we are."

Nigel beckoned to an air hostess.

"Excuse me, we're meant to be going all the way to London; but is there any chance of our getting off here for a few days?"

Fortunately, we were flying First Class, so everything was made easy for us; and within an hour and a half we were installed at the St. Georges Hotel on the sea-front in Beirut. We stayed there for about a week in the greatest comfort. For those who had money, Beirut was rich and wonderful and everything seemed to run like clockwork. It was amazing and dreamlike. It was Paris, New York, London and the Middle East all rolled into one, and far more sophisticated than any of them.

The influence of French culture was everywhere, from the elegant courtesans who actually spoke French to the long delightful lunches with wine. It was over one long lunch that Nigel did a portrait of me that I still have upstairs in the end room. There were beautiful views everywhere; and in the evenings we'd go out to a night-club, or to a film.

In Beirut, even going to the cinema was an exotic experience. One evening we went to see Jane Fonda in *Klute*, which Nigel had already told me was one of her best roles, starring as a high-class call-girl. The cinema was in a lovely old theatre; and before the film had started, a cornetist and a pianist rose up out of the pit in front of the screen, and for fifteen minutes they played music from Bach's Brandenburg Concertos.

Incidentally, having heard all my life about the cedars of Lebanon, I expected to see them everywhere, and one day we spent a good deal of time searching for them in vain. Finally, a restaurant proprietor, extremely suave and well-dressed, told us: "A misconception. My apologies. It was the Turks who chopped them down 400 years ago. They haven't planted any more." And then, just before he walked away, he added, almost as an afterthought, "I believe there is still a handful at Byblos." So we went to Byblos, a beautiful little fishing village on the coast to the north of Beirut. And there, near some ancient Greek ruins, I found my cedar trees.

We also visited Baalbek, which was full of Roman and Persian ruins. And all this time Nigel and I were getting on fine and having a good time with each other. Sometimes I wondered whether Nigel might be thinking that he'd got me back again; I was certainly feeling very relaxed about spending time with him, knowing that I wasn't tied to him for the rest of my life. But we never discussed the fact that we weren't committed to each other any longer. We just accepted the fact that when we got back to London we would continue to live apart. In the meantime, we were enjoying our surroundings and sharing our experiences with each other, and there was none of the marital stress which wrecks the holidays of most married couples.

Another day, we decided to visit Damascus, which is in Syria and only a three- or four-hour drive from Beirut. So we hired a car and a driver, and set off on one of the most beautiful drives of my life. In those days the Lebanon really was a land flowing with milk and honey. The landscape was large, but not entirely flat; and it was also rich in colour. On every side there were lush green meadows and billowing fields of golden corn and rice and vegetables; and there were also shrubs and flowers and trees here and there; and in the far distance, ranges of mountains. It was all very serene; and to my surprise I suddenly felt very Jewish, as though in some strange way I was at home.

Then we crossed the border into Syria, where everything felt different. It was much more bleak; and sometimes we would round a corner and suddenly come across a machine-gun post with a tank parked nearby. In Damascus itself, beautiful though it was, there were tanks on the street corners, and everywhere we looked there were army lorries and vans and marching soldiers.

As a woman I wasn't allowed to enter many of the temples, so we spent most of our time in the covered souk, where I bought some beautiful clothes: antique embroidered waistcoats, and two beautiful antique silk dressing-gowns which had in fact been men's wedding-gowns, worn as over-shirts. I also bought damask and other fine materials; and a few knick-knacks, including an Aladdin's lamp that I still possess.

After the sophistication of Beirut, it was strange to find that instead of being offered local food, our hotel plied us with dishes such as Heinz tomato soup, semolina pudding and spotted dick with custard. Even when we went out to a restaurant, we were offered Brown Windsor Soup, there was an air of foreboding, and the restaurant was full of soldiers. It was a relief when the time came for our drive back to Beirut. And then we flew back to England, where we said goodbye at the airport, and took separate taxis: Nigel's for Glebe Place and mine for Mallord Street.

CHAPTER TWENTY-FOUR
Travelling with Christopher Gibbs and Bill Willis

L ooking through the windows of the taxi that was taking me home, I could see signs of Christmas everywhere. Excited shoppers with bundles of parcels, Christmas decorations in all the shop windows, even one Father Christmas walking rather disconsolately down Mallord Street, as though he should have been up in Knightsbridge but had somehow lost his way; and as I stepped into my front hall, I found that Rita had decorated it with holly.

I would have liked to telephone Victoria Brooke but I realised that it was too close to Christmas and that she and all my other friends would already have arranged their celebrations, so I tried members of my family instead. Nigel was the only one I could reach, and he gave me the unwelcome news that Jasmine had moved back in with him. Worse was to come. "Why don't you ring up Arnold?" suggested Nigel. "He'll probably have some bright ideas for Christmas. By the way, did I tell you that Jasmine's pregnant?"

In a state of considerable shock, I telephoned Arnold Goodman. "What shall we do over Christmas?" I asked him. "I could have Nigel and Jasmine here, but I don't want Rita to be bothered on Christmas Day."

"Highly commendable", said Arnold, who sounded very evasive. "The sad fact is that I won't be able to join you. Despite your recent holiday together, and by the way I'm glad you got out of India in time, I was most anxious about you, I gather you are not in fact spending it with Nigel-the-seaside?" When I assured him that I was not, there was a long silence. I could imagine him wrinkling his brow at the other end of the line. "In that case", he said suddenly, "I shall book you a table for Christmas lunch at Brown's Hotel." And before I could say anything else, he added hurriedly: "My Christmas present to you all!" and slammed down the receiver.

A moment later the telephone rang. I thought it might be Goody making a return call with another idea; but instead, there was silence.

"Who is that?" I asked.

Someone with a very rough masculine voice told me: "'Next time you see your brother, he'll be six feet under!" And then the line went dead.

It was frightening. I found myself sobbing, and my legs had turned to jelly. I poured myself a stiff drink and spoke to Nigel again. He seemed totally unconcerned. "Oh, take no notice of that", he said. "That's just Michael X or rather one of his friends. He's gone to the bad – Jasmine will tell you. He threatens a great deal. But it means nothing."

"But I can't stand it Nigel. It's too horrible!"

"Then telephone the police, and have them intercept your calls for a while."

I felt relieved that Nigel was still capable of giving me some sensible advice and the very next day, although I loathed her, I bought Jasmine a beautiful Ossie Clark dress as a Christmas present. She and Nigel came to me on Christmas Day before we went on to Brown's Hotel; and when she put on the dress, I had to admit that it looked beautiful on her. It was one of Ossie's feathered dresses: slinky and down-to-the ground and fitting every part of the body that it was meant to fit, and Jasmine had a great figure.

※

Then came an invitation from Christopher Gibbs to join him in Morocco, and the New Year of 1972 found us together at Marrakesh airport. "Nicky, darling!" he said. "Wonderful to see you. We're going to spend the night at Bill Willis's house in the city. It's a beautiful place, just next to where Paul

Getty used to live. I'll be interested to hear what you think of it. Then tomorrow John Michell is arriving with his Publisher."

"John Michell?"

"A brilliant young writer, with an interest in ley-lines and standing stones, that sort of thing."

Then, much to my surprise because I had never seen him driving before, Christopher drove us into Marrakesh in a somewhat battered Triumph sports-car. When I asked whose it was, Christopher said "I bought it from Bill – it's a perfect little run-about."

It was great to see Bill again; and his house was a treasure. It was the tiniest little Moroccan house turret you've ever seen, but absolutely ravishing. A boy servant opened the door to us, and there was Bill in a wonderful bedroom on the ground floor with chandeliers and mosaic tiles, and a bathroom leading off. "I see you're still dressing like a hippy!" he said, coming towards me.

"What do you mean?" I asked, giving him a seductive hug. He pulled away.

"Take a long look at yourself, baby!"

I did. I was wearing a T-shirt and jeans, some rather fine ethnic jewellery including beads and bangles, and a pair of tapestry carpet boots with three-inch heels.

"Not a bell in sight!" I protested.

"Come on, you two", said Christopher slightly crossly. "Nicky, come and see the rest of the house." The whole of the highest floor was taken up by a small but beautiful sitting-room; and although there were cushions all over the floor everything was very exact and proper and in impeccable taste. On another floor there was a miniature but beautiful kitchen, and a ravishing little spare bedroom which I was told was mine for the night. It was all very luxurious: there were even Irish linen sheets on my bed! I unpacked, and changed into the one truly glamorous thing I had brought with me: a long flowing Ossie Clark dress which did great things for my tits. When I came down again, Bill whistled at me. "Correction, baby, hippy but elegant. And sexy! You're making me want to come on to you!"

"Oh, Bill, don't be so silly!" I said; but I had a warm glow inside, and I must have been grinning like a fool. Bill was always so good to me. In the end I was up half the night yarning with him. I'm not sure that Christopher was best pleased with this; but in any case, he had soon spirited me away.

Because the next day found me sitting beside him in the battered old Triumph, with John Michell and his publisher in the back. Christopher didn't look at home behind the wheel of a car; and although it was only thirty miles from Marrakesh to his house, it was probably the most scary drive of my life. Not only were we speeding across the Moroccan countryside at what felt like a hundred miles an hour, without Christopher appearing to have a clue whether or not we were going in the right direction, but there was a frightening moment when one of the car doors fell off. In the meantime, John and his publisher were doing their best to keep up a conversation with us.

"Tell me about your house", John Michell shouted from the back. Christopher turned his head and accidentally put his foot down on the accelerator and we veered towards the edge of the road and for a moment or two I shut my eyes, certain that we were about to crash. Nothing happened. I opened them again. We were hurtling along just as fast, but now we were going straight down the middle of the road. I hoped we would meet nothing coming the other way.

"It's where Churchill stayed during the war", Christopher was saying. "He painted a number of water-colours there. It's a beautiful location, you see..."

"They must be worth a great deal of money", interrupted the Publisher, who was one of the dullest men I had ever met.

"...right at the foot of the Atlas Mountains", Christopher went on. "I'm trying to buy it, but the sale still hasn't been completed, because the house has so much land with it that legally it's considered to be a farm; and in Morocco foreigners aren't allowed to own farms!"

At last we arrived, though the house appeared at first to be quite derelict, abandoned for aeons in that vast landscape. However, when Christopher had called out and pressed the car horn a few times, A Moroccan servant called Moulet scurried out, and collected our bags. Christopher and John Michell and the Publisher stayed in the main house while I, as the only woman, was segregated into what looked like a rather lovely little cottage. However, as in the wilds of Rajasthan, everything was wonderfully elegant, but nothing worked. The bath taps were in the form of golden lions, but when you turned them on, no water came out. The bed was antique and beautiful, but hideously uncomfortable. The best thing was the fireplace in the bedroom, which meant that at night, when it was bitterly cold outside, I always returned to the comfort of a fire burning in the grate.

During the days we went on expeditions to Berber villages, and Christopher brought carpets which we could lay out for picnics on riverbanks. The only problem was that Christopher was too aesthetic to cope with anything practical, and so there was a good deal of intelligent conversation but virtually no food. I didn't like to say anything, though I was soon beginning to feel quite hungry. The Publisher sensibly disappeared back to Marrakesh after a couple of days; while John Michell and I began privately making fun of everything. John also gave me some advice which has often stood me in good stead. I had been complaining that I wasn't very well-educated, and he smiled sweetly and said: "Don't worry, Nicky: just remember to tell everyone that something-or-other is of great historical interest, and nod your head wisely, and you'll get away with it!"

Then things got worse. There were four fat women who were meant to do the cooking; but they only took orders from Moulet, and when he disappeared one day with the car, the fat women simply stopped cooking. Christopher explained that Moulet was often in jail for being drunk down in Marrakesh; and by the second evening after his disappearance, there was nothing for us to eat apart from some pâte which the Publisher had brought from London, and a bunch of bananas.

Soon the pâte had gone, and there were only three bananas left; and then there were only two, and still the four fat women were sitting downstairs in the kitchen doing nothing. "Christopher", I said at length, "Why don't I go down and boil some eggs?"

"No", he said firmly, "the servants must do it."

And then there was only one banana left. Fortunately for me, chivalry prevailed. Still more fortunately, in the morning Christopher announced that we would be going back to Marrakesh. It felt like being let out of school. The only problem was that there was still no sign of Moulet, and therefore no car. "Don't worry, said Christopher, "we can walk."

My heart plummeted into my tapestry carpet-boots with their three-inch heels, the most practical shoes I had with me, and about as suitable for a long walk as a leaky bucket for drawing water out of a well. "That'll be fine", I said, putting a brave face on it. And half-an-hour later we set off down the road.

After a while John Michell asked "Can't we hitch a lift?"

"No", said Christopher firmly. "There'll be a bus along in about half-an-hour. We can take that into Marrakesh."

We walked on for three or four miles. No bus appeared. I was in agony. The heel of one of my boots had come off, and a nail was sticking into my feet.

"Are you doing all right?" asked John Michell.

"Sure – absolutely fine", I lied.

Fortunately, he could see that I wasn't; and soon he had flagged down a car and we were hitching a lift into Marrakesh. There Christopher found us an hotel. To begin with I was terribly pleased, because at last I could have a proper bath and go to the hairdresser; but I was still more pleased when Bill Willis reappeared a few days later and asked me to go back to stay with him in his luxurious little house.

"Yes, sure, great!" I said enthusiastically.

By this time John Michell had set off for India; and Christopher was busily planning his first journey to the USA. At first, he didn't seem terribly happy about the idea of my moving in with Bill; but then Bill made another suggestion: "Christopher, you don't have to go to New York right away, and I've got some work to do in Casablanca. Why don't the three of us go down there for a while?"

So a day or two later Bill and Christopher and I found ourselves in a very seedy hotel in Casablanca. From there we went to visit the Tazis, an incredibly wealthy couple for whom Bill was working. They lived in amazing style in a mansion with dozens of servants; and Bill was building a brand-new house for one of their relatives. As usual, he was doing it brilliantly with, for example, wonderful tiles all over the bathroom; but the work was taking far longer than the anticipated three months, mainly because he was hardly ever there to supervise his workmen.

In the evenings, Bill and I would go out with Christopher, who can't have been having much fun because he was doing his best to look after me, while Bill and I were getting incredibly drunk and dancing the nights away. And I was so fond of Christopher. Once I was wearing my long Ossie Clark dress, which looked bloody good on me, and lying on the bed with Bill on one side of me and Christopher on the other, when I suddenly felt desperately attracted to him. However, I knew that nothing would ever happen between us; and in any case he was becoming more and more annoyed with Bill and me for misbehaving.

We took no notice, and went off again dancing and drinking; and when we reappeared in time for breakfast Christopher said to us angrily: "How dare you behave like this?"

Bill and I just giggled.

"I've had enough of it", said Christopher. "I'm catching the next flight out of here." Then he turned to Bill, and said: "Nicky must go home."

"No, I'm not going home yet", I said. "Don't be so mean! I'm going back to Marrakesh with Bill. The train leaves in about an hour."

When he saw that I wouldn't change my mind, Christopher accompanied us to the station and saw us onto the train. Suddenly, instead of looking angry, he looked sad, which made me feel sad too. Then his expression changed yet again, and he called out triumphantly: "Gloria in Excelsis Deo!" Glory be to God on high! And then he was gone.

※

It wasn't long after our return to Marrakesh, (where Bill was meant to be working on several more houses, including another for Tamy Tazi, and one for Yves St Laurent), when out of the blue he said: "Nicky, why not come with me to Paris?"

"Why Paris?"

"Lots of reasons, but here's just one. We can call on a very old and dear friend of mine – Loulou de la Falaise. You two have a lot in common. Then I'll come on with you to London; and then I'm going to join Christopher in New York. It's years since I was over in the States."

Feeling intrigued, and having no plans of my own, I agreed. "But tell me all about Loulou, and why you think I'm like her?"

"Wait till we get to Paris", he said mysteriously. And so we flew to Paris, where we booked into a first-class hotel.

The very next morning, Bill told me that I had to start dressing properly. "No, don't say anything. Come on, we're going shopping, baby! Let's go!" And what fun it was. It was like something out of a movie. Our first stop was Yves St. Laurent. We walked in and since Bill knew Clara Sam, the manageress, we were treated with the utmost deference.

"Point us to the silk shirts, baby!" said Bill to Clara.

One of her assistants was waved forward, and soon I was looking at a shelf on which there were about twenty in my size, in every imaginable colour. I started trying to choose between them. "What do you think, Bill?"

"They look great – have one of each!"

So I did.

We moved on, and it was the same in every part of the shop.

"Oh", said Bill, "that jacket fits, have three like that. Those trousers look good, take three pairs. And you need something for the evening – have two of those. And shoes – you could probably do with six pairs of those!"

And all this time help was surging round us: "Ah, Ma'm'selle, zese trousers need lengthening… Zees darling leetle skirt she needs shortening… Everyzing will be waiting for you demain – tomorrow – 'ow-you-say, Meed-dai!"

I had never even thought of dressing as well as this. It was intoxicating.

"And now", said Bill, when my transformation was complete, "you must come and meet the master himself. We've been invited to eat at one. Au 'voir, Clara baby!"

So on we went on to the Rue de Babylon, where Yves St. Laurent lived in a very beautiful house with his partner Pierre Bergé. Their sitting-room was stunning: every wall was dead-white, but instead of being clinical, the room simply felt very modern. It was sparsely furnished, but everything in the room was ravishing. The pictures were strange: drawings of sheep by a famous artist. Was it Henry Moore? They were all over the place: sheep standing, sheep sitting, sheep lying down, large sheep, small sheep, sheep looking away from you, sheep looking towards you.

"And will it be lamb for lunch?" I asked Yves St. Laurent teasingly.

He smiled benignly. "I think not today. Perhaps on your next visit. En tout cas, ma petite, there is someone Bill wishes you should meet. Bill, will you take Nicky up to see Loulou? Elle vous attend."

Which was how I first met Loulou de la Falaise.

It was a strange meeting, because half way up the stairs, Bill turned to me with an unusually serious face. "Now listen baby, whatever you do, don't mention Donald Cammell!"

"But why –"

"She left her husband for Donald – just like you, baby! And now she lives here and works for Yves."

So that was what I was meant to have in common with Loulou. Going to bed with Donald Cammell! And Donald had never even mentioned her name to me! I felt furious with him, and terribly jealous of Loulou.

That jealousy vanished the moment I saw her. Although Loulou had been ill, she looked devastatingly beautiful, and full of life. She greeted me in a very friendly manner, and said that she would be up the next day, and would go clubbing with us. "That is, if you don't mind the sort of places Bill likes!"

We visited Yves St. Laurent a couple more times during our visit, and I found that he had a very small inner circle of friends. It chiefly consisted of Pierre, Loulou, Clara, Bill, the French writer Thadée Klossowski de Rola (who was then living with Clara but who later married Loulou); and now, for some extraordinary reason, I too was included.

Numerous others came and went: people like Kim d'Estainville, entrepreneur playboy lover of Hélène Rochas, the parfumier; and in the evenings, just as Loulou had promised, some of us – though never Yves – went night-clubbing. We'd choose clubs where we could eat, and then there would often be a drag show, with gorgeous men dressed up in stockings and high heels and looking absolutely ravishing.

Bill was a night-owl, and if in the early hours I dared to suggest that I would like to go to bed, he was liable to become genuinely upset: "Oh baby," he would say, "you don't love me anymore – I can't stand it!" In the afternoons we went shopping. First, we toured the jewellery shops looking for Roman gold; and then we moved on to the antique shops. I'd already told him about my London house and had bought some old iron chandeliers from him when we were in Marrakesh; and now we found more items such as the most amazing Persian dragon.

Fortunately, when we moved on to London together, Mallord Street caught Bill's imagination, and he immediately set about improving the decoration. This was great, because he was very good on lighting, which had turned out to be Christopher's weak point. Suddenly there were mirrors everywhere, even inside the fireplace; and before long I had the most magical lighting. This came partly from those iron chandeliers, which took us hours to piece together, but turned out to be one of my better purchases. Thanks to the miners' strike, there were frequent power cuts; but with dozens of candles stuck in the chandeliers we could make the whole drawing-room blaze with light. This was just as well, because Loulou had said she would follow us from Paris in a couple of days, and Bill became determined to throw a party to coincide with her arrival.

"But we've only got twenty-four hours!" I protested.

"That's no problem", said Bill. "I'll start telephoning right away."

"And what about food?"

"No problem, baby." He had already pulled a notebook from his pocket, and was busy dialling the first number. "Put Rita on to it. Tell her to prepare lots of rice and chicken and salad and things like that. We'll do an enormous buffet. This is a long shot", he added. And then his face was filled with delight. "Hello, Robert, is that really you?" He put his hand over the mouth of the telephone for a moment, and said to me excitedly "It's Robert Fraser – he's out of that Indian gaol and back in London again!" He turned back to the telephone. "Robert, it's so great to hear your voice…"

I went off to the kitchen to find Rita. Fortunately, she took news of the party in her stride, said she would get her sister in to help, and set off almost at once to the shops to start buying what was needed. As the afternoon rushed by, and it was suddenly dark outside, Bill grew more and more excited. He was hardly ever off the telephone. 'Robert's coming tomorrow', he told me gleefully; 'and he's madly in love with some young boy who runs a dance-group called The Belles of Bengal – so we're paying them to come and dance at the party.'

'And what shall I get everyone to drink?'

'Relax, baby! Order a couple of cases of wine for anyone who isn't snorting or smoking joints. For the rest of us: lay on plenty of apple-juice, and fill one of the baths up with ice.'

By the time the party began at about nine o'clock the next evening, I had made a few telephone calls myself, with the result that Ossie Clark was one of the first to arrive. Although we were pleased to see each other, I think he was a bit miffed by the fact that instead of wearing an Ossie Clark original, I was in a black Yves St Laurent dress with tassels all over it, and masses of Yves St Laurent jewellery.

Ossie had brought with him not only Celia but also David Hockney, whom I met for the first time. Robert Fraser was the next to arrive. He was very courteous and we took to each other at once. With him was one of his close friends the actor Rufus Collins, a very gentle and beautiful black man who knew all there was to know about the ballet. Then more and more people streamed in. Records were playing, people were dancing, and everything became wilder and wilder.

That was the first and one of the best of my Mallord Street parties.

※

A couple of days later, Bill flew to New York. When I followed him on 21 February 1972, I found that he was staying in Manhattan with an old school-friend of his called Preston Smith, and had booked me into the luxurious Stanhope Hotel on Fifth Avenue and East 81st Street. By this time, I felt quite at home in New York, though it was a little strange to have both Bill Willis and Christopher Gibbs waiting for me.

As I mentioned, it was Christopher's first journey to the States. He likes to be a little mysterious, and at first I wasn't allowed to meet the man with whom he was staying, John Richardson, the Picasso expert who ran Christie's New York office. But Christopher and I met frequently and scoured the antique shops together, our best purchases being a marvellous chandelier with crystals and amethysts, and the painting of a tiger by Jean-Jacques Benjamin-Constant. However, I noticed that Christopher often seemed untypically nervous and ill-at-ease; and then he turned up at the Stanhope seeking my advice at 1.30 in the morning.

"I've got a terrible problem, Nicky", he said.

"What is it, Christopher?"

"I've come into some money."

"There's nothing wrong with that, in fact it's quite nice."

"I'm just not quite sure how to cope with it." It turned out that the Gibbs family banking and insurance company, Antony Gibbs and Sons, had suddenly gone public, and he'd come into some shares. When he told me how much they were worth, he added: "It's not nearly as much as you've got."

He didn't believe me when I told him that in fact it was almost exactly the same amount; and that was the first moment when I began to get an inkling of the fact that although I had a great deal of money, I wasn't one of the super-rich as everyone seemed to think.

As for Bill: he and Preston were always falling out; and there seemed to be nothing Bill liked better than leaving Preston behind and going out dancing with me every evening. We had a cocaine-fuelled riot, to which there was a frightening side.

One evening, Bill had a taxi-driver he knew pick us up. The driver looked at me suspiciously. 'She's okay', said Bill. The man shrugged his shoulders and we got into the taxi. Bill leaned forward, and whispered an address.

We drove somewhere down into the lower east side. We were far away from the bright lights, and I was beginning to feel scared. Then we drove down an alley with only a single street-lamp in it. The taxi-driver came to a halt under the lamp, and switched off his lights.

'Baby, you just wait here', Bill began, but I cut him short.

'Hell no, I'm coming with you.'

'It's your funeral – well, it could be!'

We walked a little further up the alley, and he knocked on a door three times. It opened a crack.

'What do you want, man?'

'I've come for the coke from Black Alice. There's $200.'

The money was counted.

'Okay, man. Now you back off round that corner and wait, and it'll be dropped off in five minutes.'

We did as he said.

'How on earth can you trust them?' I asked, as the minutes ticked by.

'Don't you worry, baby. Black Alice is reliable.'

'Black Alice?'

'She's a man, if you need to know!'

And then a car drove slowly past, and someone wound the window down. It was like a scene out of a forties gangster movie, and I half expected George Raft to leap out with a machine-gun blazing: but all that happened was that a packet was thrown out of the window, and the car sped away.

'That's it baby!' said Bill triumphantly, when he had retrieved the package. 'And now let's paint the town red!'

Another evening, Bill took me to have supper with Loulou's mother Maxime de la Falaise, and this was the start of my becoming immersed in what was for me a totally different New York from the one I had known before.

Maxime was married to John McKendry, who worked at the Metropolitan Museum of Art; and two or three times a week they used to give dinner-parties in their flat for about fifteen people from a complete mixture of backgrounds. Their guests ranged from very rich and famous New York socialites like Nan Kempner, down to the extremely impoverished Robert Mapplethorpe, with whom John McKendry had fallen madly in love. Another occasional guest was Andy Warhol, who seemed more inscrutable than ever; and an archaeologist called Iris Love who was a great friend of Maxime's. John McKendry and I liked each other, and I knew that I could learn from him, and with the Metropolitan being bang opposite the Stanhope I called on him a few times.

It was after I had told Christopher Gibbs about my meetings with John McKendry that he decided that I could meet John Richardson after all, and I was glad about that, because John is one of the nicest people I have ever met in my life. I absolutely adored him on sight. He lived in a wonderful house, its walls covered with Picassos; and when we met, the first thing he said was: "Of course, your father had some Picassos too;' and he was able to tell me which they were.

After two or three weeks in New York, spending so much time with Bill Willis had left me totally exhausted, so it came as quite a relief when, in the middle of another sleepless night, he suddenly decided that he wanted to fly down to Memphis, Tennessee to revisit his birthplace. After taking him out to the airport at four in the morning, I decided that this was my cue for a return to England.

CHAPTER TWENTY-FIVE
Partying in New York and London

When I returned to Mallord Street it was mid-March and, having given that very successful party earlier in the year, I found that I had become a much more established figure in the London social scene. Somewhere among the crowd of people who now began visiting me was the interior designer Nicky Haslam, and in due course he took me to one side and said: 'Nicola, my dear, I've been to see my friend Lady Diana Cooper…' Here he paused a moment, presumably for effect, since he had just given me the name of a very well-known English aristocrat. 'She helps with a charity, you know,' he went on. 'A very deserving cause: crippled children. Her committee have arranged an evening at the theatre with the comedian Max Wall to raise money; and she's looking for someone to hold a cocktail party beforehand to sell some tickets. Could I mention your name?'

I said that of course he could; there followed a meeting with Lady Diana, who turned out to be utterly charming, and we became good friends. She had been a society beauty in her youth; and although she was now elderly, she was still very striking. So, I held the cocktail party and sold a lot of tickets; and I attended the theatrical event in a group which included Lady Diana and Nicky Haslam and another friend of his, who was introduced to me simply as 'Tony Snowdon'.

'Nicky', I whispered to Nicky Haslam when I had a chance, 'don't tell me you've been to his house too? You've been everywhere. I'm going to start calling you Nicky Has-been!'

Down on the stage, Max Wall was as hilarious as ever, with his peculiar walk and his dead-pan expression. And afterwards Lord Snowdon invited Nicky Haslam and me back to Kensington Palace. At the time, he was still married to Princess Margaret; but their marriage must have been on the rocks by then, because when I was sitting next to him in the taxi, he began feeling my legs! True: we were all fairly drunk by this time – we might even have had a snort of cocaine; and then we went into the Palace. As an aesthetic experience, it was disappointing. The rooms were wonderful, but the decoration was hideous and the furniture was a complete jumble of different styles. At any rate, Tony found a tricycle he had bought for one of his children, and we all took turns cycling on it around the sitting-room and up and down a corridor.

※

My daily routine was flexible; but it was odd for me not to be up until at least four in the morning. If I wasn't going to a party or to Tramps, I'd go in through the back door of the Casserole at one in the morning when another new friend of mine, the artist Nicolette Meeres, would be tilling-up. Nicolette was no great beauty: she had a long face, quite a large nose, and the most protruding teeth I've ever seen in my life. She also dressed very oddly, thinking nothing of turning up in shocking pink boots, or wearing clothes that didn't match, like a bright red skirt and a pale blue top. And yet, with her long blonde hair and the depth of feeling that she showed, she always looked good. It was something kind and noble in her spirit which shone through.

Nicolette and I might share an apple crumble with the owner Keith Lichtenstein and his partner Dicky Kriss, who were also becoming good friends; and then Nicolette would come back to Mallord Street, where we would we'd stay up talking till six in the morning, and then sleep until mid-day.

After that I would go off to lunch, most often with John Stefanidis or the artist Teddy Millington-Drake, or the writer Violet Wyndham. I also visited Nigel Waymouth most days at Glebe Place; and then at about four or five in the afternoon people would start appearing at Mallord Street and everyone would party.

It was open house, so I never knew exactly who was going to come. To begin with there was one notable absentee: Victoria Brooke. She had this strange capacity for suddenly slipping away and disappearing for a while, and I hadn't seen her since our first meeting on the eve of my departure for India.

On a good night, Mark Palmer might turn up hours on end, or Catherine Tennant, or Michael Rainey, or Jane if she was in town, or Jane's sister Victoria Ormsby-Gore. Ossie Clark visited me almost every evening: perhaps partly because he knew that I was always good for a snort of cocaine! In return, I persuaded him to introduce me to Mick Jagger's wife Bianca. Gradually Bianca and I became quite pally, and before long she had introduced me to one of her few close friends, the shoe designer Manolo Blahnik. Kenneth Anger was always around; I began seeing a good deal of the artist Michael Wishart, who was pleased with me for buying one of his paintings; David Hockney had also become an occasional visitor; and Christopher Gibbs would often arrive, and have fun helping me to rearrange all the furniture.

However, even a good night could end with me feeling so unhappy that I threw everyone out; and on a bad night, when nobody came at all, I felt dreadfully lonely. The real problem was that although by most people's standards I was having a very exciting life, I couldn't get over Donald Cammell.

Donald was still the great love of my life. I went to bed with other people now and again, but that was only through loneliness. It was Donald from whom I wanted to hear, and I couldn't stand it when the weeks went by and he didn't even telephone.

One evening I was sitting alone up in my bedroom feeling particularly depressed when I heard the front door-bell ring. I decided to let Rita answer it. A minute or two later I heard her running up the stairs, and there was a knock on my door. "Madam," she said, "there is a strange gentleman at the door. He has a hat with pieces of cork hanging from it, and he says that my hair is a most interesting spectacle!"

My heart lightened. I slipped on some shoes and rushed downstairs.

"Ah, Miss Samuel – or rather Mrs. Waymouth. I have just arrived, first from Australia, where ultimately I was repelled by their colonial crudity;

and then from your estranged husband, whom I am now doing my best to comfort in his severe distress!" Beneath his ridiculous Australian hat, it was of course David Litvinoff, who had apparently moved in with Nigel.

"David, it's so great to see you. Oh my God!" I was in his arms, and crying helplessly.

Litvinoff patted me uncertainly on the back, and I disengaged myself and led him through to the drawing-room where, since I knew he was a friend of Donald Cammell's, I began telling him how much I loved Donald and how beastly he was being and how unhappy I was. I made him promise not to say anything; but of course, within twenty-four hours he'd been round to Donald's house and told him everything I'd said.

The result was that Donald did start visiting me, and he never once brought Myriam with him. It was wonderful. We only had to look at each other and we'd be practically in bed together. That was all I wanted. I only had to look at Donald and my clothes were off and I'd fuck him stupid. I'd have done anything for him. There was even one occasion when Loulou and I took him to bed! I'd have jumped into the Thames if he'd told me to.

But in the end, it was all just as hopeless as I had been warned. Whenever Donald left my bed, I knew that he would be on his way back to Myriam's. Once again, I began making tear-filled visits to his mother. Indeed, I was so intensely unhappy that I was like two different people in the same body.

On the outside I was a social butterfly, continually on show, this young ravishing beauty who was fascinating and great fun and up for anything; while on the inside I was lonely, miserable and scared. Nigel Waymouth was one of the few people who realized this, and he wrote me letters, which I completely ignored, telling me that I was messing around with the wrong type of people, and that they were all taking me for a ride.

Thoughts of suicide recurred; while the number of drugs I was taking steadily increased. Once a week I visited Dr. Rossdale, who would happily prescribe for me; but by now, this was not enough; and I was also buying drugs on the black market. I had several dealers who would bring me anything I wanted: one hundred Mandrax, for example, and they would be with me the very next day. I was now taking two Mandrax when I got up in the morning, one when I went out to lunch, two in the afternoon, and then two in the evening to keep me going; and I was also taking speed and lines of cocaine.

If ever I spent the weekend in London, I would probably stay with Ossie Clark, going on to David Hockney's flat on a Sunday afternoon, where I sometimes met Wayne Sleep of the Royal Ballet. David's main work at this time was painting a huge double-portrait showing Wayne with his close friend the antiquarian bookseller George Lawson, and he showed it to me once or twice and complained about the difficulty of getting the light just right.

From time to time there were also traditional Sunday dinners with Goody. The Sunday Club at Arnold's, we used to call it. Everyone would be there from the former Foreign Secretary George Brown downwards, and Arnold's circle included Ian Fleming's widow Anne, who was his current flame. Goody told them all I was a fool, so they assumed I was and even quite well-known politicians spoke freely in front of me about everything from the Cold War to the problems of the Third World.

But my escape, my salvation, was that most weekends I could retreat to the Cabbage Patch, by driving down to Sussex after the Casserole had closed in the early hours of Saturday morning. I would arrive at about two-thirty and, having had a very meticulous mind all my life, the first thing I would do would be to pay my bills and do my accounts for the week just ending. Then at about three or four in the morning I'd go to bed with a pot of porridge, in my Empire bed in my lovely Sussex bedroom.

I'd wake up around midday; and what really and truly kept me sane was that I could then go and ride my horse, and spend two or three hours out on the Sussex Downs. I was usually so smashed that I fell off at least once; but falls don't hurt you if you're smashed, because you're so relaxed. I loved it, in fact I absolutely adored it. Then on Saturday evening I would do my favourite things: watching television, reading very bad books, and staying on the telephone for hours.

On Sundays I had a lie-in, and then went for another ride around lunchtime. Afterwards I usually visited my mother, who was now living a 40-minute drive away at Wisborough Green in Billingshurst; and then I'd go on to dinner with Keith Lichtenstein.

Keith lived in a comfortable Victorian house in Fittleworth, with gardens which had been designed by Clough Williams-Ellis of Portmeirion fame, and an interior that was full of modern paintings, including to my great delight several by Nigel Waymouth. Keith's partner Dicky Kriss would always be there, and we were waited on hand and foot by numerous Filipino maids. My fellow-guests alternated between people like Simon Sainsbury or Robin Symes, who dealt in Roman and Greek jewellery; and people like Nicolette, or Twiggy and her boyfriend/manager Justin de Villeneuve.

Twiggy was incredibly pretty, though I was surprised to find her not quite so spectacular in real life as she appeared in her photographs. In herself she was a sweet subdued girl. She was clearly not a fool, but it was difficult for her to shine conversationally when Justin, who incidentally stank of after-shave, had dominated every aspect of her life for so long. I must admit that I didn't much like Justin. He'd certainly marketed Twiggy brilliantly, so I couldn't help being a little intrigued by him, but I thought it was a bit much when it came to his telling her what time she had to go to bed, and what time she had to get up.

Finally, at about eleven o'clock I would drive back to London and my solitary bed in Mallord Street.

※

By now I had observed that I knew many people who were almost as lonely as me, but they could turn to their painting or their work to find some meaning in their life. Perhaps that was why I sometimes dreamt of being a model, and jumped at any modelling chances I was given.

When I had first moved into Mallord Street, for example, Catherine Tennant had just started working for *Vogue*; and she rang me up, and said that as she had just looked after Nigel and helped him into Glebe Place, would I do her a favour?

"Sure", I had said glibly. "Why not?"

She wanted to photograph my new house; and I agreed; with the result was that one morning, while I was still in bed, Norman Parkinson came round. I had never heard of him, but we got on really well; and when the rest of the usual Vogue crew turned up, he sent them packing, and took some wonderful shots of me lying on my bed. I was wearing something which let through the light; and in the print I've still got on my walls, I swear you can see my slit through the material.

Another job I had for *Harpers & Queen* was the result of my going to 'Joan Price's Face Place'. a shop on Chelsea Green, to have my legs waxed. Joan herself saw me one day, decided that I had a good skin, and asked me whether I would do a beauty feature? Curiously enough the other girl involved was Nicola Pagett, who later became a film star. It involved being taken off to a studio, where I was caked in heavy make-up, and forced into all kinds of glamorous but ridiculous poses. It was an awful experience, and it was also the last time I allowed anyone to photograph me exactly as they pleased.

※

During this generally miserable period there were no special lovers in my life. It's true that I had a fling with Ossie Clark, who had become besotted by me, but it meant nothing. There were lots of other flings, but none of them were serious. Basically, I was screwing people if they wanted to screw me. I suppose it was to do with being lonely.

I had very few real friends, although I could confide in Nicolette; and I still saw my old school-friend Annie Griffiths from time to time. Sometimes I visited her and we played tennis at the Boltons. Sometimes she came to one of my parties; but she was living a student life with people of her own age, while all the people I knew were ten or fifteen years older than me.

As for me: the only person I really wanted was still Donald: I just couldn't get him out of my hair, the fucking sod! He made me so happy and then so miserable, and by September 1972 I was longing to get away from him for a few days.

※

It just so happened that I was sitting in the Casserole one evening discussing all this with Nicolette, when Dickie Kriss came up to us. "Nicky

– you look as though you need a holiday. Do you want to come over to Corfu with me?"

"Sure, great, lovely!" All my gloom vanished in a moment. "Where will we stay?"

"Robin Symes has rented a house over there – and he says I can use it and take anyone I want. Do you want to come too, Nicolette?"

But she couldn't, so Dicky and I went off to Greece alone. First, we flew to Athens where we stayed at a rather mediocre hotel, and did all the usual tourist things like visiting the Acropolis. Then we went on to Corfu, where we spent about ten days in a house on the beach.

There was nothing much to do on Corfu: there were only three hours of sun a day; and the maid cooked lousy meals. But it was a wonderfully relaxing holiday, because there was no question of an affair. It's so tedious going on holiday with someone you love: you spend the whole time arguing. Dickie and I had separate bedrooms and a sweet time together. Even when we went gambling it was all right. There was no question of one of us saying to the other: "How dare you lose so much!" Either he lost his money or I lost mine. It was as simple as that. And Dickie bought me Muffles, my toy donkey, who still sits on my bed with my favourite teddy bears.

I hadn't been back home for long (after stopping over in Rome to see Bill Willis), when I was off again: this time to Portugal with Mark Palmer who (probably much to Catherine Tennant's fury) had been staying in my house in Mallord Street. So had Michael Rainey, which must have infuriated her still more.

I certainly thought it was great having Mark staying with me. I'd always loved Mark, and now I longed to go to bed with him. Any girl would. He's everyone's dream of the English aristocrat. Not only is he the most beautiful man, tall, lean, with a wonderful face and a wonderful voice; but he has excellent manners, and that exciting rough gypsy-like edge. And like the true aristocrat that he is, he treats everyone the same, whether he's talking on the telephone to the Queen, or chatting to some wino in the Portobello Road.

Mark Palmer's trip to Portugal wasn't just for fun: he needed to see Suki Potier with whom he was negotiating to buy a house in Wales; and

Suki had now taken up with a wealthy Chinese guy called Bob Ho, who was said to be involved with casinos in Hong Kong and Macau, but who lived not far from his parents in a Lisbon suburb.

"So, Suki's onto quite a good thing?" I asked.

Mark smiled enigmatically and stroked me on the cheek. "She'll be onto a good thing if I can get this deal sorted out. Why don't you come down with me?"

Few things could have pleased me more. We flew down to Portugal together; and I found Mark the most wonderful travelling companion: he's sort of gay, he's sort of straight, but he's loving, friendly, unthreatening, sweet and kind. Negotiating with Suki wasn't easy: she seemed to be doped out of her head for much of the time, and although the house she shared with Bob was large enough for Mark and I to have separate rooms, it seemed smaller because she and Bob had their stereo constantly blasting at full volume. After a while we couldn't stand it. Mark had acquired a land-rover which he had been planning to give them as part of the deal if Suki agreed to sell him the house in Wales; and we took off in it.

It was September and pretty cold, and unfortunately we'd taken summer clothes with us; but we had a lovely holiday, driving westward to Estoril and then touring round for five or six days, staying in very agreeable hotels. Neither of us knew the area, but everyone we met was amazingly hospitable: the fact is that you could put Mark in Timbuctoo and people would be nice to him! And in the evenings, we did quite silly, ordinary things like going to the movies, or going ten-pin bowling.

※

Soon I was back in Mallord Street again, and back in the whirlwind round of London life, where things were happening so fast that it's difficult to know quite where to begin. Perhaps with Mick Jagger.

Quite apart from his wife Bianca and his former girlfriend Marianne Faithfull, Mick and I had numerous friends in common. He had remained very friendly with Donald Cammell since they had worked together on *Performance*; through Donald he had also become friendly with

Christopher Gibbs; and at one point Mick had called in Bill Willis to help him to complete the work which needed doing at Stargroves.

Anyhow, Mick Jagger began dropping round to Mallord Street in the evenings, sometimes with Bianca and sometimes without her. I liked Mick. Not only was he approachable, unlike many pop stars; but both he and Bianca, considering the amount of dope around, were pretty straight: Bianca extremely so. Mick was also clever, and did not talk about music the whole time. Since I am practically tone-deaf this was great so far as I was concerned. I must admit that I only really liked the early Stones records when their songs had what I thought were good lyrics.

Gradually Mick and I became friends. Perhaps this was partly because I wasn't intimidated by his fame. Of course, I was flattered that this man should be in my house because he was the famous man he was; but I expect that, like the rest of us, he was lonely; and perhaps he didn't feel safe in many places, fearing that most people simply wanted to use him. In those days I was the perfect answer for anyone like Mick Jagger. All I wanted was to entertain and have fun, and if famous people came through the door, I was flattered but not overwhelmed. In fact, I felt a great deal safer with the famous ones such as Mick and Bianca, because I knew they didn't need me for anything, as opposed to the great mass of hangers on.

One of the most agreeable days I had with Mick was just before Christmas in 1972. I had gone shopping early in the morning to Fortnum's and, having bumped into each other in the food department of Fortnum's, Mick and I joined forces and went round buying various Christmas presents. I noticed that at the sight of Mick Jagger, all the tail-coated staff had their tongues practically hanging out of their mouths.

Finally, we said that we wanted to buy some caviar and we were immediately taken down to the basement where they pack it into tiny pots. There was a mass of different varieties, so we spent about an hour tasting it. "That's a little salty", I would say, making a face and trying not to burst out laughing. "Let's try another one." Eventually we did buy some, and from then on, I found that an account at Fortnum's had been mysteriously opened in my name.

Then we had a very delightful lunch at Marc's, where I found that Mick was not just a pop star but an extremely civilized person in his own right. He was certainly typical of rich men in that he never carried any money and didn't like spending a penny more than necessary. But I also noticed that he had extremely good manners and always seemed to know how to treat a woman: even in small ways like holding one's chair, opening doors, and walking on the outside in the street. I've heard people call him an egotist but I never found him so. On the contrary, he was very kind.

At this stage, despite my earlier conversation with Christopher Gibbs, I was still convinced that I was much richer than I was; and over lunch we talked about money and what to do with it, about investing on the Stock Exchange and buying paintings and property. Mick even gave me an introduction to his financial adviser Rupert Loewenstein at Leopold Joseph; though when I went to see Rupert, he did kindly point out that although I was certainly well-off, I wasn't mega-rich.

※

By this time Donald Cammell had introduced me to the film director Nic Roeg, who began occasionally turning up to Mallord Street, sometimes alone and sometimes with his wife. A small unpretentious man who was usually dressed in sweaters and corduroy trousers, he was not outstandingly good-looking but he reminded me slightly of my godfather Jean Francois Bergery. He was also a great deal older than me, and for a while I leaned on him a little because I could talk to him about Donald.

"You're a fool to go on thinking of him", Nic said to me one day. "He's not the kind of person for you." I felt the tears come into my eyes and he put an arm round my shoulder and handed me a handkerchief. "I know that you love him. But he's never going to change and so you'll never be happy with him. Believe me!"

About a week later, he and Donald turned up together, and then at some point in the evening Nic came up to me and gave me such an appraising glance that my heart missed a beat. I hoped for a moment that he was going to make a pass at me, but instead he said: "That hair – it's perfect. You see, I must have a red-head!"

"What on earth do you mean?"

"I'm shooting a cinema advertisement for Cherry-B. I wonder whether you'd consider taking part? It'll be a day's work, and you might find it amusing."

"Yes, sure!" I said, happy to do anything to please him.

He scribbled an address and a date on a piece of paper. "Take this – be there at five – and whatever you do, don't say a word about not being a member of Equity! I don't want my entire film crew going on strike. Oh, and I want you in red. Could I have a look at your wardrobe?"

So, I turned up to a film studio at five in the morning wearing the bright red dress that Nic had chosen, and went through make-up. There wasn't much for me to do, not even any lines to learn because the voices would all be dubbed. I just had to look sexy sitting on a sofa for about sixty seconds sipping a glass of Cherry-B. There was a handsome blond boy standing behind me, leaning over my shoulder, and we were meant to be chatting to each other as though it was an intimate occasion. Then he had to come round and sit next to me. He really was sipping that disgusting drink. I drank Ribena instead.

There were so many retakes that filming took most of the day; but it was a great experience for me. I'd always wanted to work, and here I was not only working but also doing something I actually enjoyed. Nic seemed pleased and said he'd use me again; and then I hurried back to Mallord Street.

It was already six when I arrived and we were doing a fashion show for Ossie Clark at eight, and I was absolutely furious because the models had taken over my bedroom and nicked all my coke.

The show was a small one, in the studio at Mallord Street; but it was very exciting and Ossie encouraged me to model the last couple of items, and I went on and threw a few lilies at people in the audience, by which time I think that nearly everyone was quite stoned. It was certainly a memorable day for me; and it was also the day when Bianca Jagger had her hair cut short, which is said to have been an important moment in fashion history.

Not long after the Ossie Clark show, Victoria Ormsby-Gore was due to be married at her father's country home near Oswestry to Julian Lloyd, the father of her baby girl Poppy. John McKendry had come over from America for the wedding, and was already staying with me in Mallord Street, where he was also seeing a good deal of Victoria Brooke. He and Victoria Brooke travelled to Wales together, and I went with Nigel Waymouth and Ossie Clark.

I had arranged for Victoria Ormsby-Gore's wedding-dress to be made by Ossie, and of course he hadn't finished it on time and most of it had been made on me at the very last minute. We didn't even leave London in Ossie's Rolls-Royce until one in the morning on the day of the wedding. It was a weird ride, with Ossie being rather bitchy and queeny with Nigel, and me trying to keep the peace.

We arrived at five or six in the morning at the garden cottage where Victoria and Julian were living. David Litvinoff, who had once again been booked to be Best Man and Master of Ceremonies was already staying there, and Nigel was due to join them. But Nigel immediately said: "We can't wake them up at this hour!" so we slept in the car for an hour and a half until Litvinoff came out to find us.

By this time the wedding dress was creased and crumpled and there were last-minute adjustments to be made because Victoria tried it on there and then. It was a very beautiful maroon-coloured dress with a tight silk bodice and Victoria looked absolutely ravishing in it. Ossie and I then decamped to the Wynnstay Hotel in Oswestry, before going on to the wedding which was in a tiny little church just outside Oswestry, and was followed by a pub lunch of all things.

That evening there was a party for two or three hundred people at Woodhouse, a beautiful old mansion owned by the art historian Willy Mostyn-Owen who was also a director of Christie's. David Litvinoff was incredibly smashed and having great fun. Victoria's father Lord Harlech was there with his American wife Pam. Victoria's sister Alice was going out with Eric Clapton, so all the pop world was there as well. The local Oswestry people didn't know what had hit them.

Christmas 1972 was spent in Mallord Street with Victoria Brooke, who was still seeing Paul Getty every day but preferred staying with me for the time being. Poor Rita! The two of us didn't even start the day until seven or eight in the evening. I spent almost the whole of Christmas Day in bed with a stinking cold reading Malory's *Le Morte d'Arthur*. I felt lousy, and Victoria was sound asleep for much of the time. Fortunately, I had managed to buy a great deal of fake money from a black dealer called Eric, who had sold me a couple of thousand pounds for £100 per thousand, and I had used this to buy wonderful Christmas presents. I gave Victoria some very pretty seed pearls, and I think I bought her a Cartier watch; and in return, once she had woken up, she gave me some pearls which she'd had since her christening.

Then on the evening of Christmas Day, Mick and Bianca came over for a late Christmas lunch, beautifully prepared by Rita, who served it up at about nine or ten in the evening. Bianca, as a Nicaraguan, was very upset about the news from her country. Only two days previously there had been a massive earthquake in Managua. Most of the city centre had been destroyed, more than 5,000 people had been killed, 20,000 injured and 300,000 left homeless.

"I have been telling Mick," said Bianca, "we must go out and raise money for the victims. We can visit my family too."

"We're definitely going", said Mick. "Then we're due in Jamaica for a recording session."

"Why Jamaica?" I asked.

"Because of the interest in reggae music", Mick explained. Then he smiled. "If you know what that is, Nicky!"

At that moment Victoria intervened.

"Maybe Nicky and I will join you!" This seemed like a wonderful idea, and I left arrangements in her hands while I went down to spend a couple of days by myself at the Cabbage Patch.

Unfortunately, while I was away, Victoria asked her friend Henrietta Moraes to stay. Now Henrietta is a very talented and beautiful girl, who had been Francis Bacon's model in all his early paintings, and is a close friend of David Mlinaric. Unfortunately, in those days she was drinking a great deal (she had been completely off her head at Victoria Ormsby-Gore's wedding) and she was also on heroin.

The result was that when I returned from Sussex, Rita was practically having a nervous breakdown. "Look, madam", she said, and I knew that was a bad sign, because she only called me 'madam' when she was very angry. "Look, madam, when I go up to Miss Henrietta's bedroom in the morning there are dirty needles hanging around and God knows what everywhere. Madam, this is enough, I'm leaving. I can't stay."

Her threat, never made before or since, was entirely effective, and I kicked Henrietta out in short order.

By this time, Victoria's arrangements had fallen through but I decided that she and I would go to Jamaica anyway. We flew to Kingston where, for our first night, Victoria and I shared a room in an hotel where a girl had been raped within the past twenty-four hours; but the next day we flew by helicopter to a far more salubrious hotel, the Sans Souci in Ocho Rios on the northern coast.

Keith Richards and Anita Pallenberg were already staying over there in a rented house which they were sharing with my black friend Rufus Collins; and Mick and Bianca decided to follow us by car. By the time they arrived, some hours later than us, they must have been disappointed to discover that Victoria and I had already been given the best apartment, which was very private; while they were put in some rooms overlooking the swimming-pool and the public at large.

It wasn't long before I had met Anita: she was unbelievably beautiful; and the two of us became good friends after an incident when we were both stung by jellyfish. There was a potential awkwardness between us, because Anita had been friends with Talitha Getty, and since at the time of Talitha's slightly mysterious death Paul and Victoria had been very close to each other, Anita had no liking for either of them. Fortunately, I had never known Talitha, so I could continue whole-heartedly to support Victoria without it being a problem.

Everything became much more complicated when my brother Nigel Samuel flew out to join us. Sadly, Nigel's life was still dominated by Michael X; and when Nigel first arrived, he was completely obsessed by the idea that he must fly to St. Lucia, where he believed there were numerous lawyers and solicitors who would be able to help Michael X to deal with his various legal problems.

However, instead of travelling to St. Lucia, Nigel fell desperately in love with Bianca. Bianca for her part had soon decided that she didn't like him very much.

By this time, just to complicate matters, Victoria had begun spending a great deal of time with Nigel. I found this very hard to cope with, especially as I had no man of my own; and this was the only time in my life when, out of pure loneliness and jealousy, I thought of making love to my own brother. My Jamaican holiday had become intolerable and, knowing that Donald Cammell was in New York, I decided to follow him there. So, I told Nigel and Victoria that I had paid the bill until the end of the week, and left.

But first there was a brief encounter with a very elderly Noel Coward. He had always been a hero of mine so I was fascinated to meet him; and he gave us tea and showed us his paintings. But sadly, what I chiefly remember about him is that he was a racist. He didn't like black people; and since we had a black driver; he wouldn't talk to us until the driver had disappeared down the drive. But perhaps it was just the nervousness of old age.

Later I would hear strange stories about what had happened to the others after my departure. Annabel Birley and Jimmy Goldsmith and a few others were staying on the island at Round Hill, and Victoria, who was a close friend of Annabel's, had become fascinated by Jimmy. So, she drove off to Round Hill with my brother, and apparently they were lucky to get there in one piece, because Nigel had been talking about all the things Michael X would do when he returned to Jamaica, and people had begun to believe him, and there were police roadblocks everywhere looking for him.

CHAPTER TWENTY-SIX

Paul Getty, Nicholas Gormanston and Harry Hyams

So sinister is it, so strange, and so full of famous people that I often think that it will be impossible for this account of my life to be published until long after I am dead and forgotten. And then no doubt there will be a blaze of publicity fierce enough to split my headstone from top to bottom in some gloomy God's Acre, some haunted field of skulls. Which reminds me: Christopher Gibbs and John Michell and I once thought of converting disused churches into houses. We were going to start a company and it was going to be called 'God's Acre Property Company'; but I went to New York instead.

※

On this occasion, from the Sans Souci in Jamaica I went as directly as possible to the Stanhope, where I resumed the life of a wealthy New Yorker. I was soon being asked out to numerous social events, although my main interest lay in seeing Donald Cammell.

Donald had temporarily broken up with Myriam and was working on a movie with the Maysles brothers, and having an affair with a very beautiful Chinese girl called China Machado. She was a very smart and sophisticated New York lady who worked hard in the fashion business but was no hustler. She also had a couple of young children with whom she lived in a beautiful apartment on the river in Manhattan.

I was only in New York for a few weeks, until mid-February 1973, but during that time my life would be dominated by yet another sexual threesome involving Donald Cammell. Fortunately, it was very different from the Myriam threesome, because although China was fond of Donald there were times when I think she found him a bit of a pain in the neck; and since she could see that I was completely besotted by him she was always kind and sympathetic to me. I don't remember a great deal of sex involving China; but sometimes she'd ring up and say "Come over to dinner" and the inevitable would happen. More often I'd go somewhere like John and Maxime's, or John Richardson's, and then call in on Donald on my way back to the Stanhope.

Before I flew back to London, I also had two life-changing meetings, one of which would lead to a massive increase in my status within New York City, and the other of which would set in train a course of events that almost destroyed me.

The first of these meetings was with Bob Colacello, one of Andy Warhol's inner circle, whom I met at one of John and Maxime's dinner-parties. We got on well, and he was one of those rare people who mean it when they say that they will ring you the next day. In retrospect, he may have been partly interested in securing a commission for Warhol; but in any case, we started partying together, and once he had decided that I was a useful person to cultivate he arranged for *Women's Wear Daily* to interview this so-called 'fascinating English red-head.' It was a successful ploy on his part, because overnight it turned me into someone whom Andy and his circle wanted to meet. The article, by Rosemary Kent, appeared on the front page and featured me running along outside the Met in midwinter wearing a summer dress.

At the time, I didn't realize how socially important this interview would be. I thought the WWD was just some fashion rag, not the paper in which every New Yorker wanted to be seen. So, I gave truthful answers, none of which were edited out. I admitted to taking drugs. I admitted to hating the English class system. I admitted to being rich and left-wing. I even admitted to loving New York. As I would discover on my next visit to New York almost a year later, it was the best thing I could have done.

The second meeting, once again in the McKendry's apartment on Riverside Drive, was with an extremely talented jewellery designer called Kenneth (more usually 'Ken' or 'Kenny') Jay Lane. Most things were as usual: no servants, just the wonderful and beautiful Maxime cooking endless dishes of rather strange sixteenth century English food which we would all acclaim; and a mixture of writers, artists and socialites, with an occasional English aristocrat thrown in for good measure.

But one thing was most unusual; and that was the presence of Ken Lane. I can honestly say that I had never come across anyone quite like him. He was so good-looking and charming and entertaining. I remember that he was wore a black silk polo-necked shirt and jeans and I was fascinated by the wonderful rings on his hands; and instead of being captivated by the other guests he only seemed to have eyes for me. It never dawned on me that he might be the slightest bit gay, because he had a way of desiring me that was overwhelming; and although I was a little frightened by this man who seemed to have everything, I almost fell in love with him on the spot. Here was Nemesis sitting by my side and sizing me up and I was bewitched.

As usual I was stoned on cocaine and Mandrax to conquer my fear of being with people, and so I was able to talk easily throughout dinner. Afterwards we went dancing. Then he dropped me back to the Stanhope, and a few days later he asked me to lunch at his house which was extraordinarily elegant. This made him still more attractive to me, though I was so much in awe of him that I never dared allow myself to think that Ken might take any serious interest in me.

In any case, despite his attachment to China Machado, I was still impossibly in love with Donald Cammell. At the same time, once I was back in London, I found myself being drawn into another curious friendship involving Victoria Brooke and Paul Getty.

At that time, Paul was practically a recluse. Apart from Victoria, almost the only two people who saw him regularly in his house in Cheyne Walk were Alastair Londonderry, whose Italian house Victoria had lived in for years before she came back to England; and my friend Christopher Gibbs.

"It's strange, isn't it", I said to Victoria one day, "how many connections there are between me and Paul."

She looked at me a little oddly. "How do you mean?"

"Well, there's you, and Christopher. And Nicolette used to work for him. And Bill Willis who knew him when he was with Talitha, and heaven knows who else!" Victoria's eyes darkened, and I thought it had probably been a mistake to mention Talitha. But I was intrigued and I wanted to know more. "He does like Bill, doesn't he?" I went on. "Bill certainly adores him! Did Bill like Talitha too?"

And then at last she told me what she knew about Paul and Talitha, and Bill and Paul's early life, and a thousand other things.

Paul's father, John Paul Getty Sr., founder of the Getty Oil company, was one of the richest men in the world. and Paul had been taken into the family business. But first, at the time of the Korean War he had been drafted into the Army.

"He had a terrible time in the army", Victoria giggled, "because he'd never actually pissed in public and things like that, and now he suddenly had to piss in a public loo. He hardly went to the loo the whole of his first week! And of course, he happened to have an income of something like a million pounds a day, which doesn't help if you're in the army with people on £2 a day!"

By 1966, when Paul married his second wife Talitha, he had become such close friends with Bill Willis that he and Talitha spent their honeymoon with him in Marrakesh, where in due course Paul bought a wonderful house which Bill did up for him. And when things went wrong between Paul and Talitha, Paul had begun living out in Rome where he had become friendly with Victoria.

In the meantime, Talitha had bought a house in Cheyne Walk, which Christopher Gibbs furnished and decorated. Her idea was that Paul should come back to London and live with her there; but he stayed in Rome and never ever flew back to see what the house looked like. Eventually, in despair, Talitha had gone out to Rome and given him an ultimatum; and when that failed, she took an overdose and died.

This made Paul desperately unhappy and, full of guilt, he went to live in the house Talitha had prepared for him. There he had been joined by Victoria and there he lived almost like a hermit.

"Of course, he's desperately stoned most of the time", said Victoria. "But you can understand why." She was standing by the large fireplace in Mallord Street, turning the pages of one of my first editions, before replacing it on the mantelpiece and giving me a speculative look. "Perhaps you should meet him, darling! After all, just like you he's mad about books."

So it was that one evening at about eleven I finally met Paul Getty. He was plump, like a teddy-bear, much older than me, wearing a short dressing-gown, and sitting on a sofa surrounded by books, in a sitting-room which was piled high from floor to ceiling with books and opera records. He smiled sadly at me and although he didn't look particularly well, he talked brilliantly about books and bindings and soon I began going over to Cheyne Walk quite regularly at eleven or twelve at night to see him and Victoria.

Soon we had become such close friends that Paul gave me a key to the house and I went in and out as I pleased. Victoria and I were usually in her rooms on an upper floor, and we would sometimes go down and spend time with Paul, who never left the sitting-room.

Then one day Victoria announced that she would be going away for a while, to Mexico. She asked me to keep an eye on Paul until she returned; and so began one of the stranger episodes in my life.

It was late one night, only a couple of days after Victoria had left for Mexico, when a large chauffeur-driven car parked outside my house. The chauffeur knocked on my door and announced that Mr. Getty was outside in the car and would Mrs. Waymouth please join him at her earliest convenience? And there in the back of the car was Paul, stuffed miserably into one of the suits that was far too small for him, but undeniably dressed and out of the house probably for the first time for months. He and I were driven back to Cheyne Walk, and soon his clothes had come off again and we were on his sofa making love.

It wasn't a passionate love-affair, and everything took place on that same wretchedly uncomfortable sofa, huddled against Christopher Gibbs's cushions. But considering the state of his health, Paul was remarkably good at sex, and in Victoria's absence our relationship became quite frisky.

Apart from me, he was seeing almost no-one except for Alastair Londonderry, Christopher Gibbs, and Gordon and Tom, his main drugs suppliers, who were mini-cab drivers. Oh, I nearly forgot his secretary Miss Gadstone, whom Victoria and I called the dragon. There was also a wonderful nurse called Jaggers who would appear once every two months or so to get Paul off dope by substituting morphine for his normal heroin. But these efforts at detoxification never achieved much. Jaggers helped to run a pub and was an alcoholic into the bargain; and I well remember having to put the two of them to bed one night, as they were both so stoned that they had collapsed on the floor.

As for Paul and me: with Victoria away, we became like two naughty children. I'd say: "Paul, look, it's 11.30. Christopher's going to turn up in an hour. Let's be screwing, because Christopher never knows where to look when you've got nothing on!" What made it more exciting was that video cameras had only just come out, so Paul and I pretended we were making dirty movies. And when Christopher or Alastair did turn up, we'd tease them by not answering the door for ten or fifteen minutes.

I remember Christopher coming in once and asking rather angrily: "What are you doing, children? Nicky, shouldn't you be at home?"

To which I replied: "Yes, okay Christopher, I'm just going up to bed."

Seeing me go upstairs instead of leaving the house made him even more angry, because he adored Victoria, and for her sake he was very confused and anxious about what was going on between Paul and me.

I think I was pretty confused and anxious myself, because although I adored Victoria, and I knew that she and Paul would almost certainly be together for life, somewhere at the back of my mind I harboured the wicked hope that Paul might fall for me and forget Victoria. Not that I was ever sexually in love with Paul; but I did want him very badly for a while. This was partly because I still believed that I was an incredibly rich woman. So, what we had in common, I thought, was that we were on an equal footing, and therefore neither of us could ever hurt the other. But it was also because I had begun to want him as a replacement for the father I had lost.

This wasn't altogether surprising. My relationship with Paul had begun with books, a good deal of it remained about books, and books had been one of my father's principal passions. Listening to Paul on the subject of old and rare books was an education, and I loved it. Occasionally, he would even sell me a book: not to make money out of me, but because he would discover that he had two copies of a book that he genuinely thought I would like to have in my own collection.

Once a week or so, if he was feeling well enough, Paul would phone up from downstairs and say "I'm coming up to the bedroom!" And about an hour and a half later, by which time I was usually sound asleep, he would appear with a pile of books, and say generously: "Look, you can have any of these three books you want!" And I would take them and always give them back to him the next day, to show that although I enjoyed his knowledge and his affection, I wanted nothing material from him.

In fact, because he appeared to be so lonely and hopeless, I was not only buying books from him and giving him money when he needed any for incidental expenses, but doing whatever else he asked. I'd go and buy his clothes from St. Laurent, I'd get him dressed, I'd get him to the doctor's, I'd get him to the book-dealers; and it was all hellishly hard work.

As for Paul's being a junkie: that just made life more difficult. Smack was on the table the whole time, but he never once offered me any. He knew that I took cocaine, but that's relatively harmless; and I think that if he'd ever seen me take any smack, he would have thrown me out immediately. He knew how dangerous it was.

I had already started nicking a few flakes of heroin from the table for myself. It wasn't exactly as if I was going into someone's safe and stealing it! But that was how my heroin addiction began. And now that I was dealing on Paul's behalf with Gordon and Tom, I began asking them to give me small amounts of heroin as a commission. This wasn't Paul's fault, and neither he nor Victoria ever knew what I had done.

Wanting Paul as a father-figure was certainly a terrible mistake. One night while Victoria was still away, I went to him one night, crying and saying: "Look, Paul, I have to have you. I've got no-one! I need a father!" And he froze.

※

I began thinking about Donald Cammell again; and I was still thinking about him when I began receiving a new visitor at Mallord Street. This was 34-year-old Nicholas Gormanston. The first time I saw him I asked him to sit down next to me and tell me about himself. He claimed that if there was a King in Ireland, it would be him. I teased him about this; and then we talked about India, because it turned out that he had spent a great deal of time there, and had occasionally sold pieces of Tantric Art in London.

It also turned out that Nicholas was indeed the Premier Viscount of Ireland, though he clearly had no money worth mentioning, only just enough to live on without having to work. Despite this, I was intrigued by him. Compared to some of the much older men I had been out with, Nicholas seemed like such a very nice gentle boy.

It was at the beginning of June 1973, when I was partly living with Paul and partly spending time with Nicholas Gormanston, that Goody telephoned me and said: "You know it's the Derby on Wednesday? If you'd like to come with me, we'll go and see my friend Harry Hyams. You know, um, the property developer – Centre Point? Anyway, he's got a box at the Derby, d'you see, and he's invited me to bring a guest."

So, I bought a new hat and dress and we motored down to the racecourse at Epsom Downs and joined the merry throng. The racecourse box turned out to be a long narrow room with an enormous table covered with champagne bottles and lobster lunches; and Harry Hyams was holding court to twenty or twenty-five people, including his wife and all their closest friends, while waiters surged round waiting on us hand and foot.

I knew from what Goody had told me that Hyams was an extraordinary man, a property developer who was just as successful as my father had been. When I met him, he seemed both powerful and protective; and because he adored Arnold Goodman, I was made incredibly welcome, and I began to think he was nice in a funny sort of way. But then, having manoeuvred me most charmingly into a slight corner, he suddenly changed tack. "I wonder whether I might have your telephone number", he said, placing a hand on my arm. "I would so much like to take you out to dinner one evening. Any friend of Arnold's…"

'Any friend of Arnold's' bullshit!' I was thinking to myself. His wife was standing only a few yards away, and this man was definitely coming on to me.

"No, I'm sorry Harry", I said, smiling at him, but turning just enough to shake off his hand. "I never give my number to any Tom or Dick, so why should I give it to you? And I'm ex-directory, you know. And I think that Centre Point is the ugliest building in London."

My refusal only made him even more determined, and somehow or other he succeeded in obtaining my telephone number. I wouldn't take his calls, and Rita became quite tired of announcing that Mr. Hyams was on the telephone, and being instructed to tell him that I wasn't available. Then he began coming round to Mallord Street, and I had him turned away at the door.

Eventually, however, his persistence wore me down, I let him in, and he persuaded me to go out to dinner with him. We went to Wilton's in Jermyn Street and afterwards we walked around St. James's. It was all frightfully romantic, and Harry began saying: "You're just so beautiful, and all I want to do is to touch your wonderful body". At one point I even stood with him in a dark passage in St. James's and let him run his hands over my body. After that I didn't see him for a while; but I knew that he was hooked.

In the meantime, Nicholas Gormanston had a house near Cambridge which he was sharing with several other people; and one June weekend, he asked me to go down there to stay with him. It was a beautiful old sixteenth-century house, with a very odd household. Nicholas's brother Rodney was living there; so was Tom Keays, whom I had last seen in California and who was busily writing a film-script; so was a journalist called Jenny Fabian, who back in 1969 had co-authored a book called *Groupie*, and had once been a good friend of Donald Cammell.

News of this, which she mentioned with a happy smile, left me feeling very hollow inside; and then at nine o'clock that evening another woman visitor who had just arrived, I don't remember her name, suddenly asked me: "Do you want some acid?"

Without even thinking, I said: "Sure, of course!"

So, we went up to my bedroom to take some together. It was a large bedroom and it must have been quite cold, because even though it was the summer there was a fire blazing in the hearth.

We took the acid, and everything was fine for half-an-hour, because acid doesn't work straight away. You take it and think nothing's going to happen, and then suddenly it all starts moving around and your brain's going at a thousand miles a minute! Every little detail becomes so important, and big, and depending on whether you are basically sad or happy, things can look ghastly or they can look wonderful. It's not a drug ever to be taken if you're in a bad frame of mind, which for some reason I was.

And after that first half-hour of nothing happening, I completely flipped. I just went off my head.

My companion was terribly scared, because she'd never seen anyone having such a violent reaction. She dashed out of the room to get help, and when she came back in with Nicholas and the others, I was trying to climb into the fireplace.

They pulled me away from the flames, but all I wanted to do was to die. How lovely it would be not to exist anymore. Now there was a sea of their horribly elongated faces all around me, all wanting to destroy me. Everyone I saw seemed to have some involvement with Donald, and it was their fault that everything was wrong between him and me. There was a sea of faces round about me, all elongated and all wanting to destroy me. I suddenly had it in for Tom Keays and Jenny Fabian, neither of whom had ever done me any harm whatsoever. I went for Jenny, who had become an evil nightmarish monster. I was shouting and screaming and tearing at her. I wanted to pull her eyes out of their sockets. I wanted to kill her. The others had to drag me away, and the following day her face was covered in scratches.

Nicholas drove me back to Mallord Street in my own car in a kind of stony silence; and for the next five or six days I was so exhausted that I could only sleep and sleep. It was like having an incredibly bad dose of flu or pneumonia. I woke up each morning thinking that I was better; and then after about an hour I was exhausted again. That was the last time I ever tried acid; and I suppose I was lucky that I hadn't decided that I could fly and thrown myself out of the window, as many others have done. It was the end of my friendship with Nicholas, and the following year he married Eva-Antoine, a beautiful 19-year-old red-head who I couldn't help thinking looked a little like me.

Not long afterwards I saw Harry Hyams again. This time I went to his beautiful offices in Cleveland Place close to St. James's Palace. Hanging on the wall he had the most beautiful Millais I have ever seen. Although I wasn't in love with him, I was very flattered by his attentions, and I let him make love to me on the large sofa beneath the Millais. He's such a romantic, that he talked about it for years.

CHAPTER TWENTY-SEVEN
Friends and Lovers

My twentieth birthday loomed up through a haze of misery and cocaine and heroin and lilies. Yes, lilies. In an ordinary week, I used to spend £50 filling the house with lilies. In a week with a party, it would be £100; and the whole place would be filled with white lilies and tiger-lilies, and the scent was overpowering. No need for incense. Rita had been advised of my birthday, and had brought in her sister Elena, and the tables were covered with food. It was a wonderful party. Most people were snorting themselves to death, and in the morning all the tables were covered with dust, and Rita couldn't understand why the dust was white instead of black.

The party had ended suddenly at five in the morning because everyone knew that I was going into hospital at nine to have my wisdom teeth removed. I am suffering the most terrible blues, even worse than the usual post-party blues, when suddenly almost everyone has gone, and I notice that Wishart is no longer lying on the sofa complaining about the Labour Party as he does the whole time.

When I look round, only two people are left: Ossie Clark and Nigel Waymouth. So, we've even managed to get rid of Litvinoff: through a window, probably! But the last thing I want just now is Ossie Clark hanging around, so I sit down next to Nigel and lean across him so that my breast is pressing against his arm and then look up and say weepily: "Please don't leave me alone, you're the only person I've got left. Stay with me, Nigel. Stay with me and take me to the hospital!"

Ossie takes the hint and leaves, and eventually good old Nigel takes me off to the Nuffield in Bryanston Square. I am smashed out of my gonk. I've been told not to eat or drink anything overnight, but that hasn't stopped me from taking pills or snorting cocaine, so I am absolutely as smashed as a trouper. On top of that come all these wonderful anaesthetics, so I drift into the operation in a fantastic state.

When I come to, my dentist John Powell is marvellous. "How are you, Nicky?" he asks.

"I'm in terrible pain", I say, lying through my remaining teeth. I'm not in any bloody pain at all. I just want some pain-killers.

He thinks for a moment.

"I expect you wouldn't object to some synthetic opium?"

"That would be wonderful", I say as weakly as I can.

So, I was on opium for the next three days. The result is that I don't remember much, except that the Nuffield were furious with me because I had so many visitors that they couldn't fit them all into my room. And then Christopher did the most extraordinary thing. Instead of sending me a bunch of flowers, he sent a complete rose-tree! This was too much for the Nuffield, who rejected it, and so far as I know it's still growing in the garden of Christopher's house in Cheyne Walk.

Ossie waited on me hand and foot, by the way; and when it was time for me to go home, he picked me up in his Rolls-Royce, which was grand. Rita welcomed me home but I went straight on to see David Hockney. Life was like that; and within twenty-four hours I was throwing yet another party.

※

Christopher hadn't had any luck with his rose-tree, but he did something much better when he introduced me at a party to Bruce Chatwin, who was never a lover of mine but became a very good friend. Bruce had once worked for Sotheby's but had then taken up writing and was now contributing brilliant articles to *The Sunday Times Magazine* for whom he travelled all over the world interviewing people like André Malraux and writing on subjects like the Great Wall of China He was 33 years old, but looked very much younger, and he was very kind and clever. He dressed a little eccentrically at times, but although he was homosexual, he was never what we used to call a camp queen.

He was lucky enough to be married to a sweet American wife called Elizabeth who totally understood him and would move heaven and earth on his behalf. She was happy for him to lead a largely separate life from her, and he depended upon her and loved her dearly. She herself doted upon him in the way that a mother might dote upon her child; and, coming from a wealthy family, she made it possible for him to write without having any financial worries. They had a house in Gloucestershire with a small farm attached: Elizabeth was a country girl at heart and loved talking about her cows; and I think there was a flat in London too, which Bruce sometimes used on his solitary visits to London; though he had numerous friends with whom he could stay, and he began coming to Mallord Street quite often, though I noticed that he went home to Elizabeth every week-end.

For some reason Bruce Chatwin and I always got on terribly well. I found that he enjoyed his reputation as a traveller, and was amused by the idea of everyone thinking that when he went on holiday, he took a rucksack and nothing else; but in practice he really enjoyed the good life, and liked being in a comfortable room. And although he may have teased me a great deal, once he told me something that outweighs all those teasing remarks, something that I still value greatly: "Oh, it's like you Nicky", he said. "As soon as you decide to do something you make sure you do it damned well!'

In mid-July 1973 there was a bombshell in the normally calm and reclusive atmosphere of Cheyne Walk. Paul Getty III, Paul's son by his first wife Gail, was kidnapped in the USA. Paul's father, who actually controlled most of the family money, refused to pay a ransom on principle, feeling that it would endanger his other grandchildren; and Paul was thrown into a state of serious depression.

Then in mid-August, Bruce Chatwin and I went on holiday together.

It happened like this. Bruce and I had gone together to a party given by Drue Heinz, the socialite and literary philanthropist; and we were sitting chatting about this and that when Mariga Guinness came over. I had known Mariga for some while: she had an aristocratic background, had been brought up partly in Norway and partly in Scotland, and at the age of 22 had married Desmond Guinness, with whom she had founded the Irish Georgian Society, but from whom she was now separated. She was also highly eccentric and used to call herself the Queen of Ireland, though she had no servants and was always pleading complete poverty. But I couldn't help liking her, and the food she cooked at her lunch parties in Islington was really very good. On this occasion, the first thing she said was: "'Would you two like to come to Norway?'

Almost in unison, we sang out: "Yes, we'd love to, Mariga"; and then Bruce added: "Can I bring my wife?"

"Yes, sure!" said Mariga, nodding her head slightly madly and wandering off again.

First, we flew to Oslo and spent a couple of nights there in an hotel, with Bruce sleeping in a single room on his own, while I shared a double room with Elizabeth. During the day, Bruce led us round the Viking Ship Museum and all the other tourist attractions.

"You remind me of Christopher more and more!" I said to him.

"How do you mean?" he asked, sounding quite flattered.

"You both want to do a little sight-seeing every day, or you feel you've been denied your daily fix! I swear that Christopher starts getting anxious if he doesn't see at least one church every day!"

Finally, we set off by train for Mariga's house which was somewhere beyond the very last stop on the line going north. It really was at the ends of the earth; and when we reached it, we also found that it was absolutely beautiful, like something out of Hansel and Gretel: a little wooden house on the side of a fiord with a couple of chalets for guests.

Mariga was living with Hugh O'Neill, son of the second Baron Rathcavan, and the two of them came out to greet us when we arrived. "Ah", said Mariga grandly, "it's Mr. Chatwin and Mrs. Waymouth!" She was going through a phase of referring to everyone in this very formal manner. Then she turned to Elizabeth and asked: "And who are you?" Bruce explained that she was his wife; but later that evening Mariga turned to me at the dinner-table and said in a dramatic stage-whisper: "I didn't ask that woman, that can't be Bruce's wife! All she talks about is cows!"

It was all highly sociable, and Bruce must have been enjoying himself, because each evening he said that he was about to set out alone on a walking holiday with only his rucksack for company, and each morning he stayed on.

Plenty of drinking went on, and I soon saw that when Norwegians start drinking, they go on until they're completely smashed. Which probably explains why drink in Norway is hard to get, and why our daily long-distance jaunts always ended up in some museum or other which may have contained very little of interest, but which had a shop nearby selling booze. It was on one of these jaunts that I bought a sledge at the side of the road, simply because there was a notice promising to post sledges to any country in the world, and I wanted to see whether it would ever get back to England.

Then one day a telegram arrived from one of Mariga's Irish relatives. It said that he and Nicholas Gormanston were coming to stay, but that they expected me to be gone when they arrived. I did overlap with Nicholas briefly, but it put me in an awkward situation, and I left as soon as possible saying that I could no longer stand the atmosphere. Not long after I got home, by the way, that sledge arrived. I gave it away to Dr. Rossdale.

To cheer myself up, I went down to the Cabbage Patch for the weekend. I had only been there about ten minutes when the telephone rang. I didn't feel like talking to anyone, but it went on and on, and in the end I picked up the receiver and found I was talking to Harry Hyams. All he said was: "Hello Nicky. I'm coming down."

"Pull the other one Harry", I said. "It's got bells on." And I found a book I had bought from Paul, a book with the most beautiful binding in the world, and I went out and lay on the lawn reading it and smoking a joint and feeling calmer and more peaceful than I had done for months.

But then Harry did arrive, driving one of his wonderful vintage cars; and soon we were spinning across the Sussex Downs, with my hair flowing in the wind. As usual with Harry it was all very romantic, and when we were back in my bedroom in the Cabbage Patch I allowed him to make love to me.

Unfortunately, he now seemed to believe that he owned me, and although he was very amusing and entertaining, he was also the most possessive man I had ever met. He would be on the telephone four or five times a day to make sure that I was doing what I said I'd be doing, to the ridiculous extent that if I had said I was going to the hairdressers, he'd ring them up to make sure that I was there.

This made my life extremely complicated, especially as I was still spending a great deal of time with Paul. Which meant incidentally that I was now going out with two of the richest men in London!

But although Paul and I were still close, the initial excitement was over, and spending time with him had become predictable and dull and even depressing. He was asleep most of the time, and when he was awake, he worried endlessly about his kidnapped son, of whom there was still no reliable news; and he talked endlessly about his first wife Gail, who was still alive; or about his second wife Talitha, who was dead; or about Victoria, who was still away in some remote part of the world. He'd also developed a mild crush on Bianca Jagger, to whom I'd introduced him. She would never have had an affair with him, but she was flattered by the attention.

✲

In September, John Stefanidis and Teddy Millington-Drake invited me to join them for a fortnight's holiday in Greece, where Teddy had bought a house on the island of Patmos. I heard that Loulou de La Falaise was going to be there, and that was a huge incentive, as I adored her and thought we would have a great time together. So, I packed all my flashiest St. Laurent dresses, and flew to Athens where I stayed at the Grande Bretagne. Patmos was hard to reach in those days: it meant either sailing there in a small boat, or taking a large ship which would spend all day getting there, and would probably make me frightfully seasick. "Is there no other way?" I asked the hotel-manager in despair.

"One can always take a helicopter, madam. I would be delighted to make all the arrangements."

I smiled at him sweetly – I really must have thought I was Christina Onassis – and a few hours later I was flying as the only passenger in a privately chartered helicopter high above the islands of the Cyclades to the far side of the blue Aegean. Patmos, only fifty miles from the Turkish coast, was a beautiful little Greek island with whitewashed houses. My arrival by helicopter caused quite a sensation – but so far as Teddy and John were concerned it was a great joke, and I never lived it down.

I found them living in a beautiful house at the top of the town. "We run a very strict helicopter – I mean ship!" said Teddy to me that evening, to general laughter. "You'll be sleeping in one of our guest-houses down below in the town. It's within walking distance – unless you want to fly there by helicopter!" More laughter.

"And our chief rule is this", chimed in John. "You must be at the car by 10.30 in the morning so that we can all go to the beach. The other rule is: you must keep your legs covered. This is the islanders' home, not ours, and we don't want to offend them."

"You mean this would offend them?" I asked innocently, wiggling my hips and unzipping my skirt and hurling it through the air as though I were about to start one of my strip-teases. I must admit that I was fairly smashed because I hadn't dared bring any heroin with me, and to avoid withdrawal symptoms I was drugged up to the eyeballs with Mandrax.

I was also feeling a little strange because although Loulou was there, she was accompanied by another girlfriend, who had known Loulou much longer than I had, and who was fashionably slim. "It's not your legs everyone's going to notice", said this other girl, pretending to cup enormous breasts with her hands – and so the other great joke that holiday was the size of my tits.

Apart from this teasing, which hurt me more than anyone realized, it was all quite good fun. I used to call it 'picnicking in Patmos', because every morning after breakfasting in our own houses we met by the mini-mokes at 10.30 with an enormous picnic, and were driven to the harbour. There we boarded a large motor-boat, and were given bull-shots with vodka and consommé while we raced over the water to whichever picnic place had been chosen for the day: sometimes Teddy and John's own private beach, which was very secluded and had its own beach-hut; sometimes a little cove with a tiny village and a beautiful Greek church somewhere nearby.

Towards the end of my fortnight, Loulou left to return to work; and then Lindy Dufferin arrived. Born Lindy Guinness, she had married Sheridan Dufferin nine years previously in 1964. Sheridan was a sweet, quiet, gentle man who was a friend of David Hockney and sometimes came to my parties at Mallord Street. He was also the fifth Marquess of Dufferin and Ava, and would sadly be the last, because he and Lindy were unable to have children. I say sadly, because he had a great gift for friendship; but he always looked as though things weren't quite right for him, and probably came to my house such a lot because it had turned into a meeting-place for gays, and Sheridan had a number of boyfriends as well as a wife. Lindy adored him, but allowed him to lead his own life when he wanted, rather as Elizabeth Chatwin did with Bruce.

I was a little alarmed by Lindy, because she had a very strong personality – she's a Grande Dame in her own right – and I didn't think she liked me very much: perhaps because her husband visited me so often, perhaps because she had had an affair with Harry Hyams years before, and may have been annoyed with me for being his current favourite. She was also an artist, who insisted on being up at four in the morning to see the sun rise, and would then walk up the hill to another house where Teddy had his studio, so that she could paint her watercolours there. Fortunately for me, she couldn't be too dominating during the brief time when we were both in Patmos together, because on her very first day she made the blunder of walking round the town in shorts, to the scandal of the villagers and the terrible indignation of both John and Teddy.

※

Not long after I returned to England, Victoria reappeared. Paul was now really quite ill, and he became worse when in mid-November the severed ear of his kidnapped son was sent to an American newspaper office. Eventually Paul's father paid the necessary ransom, and John Paul Getty III was released, minus his ear, in time for Christmas.

It was a very confusing time for me. Possibly, Victoria thought that I had moved a little further onto her territory than she had planned, because she began becoming extremely friendly with Bianca, who had been my friend first. However, the two of us had an amusing weekend down at Tony Lambton's home in Northumberland. The point was that Victoria and the Lambtons and the Londonderrys had been close friends since their days in Italy, and Victoria wanted to be present at the christening of Alastair Londonderry's first child by his second wife, who as Doreen Wells had been principal dancer at the Royal Ballet.

The christening was a hoot, because in one room were Doreen's friends, dozens of little ballet-dancers, none of them more than 4 foot 6 inches in their rabbit fur coats; and in another room were all the grand Londonderrys, none of them less than 6 foot; and neither group would talk to the other, though everyone was pretending to be deliriously happy.

I spent Christmas 1973 with Christopher Gibbs at Davington Priory, the beautiful country home just outside Faversham in Kent that he had bought from the Church of England the previous year. The Priory was physically attached to the church, and on my way down to breakfast I once opened the wrong door and found myself in the middle of a church service.

It was full of the most ravishing things but apart from the sitting-room (off which he had built a handsome library) it was never totally comfortable. The problem was that although Christopher had spent a vast amount of money in an effort to make Davington warm and livable, he simply didn't notice things like the beds being hard.

In many ways, Christopher's life continued to be thoroughly eccentric. Faversham was a substantial town, yet he called it the village; and it was only a five-minute walk away, yet he talked as though he was living in the heart of the countryside. In addition, the quality of the food on offer was almost as weird as it had been on our Moroccan trip, partly because he was employing as his chef a crazy man who could never produce anything on time.

On Christmas Eve I went with Christopher to midnight mass, and on Christmas Day I joined him in just one of the numerous services that he attended that day. David Litvinoff was in residence; Michael Wishart came for Christmas lunch, which was the usual turkey; and his business partner and close friend Peter Hinwood was there too.

When it was time to open our Christmas presents, I found that Paul Getty had given me a beautiful gold ram's necklace which had once belonged to Talitha; while Christopher's present turned out to be a pair of snakeskin gloves so large that they would have fitted a man, and a tourist drinking mug from Canterbury Cathedral. In the afternoon, we watched the Queen's Speech on television, the vicar came to tea, and there was Christmas cake. It was all very low-key, and the day was full of long silences.

On Boxing Day Mick and Bianca turned up, five hours late as usual. I enjoyed a long conversation with Bianca, who was frightfully proud of a lovely diamond bracelet that Mick had given her. In exchange I showed her the necklace given to me by Paul; and the following day I said goodbye to them all and drove away to Sussex.

The best part of my stay at Davington had been going walking with Christopher. He loves long rambling walks, and it was always wonderful walking with him, because his artistic sensibility is so acute that he would make me see things I would never normally have seen, and manage to convince me that a countryside of swamps and marshes was actually extremely beautiful.

After that first visit, I spent many weekends at Davington, arriving there on a Saturday afternoon and leaving just before lunch on Sunday, and fitting in at least two walks during my visit. Secretly I was always in love with Christopher, and I would dream about what it would be like being married to him. But I never said anything for fear of frightening him away.

※

One day early in January 1974 I was back in London having dinner with John Stefanidis at his place in Chester Square, when he said to me, completely out of the blue, "Oh, do you want to come to Mustique with me?"

"Well, sure, lovely, why not?" I replied. "I'll pay my own way of course!"

So, we flew out to the Caribbean, stopping off in Barbados at the famous Michael Tree Hotel, before catching a rickety-looking plane which took only an hour to reach Mustique.

The entire island, as everyone knows, was owned in those days by Catherine Tennant's brother Colin. Mustique was like his private kingdom; and it was he who had put up the only hotel, in which he was living while having a new house built for himself.

I had been anxious about seeing Colin again, because there had been an occasion when Catherine and I had turned up at the family's Scottish Estate on the very day when the BBC were there to do some filming. We shouldn't have been there, and Colin had lost his temper and been absolutely furious with us both.

Fortunately, he's the perfect English gentleman, and when I arrived with John, he was absolutely charming, and nothing was said about our earlier meeting. Indeed, by eleven o'clock on our first morning on Mustique John and I were sitting with Colin in the hotel bar when he said: "If you like, I'll take you both around the island."

Although nowhere on Mustique is more than a mile from anywhere else, and in ten minutes one could drive right round the entire island, Colin took us on a jaunt that lasted for almost three hours. By showing us everything on the island, including all the different beaches where we could swim, he somehow managed to make Mustique (which he evidently loved) seem enormous.

There were a number of large houses, most of which had been designed by Oliver Messel, and had stone lions and statues outside and looked like fantastic stage-sets, but it seemed odd to me to have so much grandeur on a tiny Caribbean island which doesn't even have any drinking water except what can be brought in by boat.

Colin had his own set of keys to the house of his friend Princess Margaret, which he opened up for us; but instead of being impressed by it, this had me in complete hysterics. The furnishings were absolutely frightful, and instead of having pictures on the walls, she had ostentatiously covered them with hundreds of the commemorative plates she had been given when on her official duties. And incidentally it was next to the most dangerous beach on the island.

The hotel was no larger than a moderate-sized house with a restaurant outside and a swimming-pool; but John and I were in a rather nice little apartment at some distance from the main building. We each had a large bedroom, a maid brought us breakfast at eight or nine in the morning; and then we would wander off to the beach with the picnic-lunch which had been made up for us. John and I were alone a good deal, and he teased me a great deal; but it was all very affectionate. He didn't seem to mind the fact that I was stoned most of the time; and one day we went out in a boat to see the remains of an ancient wreck, a wonderful old sunken ship of which at low tide one could see the remnants sticking up above the waves.

There were horses on Mustique: so in the evenings I sometimes went riding. Afterwards a large black man called Basil might organise a barbecue on the beach, where there was a bar by a little jetty that ran out into the sea. Or we might go to dinner with some of John's friends, in whose company I met the publisher Andre Deutsch, who had known my father; and Bryan Ferry, who was very good-looking, but so self-opinionated that I found him a total bore. Fortunately, Bryan was then going out with Gaylor, who had once been one of Ossie Clark's models; and I thoroughly enjoyed talking to her, because she was part of a world into which I fitted better than into the self-styled Mustique aristocracy.

And then after ten days or so of this pleasant holiday jaunt, John announced that he had to return to Europe. So I said: "All right. In that case, as it's January, I think I'll go to New York."

"Just ring up Maxime", said John, "and that's your New York social calendar arranged."

So that was exactly what I did.

CHAPTER TWENTY-EIGHT
Andy Warhol and his set

Almost as soon as I had reached New York, which I did on 12 February 1974, I found that my interview in *Women's Wear Daily* the previous year had made me highly desirable to the Andy Warhol set. Andy himself had been worried by my admission that I had taken drugs, but couldn't resist the fact that I was said to be an heiress; while Bob Colacello and Fred Hughes (Andy's business manager) were practically baying at my feet with excitement.

Fred began asking me out to dinners at which Andy would be present, mostly at Maxime's; and one evening, when he and Andy were conspicuous by their absence, I asked my fellow-guest John Richardson about them.

"Didn't Fred tell you?" he asked in some surprise. "He's already gone on ahead to Paris. You know Andy's got an exhibition opening there on the 22nd – his Mao-Tse-Tung pictures. Several of us are going – why don't you join us?"

"It sounds great, but would I be welcome?"

"As it happens, I've already talked it over with Andy. He's happy and you'll have a lot of fun. Bob's going, so is Paloma. We should have a ball."

Paloma was Paloma Picasso, daughter of the artist and another of the Warhol set whom I'd begun seeing. She had a classically beautiful though at that time very unfashionable figure, and a stunning face on which she wore fairly heavy eye-make-up around her dark eyes, and the reddest lipstick imaginable on her lips. She also wore a good deal of jewellery, most of it designed by herself; and she always looked so stunning that although Yves Laurent gave her lots of his clothes to wear, she could get away with attending some grand function in a second-hand ball-gown bought from a thrift shop, and still look absolutely fabulous.

Paloma was indeed a great deal of fun, and when I told her that I was coming with them on the plane to Paris, she and I decided that we would dress for dinner, which for anyone travelling first-class was in a special upstairs cabin. That was all right for the two of us and for Andy, John Richardson and David Whitney the art curator, another close friend of Andy's who was in our party; but not for Bob Colacello, who was the only one of us flying second-class. Andy (who had been too mean to pay for Bob to travel first-class) egged on Paloma to tell the stewardess that Bob was her fiancée, and to beg her to allow him to come through to dine with us; but she wouldn't bend the rules, so we had a very boisterous dinner without him.

After dinner, Andy very wisely disowned us all and went downstairs to sleep. The rest of us stayed upstairs; and it was only at about five or six in the morning, when we were about to land at Le Bourget, that we all realised how tired we were; so, David gave us some B-12 vitamin pills to give us a boost: though in my case they simply made me turn bright red, which reminded me of my schooldays.

Fred Hughes was waiting at the airport to greet us, and he quickly shooed Andy and Bob into a waiting taxi and drove off, leaving the rest of us to fend for ourselves. Paloma, who lived in Paris, simply went home. John was staying with a very old and nearly blind friend of his, Virginia Chambers, a great lady who was poor but extremely stylish, and who had a wonderful apartment in the palatial seventeenth-century Palais Lambert in the heart of the city on the Île Saint Louis. When we had dropped him off, we followed Andy and Bob and Fred to the Hotel Crillon where they had an enormous suite, and where David and I booked ourselves into rather more modest rooms.

It was a wonderful time. Every day began with a champagne breakfast, and there were numerous lunch-parties and dinner-parties. One lunch was given by Yves St. Laurent, where the party included the usual members of his inner circle: Pierre Bergé, Loulou de La Falaise, and Thadee Klossowski de Rola with his girlfriend Clara. Having met them all through Bill Willis, I felt perfectly at ease – in fact I knew them much better than Andy and his entourage. I sat next to Andy on this occasion, and we talked a great deal. Or rather, I talked and Andy listened. He always seemed far more interested in what I could tell him than in ever telling me anything about himself.

We were also invited to several lunches at the Palais Lambert. This was owned but not yet occupied by Baron Guy and Marie-Hélène Rothschild; and they joined us in the huge apartment of the Baron Alexis de Redé, where we ate off gold plates with gold cutlery and had footmen waiting behind every other chair. It was undeniably impressive, but very ostentatious; and I much preferred a simple lunch given in the same building by Virginia Chambers, who offered us only two courses, one of which consisted chiefly of poached eggs.

On other days there were drinks with São Schlumberger, wealthy wife of a disabled oil-equipment magnate. She and her husband Pierre lived near the Luxembourg gardens in a house filled with wonderful pictures, among which Andy's portrait of her was given pride-of-place.

We also visited Douglas Cooper, an elderly homosexual with whom John Richardson had once lived for ten years, and who owned not only the most amazing collections of Impressionist Art that I have ever seen in private hands, but also a splendid collection of books – in which context he claimed to remember my father. Other than that, I chiefly remember him for his fund of malicious stories.

At night we would usually dine at Maxim's, and then some of us would go on to Club Sept, the fashionable Parisian night club of the time.

One evening, however, I felt I needed a break from this close-knit society and in any case, I was longing to see my Godfather Jean-Francois Bergery. So I called him, and he came to my hotel and took me out to a restaurant for dinner. For once, he didn't have his girlfriend Catrine in tow, so I had the best conversation with him that I had ever had in my life, though he reproved me in a somewhat godfatherly manner for leading a very shallow life as one of Warhol's camp-followers. I smiled and took no notice: I was enjoying myself too much.

Afterwards, we went back to the Crillon, and we had hardly reached my room before Bob and Andy were on the phone asking me what I was doing, and why didn't I join them with my Godfather? Andy hated anyone in his circle to be up to something he didn't know about, especially if it was with someone who might be important but whom he hadn't met.

We didn't join them; and then one of my childhood dreams came true, and Jean-Francois and I took each other to bed. It was one of the best experiences I have ever had with a man, partly because I hero-worshipped Jean-Francois and partly because of his close links with my father. After we had made love, Jean-Francois confessed that when he was visiting London as a seventeen-year-old schoolboy, it was my father who had introduced him to sex, by producing a beautiful professional prostitute at a flat he owned in Mayfair.

"Was it a good experience?" I asked.

He smiled. "My dear Nicky, it was a long time ago; but it must have been quite good. We managed to break the bed!"

My own evening with him had been perfect: sexual and very loving, but with no strings attached. Not that I didn't secretly long for those strings; but sadly, I only saw Jean Francois once more after that, and then it was at a large dinner at which both Catrine and their children were present.

Finally, Andy's exhibition of the Mao pictures had its grand opening and there was a large party afterwards at the Crillon. Loulou lent me a dress from Yves, one of the ones that was kept in the archives. It was beautiful: shimmering black with silver threads, very twenties, but shorter. The evening was fun, and as usual we went dancing at the Club Sept afterwards. The next day I returned to London and the others went back to New York.

However, I kept in close touch with the Warhol circle, because Fred Hughes started coming to stay with me whenever he was in London, and we became close friends. He was a marvellous house-guest, because he had beautiful manners and always came bearing gifts, not only for me but also for Rita, who grew to adore him almost as much as she adored Christopher. Fred always made me laugh; and he knew exactly what I needed from him: he loved to be close to me and to give me a cuddle in bed, but he never pressed for more and then at just the right moment he would discreetly return to his own room to sleep alone.

In April I travelled again to the Stanhope in New York, where I was beginning to enjoy myself much more than I usually did in London. I remember in particular one dinner at La Côte Basque when my blind date for the night was the famous viola player Michael Tree, while John Richardson was escorting the elderly Loelia Lindsay, who had once been the Duchess of Westminster.

I was wearing a very complicated Ossie Clark cream silk suit. The skirt was cut like a lily, and the top was a jacket with thousands of tiny little buttons all the way down. It took half an hour to get into and half an hour to get out of. Unfortunately, when I disappeared to the ladies half way through dinner for my normal snort of cocaine, I noticed that one of these buttons had broken, and I was too stoned to cope. At first, I was simply anxious that one of my tits might be showing; but then for the next half-hour every stranger who came into the ladies was greeted with my despairing cry of: "Which tit's bigger, the left tit or the right tit?" As my cries penetrated beyond the intimacy of the ladies' loo, some of the restaurant staff came to see what on earth was going on. And then, just when a minor riot seemed about to break out, I reappeared at the dinner-table as if absolutely nothing had happened, and I couldn't for the life of me understand why half the people in the dining-room were smiling at me, while the other half were looking distinctly cross.

It was on this trip to New York that I met Jan Radziwill. He was the very good-looking son of John Richardson's friend Grace, Countess of Dudley, by her first husband Prince 'Stash' Radziwill, a Polish nobleman; and we started spending time together. Jan did have a girlfriend whom he later married, and whom his stepmother Lee Radziwill much preferred to me, but they were having a break from each other.

One evening, I was at the Stanhope when Jan rang me up and said: "Can you be ready for dinner at 8.30? We're going to dine at La Côte Basque with the Duchess of Windsor."

I just burst out laughing, thinking he was joking, and put the receiver down. Then I thought I would check it out with John Richardson, so I rang him and said: "Look, Jan Radziwill's just rung me and told me we're having dinner with the Duchess of Windsor."

"Yes, that's right," he said calmly. "Are you coming?"

"Yes, apparently I am!"

"Oh God how exciting! You'll make the evening go off with a bang!"

I still didn't really believe it was true; but two hours later I found myself sitting next to the Duchess of Windsor, who turned out to be Grace Dudley's best friend.

Sadly, she was also elderly, and pretty gaga. There we were sitting in the middle of a well-known New York restaurant, when about halfway through the evening she suddenly burst out with: "Oh, what a lovely house this is, and the servants are so well trained!" She was perfectly friendly to me, but all she could talk about was her dogs, and I remember her showing me the wonderful bracelet she was wearing, to which were attached numerous little charms of her various pugs.

It was a curious occasion altogether. For one thing, the President's daughter Tricia Nixon came to have dinner in the same restaurant, so there were bodyguards everywhere. And by a strange coincidence, Christopher Gibbs was also in New York and he too was dining at the La Côte Basque. I'll never forget the moment when Christopher came over to our table and knelt at the Duchess of Windsor's feet, quite overcome by the sheer honour of meeting her. As for me: I was so young and naïve that I took it all rather casually, not realising what a unique occasion this was. Indeed, it may have been one of the last meals the Duchess ever ate in public.

※

At this time, I was also seeing something of Kenny Jay Lane, with whom I was becoming more and more besotted. He in his turn obviously liked me, inviting me to his house for lunch, and even occasionally taking me out in the evenings.

Not that I always pleased him, because I am afraid that when it came to Ken I was often like a child, one who was hoping to be offered a golden egg. His lifestyle was so elegant that it was just what I had always wanted for myself. However, I managed to arrange for Kenny to be given some valuable publicity in the British edition of *Vogue*. It happened like this: a woman from their New York office with a heavy southern accent rang me at the Stanhope and asked: "How much longer will you be stayin' over here, Mrs. Waymouth?"

"I don't know", I replied. "Another week, perhaps two. It all depends."

"We wondered whether you'd consider doin' a spread for us?"

"Sure, but can I choose the photographer?"

"Well… Okay, darlin, but who do you want?"

"Eric Boman", I said.

"Sure, if that ain't just who we wanted to do it for you anyhow! He's on his way over from the United Kingdom in two days."

"The other thing is", I added, "I must be allowed to choose what I wear, and where the photographs are taken."

There was a long pause, and then the woman said: "Okay, honey, just so long as the clothes are all by American designers".

Eric Boman took some brilliant pictures of me: one of them at the Met; one in the Quo Vadis restaurant with Jed Johnson, Andy Warhol's live-in boyfriend; one at the Stanhope, with some goldfish that were the same colour as my hair; and, most important of all, one with Ken and me in Ken's house. I had insisted on this, and he was very pleased, because he wasn't nearly as well known in England as he was in New York, and appearing in British Vogue would be extremely good publicity for him.

As a slight tease I presented Kenny with the goldfish, for which we had had a huge amount of trouble persuading Vogue to pay; and there was something about the manner of his acceptance which suggested that our relationship was becoming more significant.

By this time, he had already introduced me to his elderly friend Diana Vreeland. Like other elderly New York widows, Diana needed an occasional 'walker', as they called single men, often homosexual, who would escort them out in the evenings, and later I realized that Kenny J. Lane had fitted the bill admirably.

Diana herself was a remarkable woman who had been editor-in-chief of *Vogue* for eight years, before being sacked in 1971 and moving on to the Metropolitan Museum of Art. There she became a consultant to its Costume Institute, and put on the most wonderful exhibitions of clothes by fashion designers like Cristóbal Balenciaga, with informative historical notes. She once gave me some of the wonderful red material, almost unobtainable, from which tunics are made up for the guards at Buckingham Palace, and which Tommy Nutter used to make a jacket for me.

Diana didn't have much money, and her apartment was very small, but she lived tremendously well; and she started inviting me to come alone to her apartment for dinner. Gradually, she became a confidante of mine. After doing the photographs for *Vogue*, I told her how much Ken was beginning to mean to me, and she said in a very American manner: "Oh darrling how wonderful! He's such a good man!"

Apart from all these dinners with Maxime de la Falaise, Jan Radziwill, John Richardson and Ken Lane, and occasional lunches with Diana Vreeland, Bob Colacello and Fred Hughes were still taking a keen interest in me: so life was highly sociable. Paloma was in New York again, and we would often see each other with the rest of the Warhol gang, sometimes at dinners with Bob Colacello's friend Adriana Jackson, whose husband Brooks had helped to give Andy Warhol his first gallery show back in 1952; and sometimes at dinners with Andy at the Quo Vadis.

I also joined Andy and Fred in occasional outings to the Iranian Embassy. In those pre-revolutionary days, with the Shah of Iran still in power, we were royally entertained. Mountains of caviar were served both before and during dinner, at which Andy was always the star of the occasion though I noticed that he said (if anything) less than ever.

My association with the Warhol set wasn't all fun. Andy had a passion for early American furniture, and Jed Johnson had a very good eye. So Jed and Fred and I, usually joined by Paloma, were expected to do a great deal of travelling round Washington and Pennsylvania and other places looking for furniture.

※

Then in June 1974, when I had been back in England for a few weeks, Fred Hughes rang me up and asked me to join him, Andy, Bob and Paloma on a trip to Italy. "Do come with us", he pleaded. "We're off to Boissano." I thought it sounded great. Ken was still stuck in New York, and almost the only communication I had with him was through his servant Mustafa, who used to ring me up from time to time to tell me solemnly that another of the goldfish had died. So why not show my independence with a journey to Italy, in the company of one of the most famous artists of the day?

"Where do I meet you?" I asked Fred.

"Andy and I have got an apartment in Paris now", he told me. "It's still being done up, but it'll do for a night. So, fly out and join us here on Wednesday. Give me your flight number, and I'll pick you up at the airport."

So I flew to Paris and then the next morning the four of us flew south to Monte Carlo where we had a frightfully grand breakfast with someone whom Andy was hoping to paint, before being driven to Boissano.

This was a little town about an hour from Monte Carlo, just over the Italian border. Some Swiss art gallery with whom Andy dealt, had discovered that if they set up and ran an art college, they could reclaim a great deal of the tax which they were currently paying on their imports and exports. But it was all a scam. There were no students and no real art collage, just a ramshackle collection of buildings not far from Boissano on the side of a hill just above the motorway. Andy had been invited along to their so-called grand opening to lend a spurious credibility to their project. His presence was quite enough to guarantee plenty of favourable publicity; and having Picasso's daughter in the offing made it even better for the reporters and photographers.

In the meantime, we weren't being properly looked after. We were used to champagne and caviar, and we were eating really badly. We were used to the best hotels, yet Paloma and I were sharing a dormitory which had eight beds in it, and one shower. Andy himself was in another room with a single tin bed.

Fred, having taken one look at this place, had immediately recalled that he still had very important business in Monte Carlo and decamped. So the rest of us were stuck in this dreadful place. Andy would appear at meals and complain that he even had to wash his own underpants and change his own wig.

It was at that point that Andy Warhol admitted to me that he couldn't paint to save his life. "I don't really know how to paint anything", he told me. "And I never learned how to draw." There may have been some truth in this: he certainly couldn't draw a decent map of England when I asked him. But he was a consummate businessman.

Andy also had a gift for getting people to tell him anything he wanted to know; and so long as I was talking either about sex or about someone famous, he became totally fascinated and absorbed. He was particularly driven by wanting to know precisely what you had done in bed with someone and what it felt like. "Nicky, what size was his prick?" he would whisper to me greedily. "What size were her nipples when they were erect? What colour was her hair? What did it feel like when you were sucking her cunt?"

In his own everyday life, he appeared to be almost unbelievably shy and reserved. Sometimes he would hold my hand; but when he kissed me it was only on the cheek, and he didn't seem to like being touched. He was also totally impractical. He was always complaining about the marmalade at breakfast and I sometimes wondered whether he could even have made a cup of tea for himself.

During the day, it was almost like being back in school, because we were kept in like prisoners, on the off-chance that someone might be turning up to interview Andy. In the evenings Paloma and I would play truant, sneaking out and then driving off to Genoa in a car which Paloma had acquired. Once in Genoa we went to some quite low dives just for the hell of it. Later on, we sometimes took Bob down to Boissano. It was a real dump, but we made the best of it: the evenings were warm and we went dancing at the out-door night-clubs.

After five or six days, Fred reappeared looking guilty and sheepish because he hadn't been in touch with us at all, and he must have known what a terrible time we had been having. In any case he brought us the most incredibly lavish gifts, and added: "It's all right, you know. We're leaving for Monte Carlo tomorrow. It's all arranged".

At Monte Carlo, Fred put us up in a private annex to the Hotel de Paris. Andy had soon become fascinated by some frightfully rich young boy and made me have an affair with him. At night Andy would ring my room to ask if the young man was there; and the next morning he would want me to give him a blow by blow, suck by suck account of our lovemaking.

Andy also introduced me to Truman Capote, who scared me. I began by having long conversations with him, and found that he had an extraordinarily good memory combined with a very malicious streak. This meant that he forgot nothing I said, and would then give it a nasty twist when he repeated it to others. It was as though he could only find relief from his deep-seated anxieties by being thoroughly cruel.

Finally, we returned to Paris, where I checked into an hotel for a night before flying back to London in time for my 23rd birthday.

CHAPTER TWENTY-NINE
Kenny Jay Lane

"So, you were the person who bought that painting!" Kenny Jay Lane was so surprised that he almost fell over. He and I were in Mallord Street, standing together in the gallery to the balcony, and he had just come face to face with my vast Jean-Joseph Benjamin-Constant painting of a tiger. "I wanted it", he went on, a little breathlessly; "and when I went to the Shepherd Gallery in New York they said a young English girl had bought it!" At this point, something so extraordinary happened that after our wedding we would joke that our marriage had been a marriage of two people with a painting between them. "May I buy it from you?" he added.

"No", I replied flirtatiously. "But should we ever marry, then you can have it!"

It was July 1974, Ken had come over from New York at last, and was visiting me for the very first time. After this incident with the Benjamin-Constant we became much closer, and began seeing each other daily. Then he announced that before returning to New York, he would be visiting Athens for a short holiday: would I care to join him there?

I agreed; but first, I told him, I would be going to Paris for the Summer Collections. This turned out to be a big mistake. When I arrived back in England one Friday afternoon holding a brand-new hat box marked 'Yves St. Laurent', I very foolishly went through the passage marked 'Nothing To Declare'. I should have known better; but I was in a hurry and I had become used to ignoring authority. A customs official took one look and pounced. Everything of mine was searched; and once he and his colleagues had found some new clothes designed by Yves, they insisted on coming back with me to Mallord Street.

When we arrived, I rushed in shouting: "Rita, I'm home!" and before they knew what was happening, I had dashed straight upstairs and thrown all the cocaine I had in the house straight out of the window. More's the pity, as they weren't after the drugs!

Methodically they went through my drawers and cupboards, seizing every item of clothing with a foreign designer's label. Most of them had been bought in England, but I had kept no receipts, so was unable to prove that they too hadn't been smuggled in.

In desperation I rang Arnold, who calmly told me there was nothing one could do with Customs and Excise: they had different powers from the police; and I must put it down to bad luck and let them seize whatever they wanted. By the time I had to even take off the clothes I was wearing, in front of a customs lady, I was weeping copiously; and the upshot was that I lost most of my clothes and had to pay a huge fine of around £3,000.

My luck had certainly been at a low ebb that day. While the customs people were with me, Jan Radziwill had telephoned asking me to have dinner with his mother, and I had declined. Then a little later, Harry Hyams had asked me out and I had agreed; but as soon as we had sat down for dinner at Prunier, which I loved because it was always so dark, there at another table very close by, I saw Jan and Grace.

※

By the time I had reached the reception desk of the Grand Britannia Hotel in Athens, all my troubles were forgotten and I was feeling ridiculously happy at the thought of Ken and me being two lovers on holiday in Athens. I asked the reception clerk for the number of Mr. Lane's room, and she looked in her book. "Mr. Lane – he is in the blue suite." She picked up an internal telephone. "But I must tell him you are coming. Your name, please?"

"Mrs. Waymouth", I said, my heart leaping with excitement at the thought of sharing a suite with Ken.

"Ah, Mrs. Waymouth." She put the telephone down again. "Mr. Lane, he has booked you into room 403." She beckoned to a porter. "Aristotle, take Mrs. Waymouth's cases up to her room." She turned to me again. "You will find the blue suite on the second floor."

It was disappointing to be taken up to a single room so small that there was hardly room for all the baggage I had brought with me. But the main thing, I told myself, was that in a few minutes I would be with Ken. I showered, changed into something light and I hoped appealing, took some Mandrax to make sure that I would be just high enough to be amusing, and more or less ran down to the blue suite two floors below.

When I knocked on the door, there was no answer. I tried the handle. It was open. I walked in joyfully. "Ken!" I called out. "It's me!"

"We're in here!"

I dashed into the bedroom, and there was Ken lying in a large double-bed with his arm around a boy of about sixteen.

"Hi Nicky! It's really good to see you! Oh, this is Andreas."

"Hello, Andreas", I said, feeling both nervous and surprised but also excited. "Would you boys like to come and undress me?"

"You go", said Ken to Andreas. "Come back and join me when you're ready!"

Andreas got out of bed. He was absolutely naked, and although he was young, he had a prick which was enormous even when limp. He came over to me and put his hands on my tits. He was very close to me, and I could feel his prick hardening against me. Then he pulled my pants down and pushed me onto the bed. God, I was so moist. His huge prick slid into me and he began pumping away and then Ken was behind him, and screwing him up the bum.

A little later Ken gave Andreas a few drachmas and he left. Ken turned to me. "Thank you darling", he said, and began kissing my tits and running his fingers over my pussy. I put my hand on his prick, which had soon sprung to attention again. And then, bliss oh bliss, Ken was inside me and taking me, and I soared up into a region of joy.

By a coincidence Fred Hughes was also staying in the hotel; and that evening the three of us went out to dinner on the Plaka Steps where there were numerous out-door restaurants. By another coincidence, we bumped into Dickie Kriss, with whom I had enjoyed such a lovely holiday in Corfu only two years ago, and I am sorry to say that I was so proud of being with Ken that I treated Dickie in a very off-hand manner.

I should have known who my real friends were. It was already clear that Ken's sole reason for coming to Athens was to be able to pick up boys; and I was there to help him, because it was so much easier to attract the straight young boys he preferred when you had a pretty girl who was prepared to come on to them. But I was so besotted by Ken that I would do anything for him if I felt that it would make him love me more.

During the late afternoons, we would behave like normal tourists, going round and seeing the sights. Then, after much dancing and drinking, the nights would be spent back in the hotel in Ken's large suite, where our meetings with the young boys I had picked up followed an invariable pattern. I would fuck them for Ken; then he would join in; and then he would be wonderfully loving to me, which was all I wanted.

I didn't want to see how I was being used by Ken, who could do no wrong in my eyes, so I took more and more Mandrax, and after a couple of days it was only by being completely stoned that I could face yet another horny young Greek in Ken's bed. Soon I had had everything, including their pricks up my ass; and sometimes Ken wanted me to lure two or three of them a time into his bed. It was very exhausting physically and mentally; but although part of me hated it, part of me thought anything was worthwhile just for Ken to finally make love to me, which he usually did at the end, though increasingly often while the young men were still there to watch.

Finally, Ken would throw them out. We would talk a little, then he would throw me out too – or rather he would say: "That's that. Let's get some sleep. See you tomorrow." So I would go to my room, not knowing whether to laugh or cry, barely able to sleep, but knowing that at least he wanted me around.

After only four or five days – it had seemed much longer – we flew back to London.

The next morning, we both felt very tired, but Ken insisted on our driving down to Sudeley Castle in the Cotswolds, where his old friend Liz Dent-Brocklehurst had invited us for the weekend. We were put in separate rooms, and everything was extremely well-behaved and very English, with a fine display of country house manners.

On the Saturday evening, still feeling utterly exhausted, but buoyed up (in my case) by Mandrax and cocaine, we went over to Warwick Castle for dinner with Lord Brooke, a very old friend of Ken's, and the son and heir of the Earl of Warwick who owned the Castle. There were a great many people there, including Nicky Haslam; and a few days later Ken flew back to New York.

※

My London life was now in a state of turmoil. Rita had decided that she had had enough, and wanted to retire to Portugal. As for me: I was no longer interested in my London entertaining, having felt lonely too often in Mallord Street, so I was planning to sell it, and buy from Christopher Gibbs the lease on his flat at Lindsey House, 100 Cheyne Walk. This was the most wonderful apartment in London. Whistler was reputed to have painted there, and it included a great deal of wood, especially round the fireplaces, which had been carved by the great Grinling Gibbons.

About six weeks after Ken's departure, I followed him to New York where I stayed, as usual, at the Stanhope. This time Ken was definitely the chief reason for my being in New York; and in retrospect I suppose that this was when I should have taken more notice of the way in which he lived; and realised that he liked me so much largely because I seemed to be happy to join in with and support his gay lifestyle. After a while it became rather boring: the only element of excitement being that at the end of the evening I was usually able to sleep with Ken; and occasionally I was even allowed to stay the night, once the boys had been sent away.

I wasn't in New York for long on this occasion, but I did my normal social round, seeing a great deal of Fred Hughes, Bob Colacello, Maxime McKendry and John Richardson.

Back in England, I had a brief three-night affair with Henry Pembroke. He was very good-looking, suave, debonair, kind, an Earl and safely married. When I told him that I was moving out of Mallord Street into somewhere smaller, he bought a good deal of furniture from me, including a wonderful big sofa which had been the setting for many of my most exciting sexual adventures.

I also saw something of the fabulous dress designer Zandra Rhodes. I could telephone her at her home, say: "Zandra, I want a dress for a dinner-party I'm going to next week", and she'd turn up the following afternoon with her hair dyed green or purple, in a complete flap and in the throes of artistic creation. It's not very common to find a woman who wants to make other women look beautiful, but she created the most stunning clothes in her studio in Notting Hill Gate, and although she always liked to appear to be totally off the wall, she had a very sound business sense.

※

Then towards the end of 1974 I returned once again to New York, which was now the centre of all my hopes and fears. Ken had asked me to go with him to South America for Christmas; but that somehow fell through, and then Ken succumbed to a severe dose of influenza, and was ill in bed over Christmas.

I was still spending a good deal of time with Andy Warhol and his circle; with the result that I found myself celebrating New Year's Eve with Rudolf Nureyev. The point was that Baryshnikov had recently come over from Russia, and some of us had gone with Nureyev to watch him dance. Nureyev was in a frightfully bad mood afterwards, because he had recognised Baryshnikov's brilliance. Then I found that we had something in common: I knew Paul Getty intimately, and he was still carrying a torch for Paul's second wife Talitha. "She was the most beautiful woman I have ever met", he enthused, not very tactfully. "I loved her so much – I never stop thinking about her."

When Ken had recovered from his 'flu, we went off to a cottage in Connecticut with Ken's current boyfriend, an incredibly good-looking and extremely tough taxi-driver known as Baby. However, Ken and I were sharing a bed, while Baby was exiled to another part of the cottage, and gradually Baby became more and more upset by this arrangement. Finally, there was a dreadful row which ended with Baby storming off, taking the car with him.

To make matters worse, we then had a heavy fall of Connecticut snow. The telephone lines went down, and we were snowed in. Our only adventure lay in walking across to the big house, owned by Diane von Fürstenberg, the fashion designer from whom Ken was renting the cottage. There we played scrabble together; and it was there that Ken suddenly asked:

"Do you want to marry me?

And I said "Yes, sure!"

That's how it all happened. I wondered later on whether Baby's departure had been cleverly stage-managed, but at the time I was head-over-heels and couldn't believe my luck. The next day we spent making plans, and at one point Ken asked me exactly how much money I had. I think he was slightly shocked that I wasn't as rich as he thought I was, but he passed it off with a joke.

Then we went back to New York, our engagement was announced in the papers the very next day, and we decided to get married in London the following month.

CHAPTER THIRTY
A Cabinet of Skulls

I went on ahead to arrange everything. I stayed at Blake's Hotel, because I'd sold Mallord Street, and my new apartment in Cheyne Walk was still being done up by the interior decorator David Mlinaric.

Our wedding day was on 17 February 1975; we were married at Caxton Hall Registry Office in London with Lord Brooke as our Best Man, and Elaine Kaufman of the New York restaurant Elaine's as our Matron of Honour; and then there was a massive reception.

I had very much wanted Ken to meet Paul Getty. Naturally enough, he wouldn't come either to the wedding or to the reception; but on our wedding night we partied until about two in the morning, and then, since it was roughly Paul's getting-up time, I said to Ken: "Let's go round and see Paul." It was rather a touching meeting, because Paul seemed to be genuinely pleased about our marriage, and he even found an American beer-jug which he presented to Ken as a wedding present.

When Paul retreated into his den, it was the first time that Ken and I had been left alone all day, so I said "Oh come upstairs to the bedroom, Ken", and we made love for the first time as a married couple and it was really wonderful. However, we then had to return to Blake's Hotel, where Ken's latest boyfriend was waiting for us, and that was not wonderful at all.

The following day we rushed off to Paris for our honeymoon, taking Elaine Kaufman with us. We stayed with her in an extraordinary suite in the Crillon Hotel, where I had a touch of food-poisoning, and had to spend a day in bed, though I was soon well enough to share a sexual scene with Ken and some boy whom he had picked up.

Back in New York, we were wined, dined and fêted everywhere, not only by people I knew well, like Maxime de la Falaise and John Richardson, but also by Ken's wealthy friends whom I hardly knew at all, the cream of New York Society, the Heinzes, the Paleys, the Fürstenbergs, Kitty Miller, the Erteguns, the whole bloody lot. I was also subjected to a strange Greek orthodox wedding-blessing ceremony which was held in a singles bar and went on well into the night.

※

Now, I had to settle down to living in Ken's very grand house on Park Avenue and East 38th Street. To my surprise this wasn't at all easy. I had assumed that because it was such a wonderful house, it would be difficult not to be happy within its walls. Events proved me wrong. For one thing, I had completely lost my independence. For another, I had lost the services of the wonderful Rita. It had been arranged that the wife of Ken's Moroccan manservant Mustafa should take her place, but this was impossible because not only was she monumentally lazy, but she spoke not a word of English.

The plan was that in due course the top two floors should become mine. Ken had never lived in them, reserving them for his driver and his secretary, who had both been expelled without anything being done to convert them for my use. As for the lower floors: now that I was living in them, they felt more like a museum than a home; but because Ken had been there for ten or twenty years, he insisted that almost nothing should be altered.

I did manage to persuade him to sell two dreadful modern sculptures in the hall. They were of women's busts with black leather zips down them. Fortunately, I had given him the Benjamin-Constant tiger by then, so that was able to go into the hall in their place. But everything else was Ken's, and everything else was sacrosanct.

Worst of all was our bedroom. It should have been a safe haven away from the rest of the world, somewhere warm and welcoming. Instead, it was full of exhibits, and right next to my side of the bed was a glass cabinet with the most sinister exhibits of all: a collection of shrunken human skulls. I hated waking up next to them, but it turned out that Ken had a mania for skulls, and these were his pride and joy.

With very few of my own things around me, my sense of personal identity and my emotional stability both began to weaken, and I became more and more dependent upon Ken. To make matters worse, I learned for the first time that he was in considerable financial difficulties. His core business, costume jewellery, wasn't as fashionable as it had been; and in an effort to diversify his way out of trouble, he'd made some bad business decisions. He'd gone into watches, he'd gone into making sheets and shirts, he'd started dealing in franchises, and none of these ventures was profitable. Almost every week he seemed to have trouble paying the wages, and almost every week I found myself being expected to write out large cheques simply to keep things going, though Ken told me that these difficulties were only a passing phase, and that I was investing in our future.

Another difficulty was that although I had been taking heroin on and off for more than a year, I had no American supplier; so I relied heavily on Mandrax pills of which I had a considerable store. Ken knew that I took cocaine, and would occasionally have some himself; but I had managed to keep the Mandrax a secret from him; and since in itself it was never quite enough, I also started drinking far more heavily than I had ever done before. Fortunately, Ken didn't notice this, because he drank fairly heavily himself; and it helped me to get through the days.

These days were often long and exhausting. It wasn't just that there were endless parties – I was used to that; but I couldn't relax as I had done in London. I was constantly on display as a model for Ken's jewellery, so I always had to look my very best; and I also had to be extremely careful what I said at the dinner table, because all our social doings were reported minutely in *Women's Wear Daily*.

I was also feeling lonely, because despite all the partying, Ken's friends were twenty years older than me, and now that I was moving in such high society, the younger friends that I'd made when I was part of the Andy Warhol set were neither valued nor welcomed by Ken, and so faded out of my life almost completely. I could still talk freely to John Richardson and to

Maxime de la Falaise; but they too were much older than me, and Maxime herself was very unhappy since the death of her husband earlier in the year.

I did make one real friend of my own age, Delfina Ratazzi, the daughter of Ken's wealthy friend Susanna, or 'Sunni' Agnelli. Delfina, who was studying photography and film-making, was beautiful in a pre-Raphaelite kind of way, slightly neurotic just like me, and she had a heart of gold. She was on an allowance at the time, and we used to go around the big stores like Bendel looking for bargains. She was a pal with whom I could relax and have fun, and because she had the right social status Ken didn't mind having her in the house.

Someone else who became a friend of mine was Berry Perkins, wife of the actor Anthony Perkins. Ken knew Berry and Tony, and when we were first married, they came to a couple of the parties that were given for us. One was at Elaine's, where I took to Berry at once, because she was so laid back, much more like my English friends, and not so much concerned about how she looked and what she wore – though she was in fact extremely attractive.

"Loulou tells me she's a great friend of yours", said Berry. "That's so lovely, because she's a close friend of mine, too. Listen, Nicky", she said, and here she scribbled her address and telephone number on the back of an empty packet of cigarettes, "Ken will have all these details – but this is for you. Come and visit us anytime. You've got to meet Osgood, anyhow! He's just so adorable!"

They lived in down-town New York; Osgood was their child (they soon had more); and it was wonderful visiting a real family home where everything was in slight chaos. I knew I could go there in jeans and a T-shirt and have a proper conversation and be reminded that there was more to life than superficial social gossip. And if Loulou was in New York, she would pop by, and we would all have a lovely, relaxed time together.

I would have liked to see much more of Berry, but she took Osgood around with her whenever she could. This meant that sadly I couldn't say: "Berry, do come round for the afternoon", because Osgood might have moved an ashtray or broken something, and I knew that in Ken's eyes his house and its contents were far too precious to be endangered by children running around in it.

Tony was basically gay just like Ken; and how I envied the lifestyle that Berry shared with him. They adored each other and Osgood, and were perfectly happy to spend an evening at home together.

Ken, by contrast, seemed incapable of spending any time alone with me. How I longed for him to say, just once in a while, "This evening, Nicky, we're going to sit and watch a movie on TV". If we hadn't got something arranged, we went out to the cinema, or round the corner for a Chinese meal. Once or twice, I conned him into a Sunday evening at home, but it made him very uncomfortable. He did take me to Mexico in April on what he called 'our second honeymoon'; but it was ruined for me by the fact that we were accompanied by a young man with whom Ken was totally besotted.

My next problem was that Ken was very keen for me to be like all the other New York society ladies, and have some kind of career or important pursuit. For many of them, this meant being on the committee of a charity; but I didn't like that idea, and eventually, when Ken began pressing me, I came up with the idea of a book-binding business. I did arrange for a few books to be bound, but the business never made much progress: it was just something to keep Ken quiet.

As Ken's wife, I had now become recognized as one of the acknowledged leaders of New York society. In June 1975 I was even featured by *Time Magazine* in an article on the 'New Beauties' as one of New York's 'social pace-setters'.

That was the month when, slightly to my surprise, Ken encouraged me to fly back to England in time to celebrate my 24th birthday at Cheyne Walk, which was ready for me to move in.

※

Although Rita had retired to Portugal, she had a sister who came in to work for me; and she and I had a week to get the house straight. This was a real pleasure: David Mlinaric had done a magnificent job and everything looked absolutely fantastic and beautiful and I've never loved anywhere so much. It contained most of the lovely things which Christopher had helped me collect for Mallord Street; and since David was very practical, it also had a proper kitchen and a proper bathroom and everything worked. It was also smaller and less overpowering than Mallord Street, though it had more living space, because so much of Mallord Street had been taken up with that huge studio. I was much happier here than I had been for months, with my own possessions all around me in my own home, and so many good friends within easy reach.

Ken followed me over to London before long. On the afternoon of his arrival, he and I ended up in bed at Cheyne Walk with my black drugs dealer Gordon; and the next day I learned why he had been so keen for me to revisit London. He began telling me very forcibly that it was crazy for me to keep so much of my money in a land of grotesquely high taxation; and within a few hours I had obediently removed from my bank a vast sum of money in cash. I handed this over to Ken, who assured me that it would be held securely in Switzerland, though I never saw it again.

This was only the start. The next morning, we were still lying in bed when Ken began making it clear that in his view, if our marriage meant anything at all to me, I must accept that England was over and done with, and sell everything: Cheyne Walk, all my furniture, everything.

"Can't I hang on to the Cabbage Patch?"

"That silly little cottage in Sussex? What's the point? It's not worth anything." At that moment Jane Rainey arrived and was shown into our bedroom.

"He wants me to sell the Cabbage Patch!" I blurted out.

"Now Nicky", said Ken, raising his voice a little, "you know you've got to sell everything: what are you complaining about? And you've got to sell it all this week!"

Jane looked shocked, but I was afraid of Ken when he raised his voice, so I just said quite simply:

"Yes, darling, of course I will."

For some reason I couldn't help being reminded at this point that Christopher Gibbs had been dead against my marriage to Ken. "I don't want to alarm you", he had told me, "but he plays financial games which are very strange, to say the least. Whenever I've sent him a bill, I've always had tremendous problems getting money out of him."

And now here I was, slavishly doing whatever Ken wanted, and selling up almost everything of mine except a few odds and ends of furniture destined for my New York sitting-room.

CHAPTER THIRTY-ONE
Breakdown

On 22 June 1975, I celebrated my 24th birthday with an enormous party in Cheyne Walk. It was a tremendous social success, attended by everyone from Lord Goodman to Lady Diana Cooper, from Christopher Gibbs to my new husband Kenny Jay Lane. What a shame that it would also be the last party I could hold in my own beautifully-decorated London home, with all my friends round about me, and where I was able to go to bed without having to wake up to the dreadful sight of a cabinet full of shrunken skulls.

Immediately afterwards, Ken and I travelled up to Scotland together to stay with another of Ken's wealthy connections, Molly, the Dowager Duchess of Buccleuch. This was actually rather romantic, because Ken and I were alone, he was very loving and sweet, and there was no hope of him finding any boys in the Scottish hills.

From Scotland, Ken flew straight back to New York; while I returned to London, to complete the melancholy task of selling up. Very reluctantly I put the Cabbage Patch on the market; and my heart was almost broken when it found a buyer the very next day. Events were sweeping past me, and everything seemed to be more and more out of my control.

Ken was determined that I should become an American citizen, and as soon as possible. To this end, his friend Jacob Javits, a Republican Senator, had been pulling strings on my behalf. The result was that instead of having to wait two years for the all-important Green Card, I was placed in a special category which meant that I could be given one straight away.

As soon as everything was in order, I set off for Heathrow and the long flight to New York. Fortunately for me, I had an unexpected and delightful travelling-companion in Prince Rupert Loewenstein, the financial manager to whom I had been introduced by Mick Jagger, and whom I had started affectionately calling 'the great big teddy bear'.

We were both travelling first-class on an Air India flight; when the plane was delayed for hours we just sat and drank champagne; and then we had a most amusing flight. Still better, when we arrived at La Guardia and, now that I had my Green Card, I had to go through a very complex set of immigration procedures, Rupert waited around until I had been completely cleared.

Ken simply hadn't bothered to turn up; and as soon as I had said good-bye to Rupert, and was taking a taxi back to 38th Street, all my worries about the future returned more strongly than ever. 'Oh, my God!' I thought to myself, 'Now you've really burned your boats. You've sold your homes; you've cut yourself off from family and friends. Now you've just got to stick it out and hope that Ken changes before...' I didn't complete the thought, but I was beginning to be afraid of going mad. And surely Ken would realise at long last how lucky he was to have me, and would stop wanting boys, and we could settle down happily like Berry and Tony?

To make matters worse, this would be my first extremely hot New York summer. Indoors, with air-conditioners humming away night and day, the air was so chilly that one had to wear sweaters. Outdoors, the air was hot and heavy and damp and all my clothes stuck to me. Walking across the pavement into a taxi was like struggling through a Turkish Bath where they'd turned the heat up too high. I dreamed of going riding through the English countryside on Fella in a shower of cooling rain.

Instead, I swallowed more Mandrax and drank more alcohol and, probably much to her annoyance, I began a totally unimportant fling with Diane's ex-husband Prince Egon von Fürstenberg. He had married again but behaved as though he was still footloose and fancy free. He liked men just as much as women, and was great fun to be with apart from the fact that, like me, he was always unbelievably stoned. Anyhow, one day Egon suddenly said to me: "Do you want to go to Fire Island?"

"Sure", I said. "That's great. Let's go! Having said that, I'd better check it out with Ken!"

Ken didn't seem to mind at all. So off we went over to Fire Island, which is about twenty minutes by plane or helicopter from New York, and is the place where homosexuals like to congregate. There were very few women and, in any case, it was almost impossible to tell who were men and who were women because many of the men were drag queens, who did an amazingly good job of making themselves up and dressing as women. For some of them, this was virtually a full-time occupation, and there were numerous competitions in which they could take part.

All the action was on the beach, and wherever I looked I could see all these incredibly camp people dressed in leather, or simply wearing a leather thong around their balls! There were hundreds of little huts and houses, with tiny little beach paths between them, and Egon and I moved into one of the houses, which we shared with three or four gays. At four in the afternoon tea-dances were held, at which everyone from the island seemed to be present – dressed or undressed to the nines. Often, I felt as though I had woken up to find myself in the middle of a particularly surreal movie by Fellini.

On our first afternoon, I noticed a distinctive figure with moustache, beard and considerable paunch. It was Henry Geldzahler, David Hockney's best friend – and there was David alongside him! "Henry! David!" I called out. "Great to see you!" I was particularly pleased to see Henry, who worked at the Met where he had been a close friend of John McKendry. So I had known him for some time; and when I had been living at the Stanhope he would often come over to tea after he'd finished work.

They told me they were renting a house on Fire Island for a few weeks, which was lovely because I could call on them. Compared to the others they were behaving extremely well. Because most people on the island were smashed. Some were on acid, others on coke, still others on uppers and downers: you name it, and they were on it. Egon and I were only there for about three days and I was smashed the entire time. It was quite fun in a way – a holiday pleasure-park mostly for queens and drug addicts; and the beaches were filled with pretty young boys just hanging around waiting for someone with a lot of money to pick them up. It had its dangerous side: no-one knew whom it was safe to invite back to their houses, and from time-to-time people were murdered, though this seemed to make little impact on those who were left behind.

Before we left Fire Island, someone gave me some Angel Dust. Within a few minutes I was on a double trip. As we flew back to New York by helicopter everything seemed to be flying around me. At one point I even thought that I could walk out of the helicopter, but fortunately Egon restrained me.

I arrived back at 38th Street in a slightly dishevelled state just as the first course of a formal lunch about which I had completely forgotten was being put on the table. I sat down and tried to act normally, though I was completely smashed out of my head, and as far as I could make out the food was flying around the table.

After lunch Ken went back to his office. My friend Delfina had been among the guests, and she stayed on and we were able to laugh about it all which was just what I needed. Diana Vreeland had been another guest and, not long after this, Delfina and I helped her with an exhibition at the Met. We were only putting costumes on dummies, and would go and have long lunches at the Stanhope just opposite; but I could see that Diana was a perfectionist and I was impressed by her enthusiasm and dedication.

Another evening, we were at a party where I met Jules C. Stein, the ageing co-founder of the Music Corporation of America. MCA had been the agents for a whole host of Hollywood stars, and Jules took a shine to me, and told me that he was going to turn me into a movie star. He was very plausible, and great fun, and I fell for his story hook line and sinker. He said that he wanted me to go over to California to do a screen-test, and Ken began talking excitedly about contracts.

Sometime later, I had a detailed discussion about what money I should be asking for and things like that, with another of Ken's acquaintances, Jack Nicholson, whose new movie *One Flew Over the Cuckoo's Nest* was an absolute sensation. Armed with what Jack had told me, I went to Jules's

New York office. I was then politely told by his secretary that he was rather apt to promise pretty girls a screen test, but she didn't think that anything would come of it – so that was the beginning and the end of my film career!

In the meantime, I was becoming increasingly unhappy with my New York life, and people were beginning to notice. Kenneth Anger visited and said: "There's something wrong, isn't there?"

I thought of a possible way forward, and said to Ken: "Darling, I don't mind coming into New York for a couple of days a week, but I really need to spend more of my time in the country." We started looking for houses in Connecticut, and found a very beautiful house that we both liked. However, just when everything seemed settled, Ken explained that his finances weren't very good at present, and that I would have to provide the money myself. This would have taken the last of my money and left me totally defenceless, so I pretended that I had lost my enthusiasm for the purchase.

There was another problem. Before leaving London, I'd sold my car to my dealer in return for his posting supplies of Mandrax to me at the Stanhope Hotel. The pills were hidden in books, and posted to me under the name of Waymouth. Several packages got through, but by the start of November 1975 my supplies were running low, and I realized that before long I would have to come off them.

I was still managing to hide my misery from Ken because I was still besotted with him; though my plans to change him seemed less and less likely to succeed. In the evenings we would go out to grand dinners with the best people in New York; and then afterwards he would take me to some seedy pool-hall on the lower East Side and I would have to seduce the prettiest young men into coming home with us, so that first I could take them to bed and then Ken could join us. I felt despairingly that our marriage was turning into a living hell.

And now my Mandrax was running out, and I was becoming ill as I tried to do without it. Finally, on 27 November, Thanksgiving Day, after a celebration at Maxim's, I admitted to Ken that I had been taking large quantities of drugs for many years. I also attributed much of my current unhappiness to trying to come off the Mandrax.

Ken was genuinely shocked to discover that I was more vulnerable than he had thought, that I wasn't just a young girl who was going to look beautiful at his parties and give him lots of money and seduce young men for him and be no trouble. I was another actual human being who was living with him; and he had to do his share of making the marriage work. Starting to see me as the real person that I was clearly frightened him: and it frightened him very much.

His immediate solution was that we should have a holiday together. "Look, don't worry, Nicky", he said. "We'll go to India: we'll have a lovely holiday and you'll be able to sit in the sun and relax and get all these worries and cravings out of your system."

※

So Ken and I flew to Bombay; and at first his remedy appeared to be working. By chance, our New York friends the actor Michael York and his photographer wife Pat were also in Bombay, and we spent a couple of very agreeable days sightseeing with them. Ken was behaving himself; there were no boys involved, and we were staying in lovely rooms at the Taj Mahal.

In the evenings we were wined and dined by Sunita Pitamber, Bombay's leading society hostess; and one night (keeping our car doors safely locked) we drove slowly down the notorious Falkland Road where we could see beautiful young prostitutes soliciting their clients from the so-called whores' cages. "Shall I leave you here?" joked Ken. "You'd look fantastic in one of those cages!" And I thought for a fleeting moment that perhaps I would be happier in one of those whores' cages than lying in my New York bed next to Ken's sinister cabinet of skulls.

From Bombay, we travelled on to the holy city of Puri, where we stayed close to the beach in a curious hotel which seemed to have been left over from the days of the British Raj. They served nothing but English nursery food such as white fish in a sea of milk sauce, or bread-and-butter pudding; and there were notices everywhere saying things like: 'Silence in the afternoon before tea is served'; while the Indian servants were still dressed up in their old uniforms, even if some of them were becoming rather tatty.

Every evening we'd see the fishermen bringing onto the beach mountains of wonderful sardines. Ken had a passion for sardines; and they would have made such a welcome change from the nursery food, that Ken kept asking for them. Finally, one of the staff came up to us in a state of great excitement and said: "Mr. and Mrs. Lane, we've got some sardines!" And to our horror they produced a tin of Shippam's sardines, imported from England; and we were told we couldn't eat the local ones, as they weren't safe!

At least there were no boys. Ken and I were alone, and we even made love. After a week of this, I began to feel much happier.

We moved on to Calcutta, and this was even better. Having met up with Robert Fraser, who had been living there a long time, we had wonderful bike-rides with him through the streets of Calcutta on rickshaws, racing each other all night down the wonderful broad roads of that beautiful city.

From Calcutta we went to Burma, where we were joined by two of Ken's friends, the art-dealers Harry Bailey and Adrian Ward-Jackson, and spent seven days under the supervision of an official tour guide called Dolly. Burma is an extraordinary country but I was suffering from constipation most of the time, and for me the only memorable evening came when we were visiting some wonderful lakes up in the very north of the country. Unfortunately, nobody had told us that Burma could be cold, and we had taken only light Indian clothing. So we found ourselves staying in an hotel, absolutely frozen.

"Do you have any whisky?" Ken asked.

The barman shook his head.

"I'll teach him how to make some dry martinis", said Ken. "Adrian – we seem to be the only guests here – see if you can get some of these fires lit."

Adrian arranged for every fire in the place to be lit, and the whole building began to warm up. As for us: we got unbelievably drunk. The five of us (including Dolly) were sitting in an enormous dining-room; and after a while Dolly disappeared: probably in a state of shock at the way we were behaving because we were so pissed. Then I decided to amuse the men; and soon I was standing up doing a wonderful strip-tease. Before long, every little Burmese head was peering through the slatted windows, because they'd never seen anything like it in their lives! Finally, we all disappeared to bed, where we were so pissed that we played gin rummy and went on drinking brandy until about six in the morning, despite knowing that we had to leave at seven.

The last part of our holiday was spent in Mahabalipuram: the most beautiful part of southern India. We were booked into a lovely hotel on the beach, where everyone had a small hut of their own. It should have been a wonderful time, but it was a disaster, which undid all the good effects of those happy earlier weeks. How? Because there were lots of boys who were available to come and give massages; and soon the inevitable happened, and Ken and I were back in our old familiar pattern. A boy would be asked to come and give us a massage; Ken would expect me to seduce the boy, and so on, just as before. Not surprisingly, I started to get upset and worried and freaked-out all over again.

Henry and Adrian were incredibly sweet to me during this difficult time, and there were still a few agreeable moments. But before long I was worse than ever, since I had begun suffering from dreadful panic attacks. I was still totally in love with Ken, I would do anything to be able to sleep with him, all I wanted to do was to be in his arms the entire time, and to be loved by him. But disturbing images were now constantly flitting through my brain.

I saw the surprised but then greedy look on Ken's face when he had first come face to face in Mallord Street with my Benjamin-Constant. I saw him proposing to me, and then having to disguise his huge disappointment when he realised that I wasn't as rich as he had hoped. I saw myself writing out cheques to prop up his failing businesses. There was Ken, lying in bed with his arm round a boy when I had followed him to Athens only to be relegated to a tiny little room two floors away from his suite; and there he was insisting that I sell everything that I had. I still loved him, but I was beginning to hate him too.

From India, we flew to London; and the following day, Ken went on to New York alone. I had persuaded him that I still had some loose ends to tie up. The reality was that I could no longer cope with what was happening in my life; and as soon as Ken had gone, I immediately went out and bought myself some heroin.

After one more night in London, I went down to Sussex, where I stayed with Michael Davys in the cottage in which I had been brought up while my parents were divorced; and I visited Fella, the horse I had bought from Mick Jagger all those years ago. I had refused to sell him, and he was now my very last possession in England. I told Michael how unhappy I was, but I concealed the fact that I was back on heroin, and for once he didn't really seem to understand.

Back in London, I was caught up in the usual round of parties, but I was dreading going back to New York, and I was soon taking large amounts of heroin to deaden my fears.

※

When I did finally return to New York towards the end of January 1976, I was still hoping to make things work, but I was fundamentally very unhappy, during my panic attacks I had severe pains in my chest, and I was regularly getting very drunk. The New York doctors dismissed my chest pains as psychosomatic, which didn't make me feel any less ill. Perhaps surprisingly, our first anniversary dinner on 17 February was a success: I was still able to put a good face on things in public.

But the very next day, while we were en-route for the Bahamas, I began to feel extremely ill. We were going to stay with the socialite and philanthropist Drue Heinz, a former actress who was married to the Chairman of the Board of the H.J. Heinz Company and so was fabulously wealthy. Ken was quite sympathetic to me, and when we arrived at the Heinzes he kept telling me not to swim for the first two days, as I wasn't well enough.

However, I could only survive by sneaking alcohol the whole time: not difficult when staying with people like the Heinzes. I could still keep things together in public, and in some ways our holiday was amazing: huge dinner parties full of New York celebrities, and during the day we seemed to be constantly flying from place to place in private planes and helicopters. But in private I began crying in front of Ken and saying to him: "Look I'm unhappy, I can't stand it, we've got to change things." This led to a downward spiral in our relationship. Ken stopped being nice, told me that I was being neurotic and stupid, and became more and more distant. And the more distant he was, the worse I felt and the more I drank.

It was one evening about two weeks after our return to New York that

I completely freaked out. It was almost as serious as my bad acid trip. I suddenly knew that I wanted to smash everything in Ken's house, all the wretched museum-pieces that he so clearly preferred to me. At the same time, part of me felt strangely cool and calculated. I wanted to smash everything; but I would concentrate on the objects which were really rather nasty – and I began with a sculpture of some awful silver sticks coming out of a bowl. As I smashed it, I was crying out: "I'm going mad, I'm going mad, I can't stand it!"

And then I began wanting to hurt myself. It was a very weird sensation. I didn't want to slash my writs, or anything like that; but I found a knife and began trying to mark myself physically, as if that was the only way to get Ken to understand that something was wrong.

He and Mustafa restrained me; and when he asked if there was anyone who could help, I told him that the only person I wanted to speak to was John Richardson. So he was brought along; but that did no good, and Ken's next reaction was to try to get me into a mental hospital: not the easiest thing to do in America at any time, let alone at two in the morning, and they wouldn't take me, thank God.

"Well, I can't have her back in my house!", said Ken. This was like a stake being driven into my heart, and my memories of the next few days are fragmentary.

I think I stayed a couple of nights at John Richardson's; and then someone called Oliver Musker, who had once been very close to Marianne Faithfull, was commissioned to take me back to London on the next plane, and I heard that Ken had got a message through to Michael Davys to tell him that I was in a bad way, and when to expect me.

The result was that when I arrived at Heathrow, those true friends Christopher Gibbs and Nicolette Meeres were at the airport to meet me which was wonderful. We took a taxi to the Ritz, where Michael Davys was also waiting for me. He had engaged a nurse to stay in my room overnight, and Nicolette stayed with me too.

The following morning, I moved to another room where I had what turned out to be a very severe nervous breakdown.

Eventually Ken did appear; but it was on the very day when I took a massive overdose and was rushed to St. George's Hospital. I was still in love with Ken; and I remember the worst part of it was waking up in St George's Hospital at about 8 in the morning and finding that he wasn't there.

This was when Arnold Goodman called in Sir Martin Roth for a second opinion, and I began telling Sir Martin the story of my life to date. Psychiatrists have heard it all before. They look at you sadly, listen to you patiently, and after exactly sixty minutes they remind you to pay on the way out. Nothing seems to touch them. But this time it was different. By the time I had finished telling my story, Sir Martin Roth looked pale with shock.

For weeks, I've been feeling desolate, absolutely desolate. The only life I have ever wanted is over…

Postscript

Nicky was right. Her marriage and the life she had lived for the past few years were effectively over. Annie Griffiths invited her back to stay with her parents at the Boltons for a while. When she returned briefly to New York, Ken Lane wouldn't allow her back in his house. She found herself treated as a borderline mental case; and indeed, the appalling lifestyle to which Lane had condemned her, had driven her to the very edge of madness.

Fortunately, there was still some money left which Arnold Goodman had sensibly salted away; and Nicky retreated to a remote part of North Wales where in due course she married a sensible doctor, a divorced man with several young children who needed raising; and where she could go for long walks over the hills and think about the bizarre life she had once led and the bizarre person she had once been.

The doctor, who was a good kindly man, made her well again; but she began to regret the exciting life she had once led in London and New York, and after ten years of a calm and peaceful and so far as anyone could tell happy and drug-free married life she decided, cruelly one might think, that they must part.

Nicky was now living alone in Pentre, the grand, beautifully furnished house with its own tennis-court that she owned in a remote part of North Wales. She retained a considerable portfolio of stocks and shares, the income from which was more than enough for her to live on; she had a Picasso in the bank; and although her fortieth birthday was fast approaching, she was still a beautiful woman. However, when she compared her current circumstances to those that she had enjoyed before Kenny Jay Lane had defrauded her of much of her wealth, she felt desperately poor. She was still in touch with a select number of friends from her former life, but she reckoned that she could now afford to spend no more than two or three days a year in their company, if she was to maintain the extravagant lifestyle which she felt they expected of her. So her immediate aim was to make a great deal of money.

How better, than by writing a memoir? In view of the amazing life she had led, and the large number of famous people whom she had encountered, she was certain that it would prove to be a best-seller. This would be especially true, she believed, if she was prepared to tell the whole story of her sexual encounters. It should catapult her straight up to the heights of fame and fortune currently being enjoyed by so many of her old friends and acquaintances, among whom she could once again appear in a starring role.

But although her memory was so good that it was almost photographic, Nicky knew that knocking her memories into an acceptable shape for publication would need help from an experienced writer. Now she had often visited a bookshop in Oswestry called Gallery Books, run by one Judith Williams, a thoroughly decent human-being and also a shrewd businesswoman who was well-connected locally. On her next visit to Oswestry, Nicky therefore called in at Gallery Books and asked Judith whether she could help her to find a reliable ghost-writer.

As it happened, Judith and her husband had become friendly with a number of local authors one of whom, Richard Perceval Graves, was now living down in Shrewsbury but until 1983 had lived not far away from them in the village of Whittington. By 1991 Graves had already published several well-received biographies including *A.E. Housman: The Scholar-Poet* (1979), *The Brothers Powys* (1983) and two volumes on his late uncle: *Robert Graves: The Assault Heroic 1895-1926* (1986) and *Robert Graves: The Years with Laura 1926-1940* (1990). As it happened, he was currently looking for work to supplement the very small advance he had received for a biography of Richard Hughes, and having received a telephone call from

Postscript

Judith Williams, he was intrigued enough to drive over to Pentre to find out what Nicky had in mind.

He found that Nicky herself was utterly charming, and that her story was certainly a remarkable one. His hopes for immediate gain were dashed when Nicky explained that she could only pay him out of the profits, but those profits looked likely to be huge, and in due course he was perfectly satisfied when she signed a contract with him agreeing that each of them would be entitled to 50% of the earnings from publication.

Richard's Agent, Andrew Best of Curtis Brown, was so excited by Richard's synopsis that he invited both Nicky and Richard to dine with him at the Café Royal; and, feeling certain that Nicky's memoir would be a massive best-seller, it was not long before he had arranged a contract for publication with a reputable London publisher.

However, some two years later when, with Nicky's help, Richard had completed all the necessary research and had written more than half the memoir, Nicky backed out. She had been advised that even though it would make her a great deal of money, her memoir could well poison her relationships with the very people among whom she wished once again to be a star. And in any case, she no longer needed the money to dazzle in London Society, because she had found a new man in her life. With him, it appeared that she would have plenty although it was rumoured that, just like her, he was considerably less wealthy than he had once been.

Nicky was of course perfectly entitled to back out: this possibility had already been anticipated by one of the clauses in the contract she had signed with Richard, which states that if she did so, he could continue with the project provided that she received her 50% share of any proceeds. In practice, however, Nicky repaid the advance to the Publisher, and Andrew Best was not happy to look for another Publisher without Nicky's active participation, so publication of the memoir was effectively put on hold. Within the next couple of years Richard had completed the text, but it would remain unseen until after Nicky's death from cancer at the age of 68 in 2019.

By this time, Richard had been out-of-touch with Nicky for many years and he has no personal knowledge of the circumstances or set-backs which had led to her living alone in Glanbrogan Cottage, Llanfechain, a very much smaller property than the one in which she had been living when he knew her. All he knows for certain is that during the months leading up to her death she had once again shown considerable interest in publishing the story of her life.

That story, Richard had originally envisioned as a classic five-act tragedy. Nicky had certainly been lucky enough with some of those whom she met: those of you who have now read this memoir may well feel that Nigel Waymouth, Nicolette Meeres, Annie Griffiths and Christopher Gibbs stand out in this respect as her truest friends, who always had her best interests at heart. Nigel in particular would remain a close friend until the day of her death; and during one of the numerous parties that were given by her and others during the final months of her life, she even suggested that before she died they should remarry. But the world of wealth and celebrity is a cruel one; and many others including Jim Haynes, Donald Cammell and Kenny Jay Lane had taken advantage of her youth, her beauty and her wealth and contributed to her mental and emotional downfall.

By the time that Richard came to know her, she was a truly damaged personality. She could still be superficially as charming and witty and seductive as ever; but somewhere at the centre of her personality there was a terrible void. It was a void that nothing could fill for long, which explains many of her later self-destructive acts such as the rejection of her excellent third husband. She was a constant prey to suicidal thoughts. Richard himself was once instructed by a doctor, in case Nicky attempted self-harm, to stay at Pentre and watch over her for the whole of one terrifying night.

Marvel at the life she led. Learn what unalloyed celebrity may bring in its wake. Weep for the destruction of the lovely human being she once was.

Finally, may it be known that all profits in connection with this publication will be duly shared between Richard Perceval Graves and Sophie Griffiths, the step-daughter to whom Nicky Samuel bequeathed her rights in her will of April 2019.

Acknowledgements

The ghostwriter Richard Perceval Graves hopes that, with the publication of this work, the spirit of Nicola Samuel/Waymouth/Lane/Griffiths may rest more easily knowing that the story she wished to tell has finally appeared in print. He also acknowledges with grateful thanks the help he received from numerous friends of Nicky's, including most notably her first husband the artist Nigel Waymouth, and the late Reg Davis-Poynter of McGibbon and Kee.

He was also given invaluable help by Kate Pool of the Society of Authors, and by Harvey Starte, Consultant at Reviewed & Cleared Ltd.; and he thanks the entire team at Troubador Publishing Ltd, and especially their Customer Services Manager Hannah Dakin and their Production Controller Joshua Howey de Rijk.

The two cover portraits of Nicky, taken within half-an-hour of each other but showing very different sides of her character and personality, were photographed for the ghostwriter by the Shropshire photographer Marianne Morris, whose present whereabouts it has been impossible to trace.

Acknowledgement of the colour photograph of Nicky is made to the copyright owners Norman Parkinson/Iconic Images and in this respect particular thanks are due to Ellie Brown their Director, Editorial and Commercial Licensing.

The cost of reproducing numerous additional copyright photographs, especially of Nicky herself, was too great for a book whose publication costs have been met in full by the ghostwriter. However, he advises readers who wish to see more, to resort to Google, where (for example) typing in Nicola Waymouth, the name by which Nicky is most remembered online, will lead them to numerous images including a portrait of her by Andy Warhol and photographs of her with Yves St. Laurent, Kenny J. Lane and many others. There is also a striking photograph of Nicky on a Facebook site about *Loulou and Yves* published by Christopher Petkanas in 2018. And incidentally, typing in Nigel Waymouth will lead you to numerous images of his superb artistic work.

In the meantime, there follows a list of acknowledgements to Wikimedia Commons to whom the ghostwriter is very much indebted for the remainder of the photographs published free of charge in the present work.

1. Ossie Clark
Ossie_Clark.png
Itzemxxly, CC BY-SA 4.0 <https://creativecommons.org/licenses/by-sa/4.0>, via Wikimedia Commons

2. Bob Colacello
Bob_Colacello_2011_Shankbone.jpg
David Shankbone, CC BY 3.0 <https://creativecommons.org/licenses/by/3.0>, via Wikimedia Commons

3. Salvador Dalí
Salvador_Dalí_1939.jpg
Carl Van Vechten, Public domain, via Wikimedia Commons
Man_Ray_Salvador_Dali.jpg
Carl Van Vechten, Public domain, via Wikimedia Commons
Salvador_Dali_A_(Dali_Atomicus)_09633u.jpg
Philippe Halsman, Public domain, via Wikimedia Commons

4. Marianne Faithfull
Fanclub1966MarianneFaithfull3.jpg
Photographer: A. Vente, CC BY-SA 3.0 NL

<https://creativecommons.org/licenses/by-sa/3.0/nl/deed.en>, via Wikimedia Commons
MichaelCooper1967BenMerk.jpg
Ben Merk (ANEFO)Rotated version of the original picture., CC0, via Wikimedia Commons

5. John Paul Getty
John_Paul_Getty.jpg
Unimates2018, CC BY-SA 4.0 <https://creativecommons.org/licenses/by-sa/4.0>, via Wikimedia Commons
Wedding_of_John_Paul_Getty_Jr._and_Talitha_Pol_(Rome,_1966).jpg
Keystone / Getty Images, Public domain, via Wikimedia Commons

6. Jim Haynes
Dworkin_Haynes_Clare_on_After_Dark.jpg
Open Media Ltd, CC BY-SA 3.0 <https://creativecommons.org/licenses/by-sa/3.0>, via Wikimedia Commons

7. Mick Jagger
Mick-Jagger-1965b.jpg
Olavi Kaskisuo / Lehtikuva, Public domain, via Wikimedia Commons
Jagger-Richards.jpg
Larry Rogers, CC BY-SA 2.0 <https://creativecommons.org/licenses/by-sa/2.0>, via Wikimedia Commons
Mick_Jagger_in_Den_Haag_(1976).png
Bert Verhoeff for Anefo, CC BY-SA 3.0 <https://creativecommons.org/licenses/by-sa/3.0>, via Wikimedia Commons

8. Kenneth J. Lane
Kenneth_J_Lane_in_the_living_room_of_his_apartment_in_the_Library_of_the_former_Advertising_Club.jpg
D C McJonathan, CC BY-SA 3.0 <http://creativecommons.org/licenses/by-sa/3.0/>, via Wikimedia Commons

9. John Lennon & Yoko Ono
John_Lennon_en_zijn_echtgenote_Yoko_Ono_op_huwelijksreis_in_Amsterdam._John_Lenn,_Bestanddeelnr_922-2302.jpg
Eric Koch / Anefo, CC0, via Wikimedia Commons
John_Lennon_en_zijn_echtgenote_Yoko_Ono_op_huwelijksreis_in_Amsterdam_hielden_pe,_Bestanddeelnr_922-2301.jpg
Eric Koch / Anefo, CC0, via Wikimedia Commons
Yoko_Ono_and_John_Lennon_at_John_Sinclair_Freedom_Rally.jpg
Unidentified (Michiganensian is the University of Michigan yearbook published by University of Michigan), Public domain, via Wikimedia Commons

10. Paloma Picasso
PICASSOS_EN_MALAGA-16.jpg
Eduardo Correa, Public domain, via Wikimedia Commons

11. Nicolas Roeg
Actress_Rosie_Fellner_and_director_Nicolas_Roeg_at_Crunch_2011.jpg
Wiki 4321, CC BY-SA 3.0 <https://creativecommons.org/licenses/by-sa/3.0>, via Wikimedia Commons
Nicolas_Roeg.jpg
che (Please credit as "Petr Novák, Wikipedia" in case you use this outside Wikimedia projects.), CC BY-SA 2.5 <https://creativecommons.org/licenses/by-sa/2.5>, via Wikimedia Commons

12. Patti Smith
Patti_Smith_performing_in_Finland,_2007.jpg
Beni Köhler, CC BY-SA 3.0 <http://creativecommons.org/licenses/by-sa/3.0/>, via Wikimedia Commons
Patti_Smith_in_Rosengrten_1978.jpg
Klaus Hiltscher, CC BY-SA 2.0 <https://creativecommons.org/licenses/by-sa/2.0>, via Wikimedia Commons

13. Andy Warhol

Andy_Warhol_by_Jack_Mitchell.jpg

Jack Mitchell, CC BY-SA 4.0 <https://creativecommons.org/licenses/by-sa/4.0>, via Wikimedia Commons

Andy_Warhol,_Jean-Michel_Basquiat,_Bruno_Bischofberger_and_Fransesco_Clemente,_New_York,_1984.tif

Galerie Bruno Bischofberger, CC BY-SA 4.0 <https://creativecommons.org/licenses/by-sa/4.0>, via Wikimedia Commons

Andy_Warhol_and_Ulli_Lommel_on_set_of_Cocaine_Cowboys.jpg

Hollywood House of Horror, CC BY 3.0 <https://creativecommons.org/licenses/by/3.0>, via Wikimedia Commons

More information about many of the characters who appear in Nicky's memoir can be found by visiting the website kindly created for Richard Perceval Graves by GWS Media Ltd. at www.theswinging60s.com

The ghostwriter's own website is at www.richardgraves.org and should you wish to purchase more copies of this work, please visit https://www.troubador.co.uk/bookshop/biography/nicky-samuel-my-life-and-loves-hb/